CHARDIN

MARIANNE ROLAND MICHEL

CHARDIN

THAMES AND HUDSON

I would like to express my thanks to Antoine d'Albis, Joseph Baillio, Georges Brunel, Jean de Cayeux, Philip Conisbee, Phoebe Cowles, Margaret Grasselli, Brigitte Margoto, Roland Michel, Tamara Preaud, Alan Rosenbaum, Pierre Rosenberg, George Shackelford, Michelle Schaetzel, Adam William and Eunice Williams, all of whom were of particular help in various ways.

Translated from the French by Eithne McCarthy

This edition © 1996 Thames and Hudson Ltd, London
and Harry N. Abrams, Inc., New York

First published in France by Éditions Hazan, Paris 1994

British Library Cataloguing-in-Publication Data

A catalogue record for this book is available from the British Library

ISBN 0-500-09259-1

Printed and bound in Italy

CONTENTS

PREFACE

Chardin is neither unknown nor underrated. He never was, either during his lifetime or after his death, and few French artists have remained so popular. He is rightly considered one of the greatest painters of his time, and his work has prompted the highest praise from both critics and novelists, from its first appearance until the present day. His *Saying Grace* has become part of our imagination in the same way as *The Forge* by Le Nain or *The Angelus* by Jean François Millet. By coincidence, his career was developing at the same time as criticism was becoming a separate field of literature and so we are able to look at the different stages of his career both in his paintings and in the writings of his contemporaries.

His painting, his colouring, his style and his touch were acknowledged as being exemplary, although he painted still lifes and genre scenes which, at the time, were considered to be inferior modes of painting. This is the first paradox about Chardin, and not the only one. This man, who was almost completely self-taught, spent time thinking about the theory and practice of teaching and, despite an inadequate artistic training, he produced learned paintings, which were praised alongside those of the most famous history painters. This remarkable artist was no intellectual, but the soundness of his judgments on painting is admired and he is linked to the best theoreticians of his time, such as Charles Nicolas Cochin the Younger, and to the encyclopaedists through Denis Diderot. His lack of any proper training meant that he drew little and badly. In spite of this, the pastel portraits which he painted in his seventies are formidable masterpieces. Although he is compared to Rembrandt, David Teniers the Younger and Gerrit Dou, his paintings are truly French and his paintings of bourgeois life were sought by the sovereigns of Europe. Finally, the superficial simplicity of his subjects is today the subject of learned and sometimes dubious analyses.

Despite a wealth of literature, and the study of various public records as well as a variety of other documents – sources to which this book owes a great deal – many questions remain. These concern Chardin's intentions, his creative methods, his choice of subjects, his pictorial technique, his 'unique execution', analysed by Diderot, and the reception of his work. How, why and for whom did he paint? What were his inspirations and intentions? Do his paintings have the significance which they have sometimes been given? How were they perceived by the public and the critics? These questions and contentious issues have, of course, been tackled before in numerous articles, catalogues and monographs, most of which are listed in the bibliography and in the notes of this book. I will simply mention here those books without which no work on Chardin could begin: *Chardin* by Georges Wildenstein, published in 1933 and much more complete than the 'revised' versions of 1963 and 1969. Also, the wonderful catalogue compiled by Pierre Rosenberg for the Chardin exhibition which he organized in 1979 in Paris, Cleveland and Boston to mark the bicentenary of the artist's death. And finally, the expansion of that work to cover Chardin's *œuvre*, published in 1983 in the series *Tout l'œuvre peint*. All references to the latter are indicated in the main body of the text as follows: [T.O.P. followed by the reference number]. In varying degrees of detail, these works gather together the many documentary sources, texts published in Chardin's lifetime, and the collections and sales through which his work passed, and they also try to establish a chronology of his paintings.

However, it seems that there may be room for a new look at Chardin's work, to try to uncover the mysterious magic of his brush, to consider eighteenth-century documents and to reflect on his paintings to try to understand the secrets or 'recipes' of the painter who was both still and vibrant, and whose compositions were simple only on the surface, their effects cleverly calculated without appearing so. This ambitious attempt to examine an *œuvre* which defies analysis, while giving enormous visual and spiritual pleasure, relies heavily on the conclusions of numerous discussions which I have had with Christian Michel. He has served as a mediator between Cochin's writings on Chardin and my own analyses, and he has helped me understand better the implications of the theories and terminology of the eighteenth century.

I would like to express my gratitude by dedicating this book to him.

Self-portrait with Eye-shade, 1775. Pastel, 46 × 38 cm (18⅛ × 15 in.). Louvre, Paris.

PART I

A PARISIAN
PAINTER

CHAPTER ONE

PAINTER OF ANIMALS, KITCHEN UTENSILS AND VEGETABLES

*He sensed that he had a spirit
urging him towards
greater things.*

Cochin

While many documents about Chardin exist – contemporary texts, public records, monographs and catalogues – there are still many questions and uncertainties about the beginning of his career, his training and his early works, which can only be answered by means of guesswork or probability.

A life spent entirely in Paris was exceptional in the eighteenth century, particularly for an artist of Chardin's stature. The product of a traditional artisan background, Jean Siméon Chardin was born on 2 November 1699 in the Rue de Seine, the son of Jean Chardin, a master cabinet-maker, and Jeanne Françoise David. The child was baptized the following day at Saint-Sulpice; his godfather, Siméon Simonet, was also a cabinet-maker and his godmother the wife of another cabinet-maker, Jacques Le Riche.

As was customary at the time, the boy was given the names of his father and godfather. However, throughout his life, he was commonly known as Jean Baptiste Siméon and his contemporaries often refer to him using all three names.[1] Jean Chardin specialized in making billiard tables, and he even made a number for the king. He belonged to that ordinary class of artisans whose children later became artists, such as Jean Oppenord, father of the celebrated architect and draughtsman Gilles Marie Oppenord. Jean Oppenord belonged to the same profession as Chardin's father; he specialized in parquet flooring and he did some marquetry design for the Petite Galerie at Versailles.

Following a well-established tradition in artisan families, Jean Chardin would have liked his eldest son to follow in his footsteps, but, according to Charles Nicolas Cochin (the author of an important biographical account to which we are indebted for most of our information about the artist),[2] this idea appalled Chardin who felt he had 'a spirit urging him towards greater things' – namely, painting. This reminds one of Antoine Watteau, the son of a master carpenter and roofer, who had been destined to follow in his father's footsteps, before the latter 'realized his son's inclination for drawing'[3] and apprenticed him to a master painter in Valenciennes. This was in about 1695. In the same way, Chardin's father accepted 'his inclination for painting', and apprenticed his son at about the age of thirteen or fourteen to Pierre Jacques Cazes, a history painter, whose studio, if Cochin is to be believed, 'was not suitable for training pupils'. Not having sufficient funds to pay models, he asked his students to copy his own work and had them draw at the Académie in the evenings. Cazes himself used these academy figures in his pictures. It was in relation to this training that the classic debate first arose concerning Chardin: should one represent 'nature' or paint 'from the imagination'? At the Cazes studio, 'one never painted from nature', Cazes himself basing his pictures on 'practice' or the application of theory, i.e., the imagination.[4] So we can understand the reservations of Chardin's contemporaries about his education. It is a fact that he was never a good draughtsman – this is not to say that he

Page 10:
The Buffet (detail), Louvre, Paris.

Opposite: Pierre Jacques Cazes, *Double Académie d'homme* (Two male nudes). Black chalk, stump, white highlights on blue paper, 60 × 43 cm (23⅝ × 16⅞ in.). École nationale supérieure des Beaux-Arts, Paris.

was a bad one – and Pierre Jean Mariette rightly wrote that 'for lack of concentrating on drawing', he was incapable of 'doing his studies and preparatory work on paper'. The only known drawing by Chardin of a nude (right), while it is close to Cazes's academy figures, is certainly no masterpiece.

Thus, Chardin barely learnt life drawing – although this type of drawing was considered the basic essential of all artistic education. He lacked training in painting from nature and he had no real theoretical or intellectual education. Later, he himself was often to complain of this lack. His father, who had a large family for which to find work, ensured only that his children had 'sufficient skills to enable them to earn a living. This is why he did not make them learn the classics.'[5]

Chardin soon became aware of his weaknesses through the painter Noël Nicolas Coypel, who asked Cazes to lend him a few of his young pupils to help him finish a commission. Chardin was given the task of painting the gun in a portrait of a hunter. Coypel placed the model in a certain light and explained to the young man how to render the light and how to draw the gun accurately. It seems that Cazes did not teach this sort of thing: Chardin was utterly astonished to learn that it was necessary to imitate life, and that this was not so simple. This episode seems to have had a huge influence on his approach to painting.[6]

This was probably the time when Chardin was painting the first pictures of which any trace remains. One is a sign-board (see p. 35) – similar to one which Watteau had painted in 1720 for Edmé François Gersaint's shop on Pont Notre-Dame[7] – which was commissioned from the young painter by a surgeon friend of his father's. Although he had been asked to represent surgical instruments in the picture, Chardin decided to paint a colourful scene, showing a man with a sword wound brought to the surgeon for attention, with several figures animating the scene. To do this, 'he assembled some of his friends in his room, put them into lifelike groups and sketched on paper the shapes and effects which they created. He then brought these sketches together in his picture, using the paving stones of the street where the scene is taking place as his scale'.[8] One of these drawings of a detail has survived, *The Vinaigrette* (T.O.P. 1b), which shows a footman pulling a two-wheeled sedan which was no doubt used to carry the wounded man (see right).[9]

It seems that Chardin hung his sign up during the night. In the morning, passers-by stopped in front of it and their praises attracted the attention of the surgeon. At first angry that the painter had not heeded his suggestions, he calmed down on hearing the admiration of the onlookers. Apparently, all those whom Paris considered to be people of taste – i.e., artists and, in particular, members of the Académie – streamed past his painting It was the first step on the way to fame.

It is also at about this time (1720–24?) that Chardin seems to have painted his *Game of Billiards* (T.O.P. 2; see p. 15) which may have been designed to serve as a sign or as other advertising material for his father. The version in the Musée Carnavalet could be a smaller copy by the artist or possibly a sketch for a bigger picture which has been lost: some details of figures on the left hand side in the background are only lightly sketched in.[10]

T.O.P. refers to Pierre Rosenberg, *Tout l'œuvre peint de Chardin*, 1983.

Male Nude (verso of *The Vinaigrette*). Black chalk with white highlights, 28.7 × 40.6 cm (11¼ × 16 in.). Nationalmuseum, Stockholm.

The Vinaigrette, 1720–22. Black chalk with white highlights on grey-brown paper, 28.7 × 40.6 cm (11¼ × 16 in.). Nationalmuseum, Stockholm.

13

Chardin was in his early twenties. He knew that he wanted to be a painter but that he did not have the traditional background for this. He experimented, probably copying Cazes's history pictures, and discovered the difficulty of drawing from life, particularly as the training he was being given was not very demanding. Years later, at the height of his fame, he asserted that no education – and he included that of doctors, lawyers and teachers in his comparison – was as long or as difficult as that of a painter. He confided in Denis Diderot that 'At the age of seven or eight, a pencil is put in our hands. We start by copying eyes, mouths, noses and ears, followed by hands and feet. Our backs have been bent over our portfolios a long time before we are put in front of the Hercules or the torso. You cannot imagine the tears which this satyr, that gladiator, this Medici Venus or that Antinous have caused…. After many days and nights burning the midnight oil studying motionless and inanimate objects, we are presented with life and, suddenly, the work of years is reduced to nothing. One is as awkward as the first time one picked up a pencil. The eye has to be trained to look at nature – and how many have never seen it and never will! It is the bane of our lives. We have been kept in front of a model for five or six years and then we are left with nothing but our own spirit, if we have any…. Aged nineteen to twenty when the palette falls from his hands, the painter is left without a profession, without resources and without morals.'[11]

This statement certainly explains why, on several occasions, Chardin took up the cause of young artists. At the same time, he also drew attention to the inadequacy of academic training (which, it is true to say, was being greatly questioned at the time when Diderot was quoting Chardin) and his awareness of the gaps in his own education. This explains why the drawings mentioned above are scarcely more than awkward preparatory sketches, simplified in such a way that they resemble one or two of Cazes's (*Pope Blessing a Bishop* or *The Resurrection*),[12] without giving any indication of modelling or volume.

The only known drawing which deals with a different subject matter is his *Head of a Wild Boar* (T.O.P. 4b) which was purchased, as were the others, by Count Carl Gustaf Tessin (see left). If it dates back, as the other drawings do, to his apprenticeship years, then it throws new light on what Chardin was trying to do and on his approach to still life.

Friends are said to have given him a rabbit, or a hare, which he agreed to paint. Never having had the opportunity before to depict fur, he tried to render it as accurately as possible. 'I had to forget everything that I had seen and even the way that these subjects had been treated by others.' In recounting this, Cochin clearly implies that Chardin was refusing merely to imitate Claude François Desportes, Jean Baptiste Oudry or Nicolas de Largillierre, who had advised that when painting an animal in its skin 'one should begin with the broad masses, laid in with a thick impasto of colour', and then work in the details with turpentine oil applied with a soft brush.[13]

'I need to place it far enough away so that I no longer see the details', Chardin continues. 'Above all, I have to ensure that I copy the general shapes, the tone of the colours, the roundness, the light effects and the shadows as well and as accurately as possible'. Mariette wrote that his friends encouraged him to continue in this direction. Chardin added some kitchen utensils to his hare

Head of a Wild Boar, c. 1725.
Black and red chalk, stump, heightened with white,
26.4 × 40.6 cm (10⅜ × 16 in.).
Nationalmuseum, Stockholm.

14

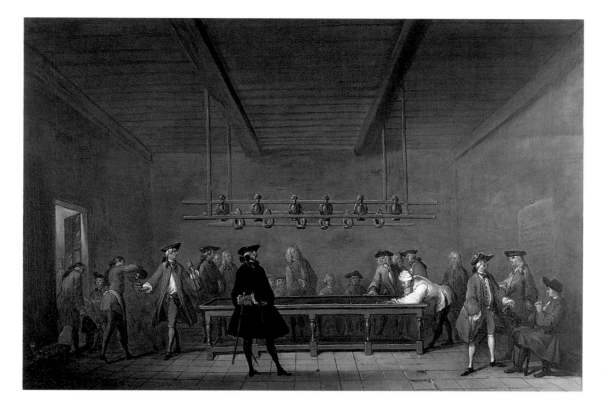

Game of Billiards,
c. 1722–24.
Oil on canvas,
55 × 82.5 cm
(21⅝ × 32½ in.). Musée
Carnavalet, Paris.

Study of a Man Sitting
(for the man on the
right hand side of *Game*
of Billiards), 1722–24.
Charcoal and white
chalk, 25.6 × 16.7 cm
(10⅛ × 6½ in.). The
J. Paul Getty Museum,
Malibu, California.

Servant Filling a Player's Glass (for the
left hand side of *Game of Billiards*), 1722–24.
Red chalk, black chalk and white highlights
on grey-brown paper, 24.7 × 37 cm (9⅝ × 14⅝ in.).
Nationalmuseum, Stockholm.

and, since the picture pleased, he was commissioned to paint a duck, to make up a pair. Cochin, meanwhile, notes that he painted all sorts of inanimate objects, and later live animals, and that these works were praised by all the artists. His drawing of the *Head of a Wild Boar* (see p. 14) was certainly part of these new experiments.

It was at around this time that Chardin met at a dance a very young middle-class girl, Marguerite Saintard, who was ten years his junior. The couple decided to marry and a contract was drawn up on 6 May 1723. However, either the girl's parents decided that their fourteen-year-old daughter was a little too young, or Chardin did not have sufficient means to start a family, as the marriage did not take place until eight years later. Perhaps it was this betrothal which prompted Chardin's father to think that his son should practise his profession in a more structured way and to make him submit his mastership documents to the Académie de Saint-Luc on 3 February 1724.[14] From that day on, as a master painter, Chardin's status was now recognized, he could receive commissions, run a studio and employ apprentices.[15]

And so here we have a twenty-five-year-old artist trying his hand at scenes with several figures, still lifes and live animals and who was doing so at the same time as Watteau, Oudry, Desportes and Largillierre. In his paintings of animals, he may also have been attempting landscapes. Was it his new skills which won him a portrait commission, or did he himself wish to try a new genre? At any rate, in 1724 he painted the portrait of Laurent d'Houry, founder of the *Almanach Royal*. The painting is signed rather indistinctly and the date appears on the endpaper of the *Almanach*, on which the subject is

Portrait of Laurent d'Houry, 1724.
Oil on canvas, 130 × 99 cm (51⅛ × 39 in.).
Private collection, Paris.

Le Peintre and *L'Antiquaire* 1743. Engravings by Pierre
Louis Surugue after Chardin.

writing (see left). One might ask why his contemporaries never commented on this picture, or indeed on *The Game of Billiards*. Why do Cochin and Mariette date Chardin's first attempts at portraiture at around ten years later? If we look at this portrait of Laurent d'Houry and compare it with his portrait of Jacques André Joseph Aved in 1734 (T.O.P. 99; see p. 119), there are features common to both. Of course the painting is the work of a young artist whose grasp of perspective is still poor – a weakness found elsewhere in some of his still lifes, even the later ones. D'Houry seems to be balancing on the edge of his chair, which itself is not level with the table – this is more or less the case with his famous *Lady Taking Tea* of 1735 (T.O.P. 101; see p. 200). But the impression of life in d'Houry's face, the way that his hands have been painted and the fabric of his dressing gown are already those of a great painter.

After this, it seems that for several years Chardin did not paint any portraits or pictures of people. However, he probably painted the first versions of his *Monkey as Painter* and *Monkey as Antiquarian* (cf. p. 17) in 1726.[16] These may have been inspired by Watteau's *Monkey as Painter* and *Monkey as Sculptor*, as they are very much in the satirical vein of the period and also reflect the contemporary craze for Flemish *singeries*. (We may recall that Watteau had been asked to paint a *singerie* to pair with Pieter Breughel's *Two Monkeys*, in the collection of the Duc d'Orléans.)

In December 1727, Chardin's name appears as a witness at the marriage of the daughter of the painter Louis de Silvestre to Louis Barère, a master painter. The other signatures are those of the bride's brothers, Louis Jacques Silvestre, a painter, and Antoine Silvestre, a draughtsman. Perhaps Chardin was only there as a friend of the bridegroom, who, like him, was a member of the Académie de Saint-Luc. But it may also have been the occasion for him to develop a relationship with an influential family of artists, who would grow to appreciate his work. The sale after the death of Jacques Augustin Silvestre in 1811 contained at least sixteen paintings and pastels by Chardin, who himself had a *Nativity* by (Louis?) de Silvestre in his own relatively modest collection.

A few months later, in May 1728, Chardin exhibited *The Skate* (T.O.P. 12; see p. 18) and other paintings at the Exposition de la Jeunesse (Young Artists' Exhibition) in the Place Dauphine.[17] It was certainly his success here that made him consider joining the Académie Royale de Peinture et Sculpture. This is worth pausing over, as it shows that Chardin still doubted his talents, which reminds us of his regret at not having had a proper academic training and thus being unable to work as a history painter.

He then devised a ploy or, as Thomas Crow puts it nicely, a 'surprise invader' strategy, whereby he arranged for Largillierre to see his work without knowing its author.[18] This is what Watteau did in 1712, if we are to believe Gersaint, with Charles de La Fosse playing the role of Largillierre.[19] It is not known whether this scene took place at Chardin's residence or at the Académie's premises in the Louvre. Cochin seems to imply that Largillierre went to Chardin's studio and the author of the *Nécrologe*[20] says that 'members of the Académie went to him'. On the other hand, Haillet de Couronne – whose text is based on that of Cochin – writes that Chardin hung his pictures in one of the first rooms and that Largillierre stopped 'to consider them before entering the second room of the Académie where the candidate was'.[21] It was

The Monkey as Painter,
c. 1738–40. Oil on canvas,
28.5 × 23.5 cm (11¼ × 9¼ in.).
Musée des Beaux-Arts, Chartres.

The Monkey as Antiquarian,
c. 1738–40. Oil on canvas,
28.5 5 23.5 cm (11¼ × 9¼ in.).
Musée des Beaux-Arts, Chartres.

here that Watteau had presented his pictures 'strong in colour and which had a certain harmony, leading one to believe them to be those of an old master'. Chardin's paintings – which included *The Skate* and *The Buffet* (T.O.P. 12 and 34; see pp. 18 and 19) – were praised by Largillierre: 'You have some very good pictures here. These are surely the work of some good Flemish painter. Flanders is an excellent training ground for colour.[22] Now, let us see your works...', followed by, once he knew the author, 'my friend, introduce yourself boldly' – the equivalent of La Fosse's 'my friend, you are unaware of your talents' to Watteau. While it could rightly have been said that members of the Académie were sufficiently generous in spirit to recognize new talents – particularly where Watteau was concerned – what did impress them about works submitted was any reference to the colour of the old masters or the Flemish artists of the seventeenth century. In fact, *The Buffet* is possibly Chardin's only still life which makes an explicit reference to Dutch painting, with its half-peeled lemon and the use of refined objects such as the beautiful glasses, the silver plate, the Chinese porcelain bowls, and so on. Before his favourable reception by Largillierre, Chardin proposed that the Académie choose from among the pictures which he had submitted. Louis de Boullogne, then Director of the Académie and First Painter to the King, who shared Largillierre's judgment, commented wryly on this proposal: 'he has not yet been accepted and already he is speaking of his reception'. Which is indeed what happened, whereas Watteau was not received until five years after his acceptance.[23] Admittedly, the still-life genre was less of a novelty than that of *fêtes galantes*.

Thus, on 25 September 1728, Chardin, 'painter of animals and fruits', became a member of the Académie and set about framing *The Skate* – which remained hanging in the Académie throughout the eighteenth century, along

Le Singe peintre.
Engraving by Louis Desplaces after Antoine Watteau.

17

The Skate, 1726? Oil on canvas, 114 × 146 cm (44⅞ × 57½ in.). Louvre, Paris.

The Buffet, 1728.
Oil on canvas, 194 × 129 cm
(76⅜ × 50¾ in.).
Louvre, Paris.

Bonaventure de Bar, *Fête champêtre* (Country Fair).
Oil on canvas, 97 × 130 cm (38⅛ × 51⅛ in.).
Louvre, Paris.

Jacques Dumont, called Dumont le Romain,
Hercule et Omphale (Hercules and Omphale).
Oil on canvas, 135 × 167 cm (53⅛ × 65¾ in.).
Musée des Beaux-Arts, Tours.

These were the reception pieces
of two artists who entered the Académie
on the same day as Chardin.

with Watteau's *Pilgrimage to the Island of Cythera* – and *The Buffet*.[24] A document in the Bibliothèque nationale gives a colourful definition of the 'talent' for which Chardin was received.[25] It is a hand-written list of the painters and engravers received into the Académie for each year between 1715 and 1734. In it, under 1728, one reads that Chardin 'painter of animals, kitchen utensils and various vegetables had, for his reception piece, painted a picture of his own taste', probably *The Buffet*.

Between 1727 and 1729 Chardin completed a number of characteristic compositions: hanging skate or mackerel, partridges and hares, fruit placed in a bowl or a basket and reflected in the silver of a tumbler, a jug, or a tureen.[26] He also grouped together vegetables, cauldrons, glazed earthenware pots and bottles in a seemingly random way.

Now that he had been received into the infinitely more prestigious Académie royale, Chardin naturally gave up his membership of the Académie de Saint-Luc in February 1729. From then on, not only could he use the title 'painter to the king', but he could also rely on more regular commissions and income. Also in 1729, he took part in designing a fireworks display to celebrate the Dauphin's birth. The goldsmith and architect Juste-Aurèle Meissonnier, who, like him, had been a member of the Académie de Saint-Luc, was the main person involved. Chardin received a payment in December which is evidence of his work, but it does not give us any precise details about it.

In February 1730, his name appears for the first time in the accounts of Conrad Alexandre de Rothenbourg, the French Ambassador to Madrid, who ordered at least six pictures from Chardin between this date and his death in 1735. Several paintings are dated 1730, beginning with *The Water Spaniel* (T.O.P. 49; see p. 21) – which seems to be the last work in which he combines a landscape with a live animal – as well as small kitchen still lifes, where he arranges some vegetables, fowl, eggs, a leg (T.O.P. 51) or a loin of lamb (T.O.P. 52) around a jug or a cauldron (see pp. 24 and 25). Also dated 1730 is an overdoor with musical instruments painted for the drawing room at the Comte de Rothenbourg's mansion in the Rue du Regard (T.O.P. 44 and 45).[27]

1731 was a turning point in Chardin's life. On 26 January, he signed a second marriage contract with Marguerite Saintard, whom he married at Saint-Sulpice on 1 February. He continued to live at his parents' home in the Rue Princesse. It seems that the family of the young girl, quite well off when Chardin first knew them and became engaged to her, had meanwhile suffered significant reversals of fortune. His contemporaries agreed to support him so that he would not be put under pressure by these financial troubles or by the poor health of his wife, who died four years later, having given him a son, Jean Pierre, in November 1731 and, two years later, a daughter, Marguerite Agnès, who probably died shortly after her mother.

There are no portraits of Chardin in the 1730s. The known portraits of him are all dated after 1750: Cochin's medallions (see p. 27) are dated 1755 and 1776 and Maurice Quentin de La Tour's pastel and his preliminary study are dated 1760 (see p. 28). The portrait by Jean-Baptiste Tiger, which hung at the Académie, has not survived and, in his famous self-portraits of 1771, 1775 and, shortly before his death, in 1778 or 1779 (T.O.P. 191, 194, 201; see pp. 8, 225 and 228), the artist is much older.

Duck with Seville Orange, c. 1729–30.
Oil on canvas, 80.5 × 64.5 cm (31¾ × 25½ in.).
Musée de la Chasse et de la Nature, Paris.

The Water Spaniel, 1730.
Oil on canvas, 194.5 × 112 cm (76⅝ × 44⅛ in.).
Private collection.

Two Rabbits, Grey Partridge,
Game-bag and Powder Flask,
1731. Oil on canvas,
82 × 65 cm
(32¼ × 25⅝ in.). National
Gallery of Ireland,
Dublin.

22

Two Rabbits with Game-bag, Powder Flask and Orange, 1728. Oil on canvas, 92 × 74 cm (36¼ × 29⅛ in.). Staatliche Kunsthalle, Karlsruhe.

23

Still Life with Loin of Lamb, 1730. Oil on canvas, 40 × 32.5 cm (15¾ × 12⅞ in.). Musée des Beaux-Arts, Bordeaux.

Still Life with Leg of Lamb,
1730. Oil on canvas,
40 × 32.5 cm
(15¾ × 12⅞ in.).
Blaffer Foundation,
Houston.

Cat with Salmon, Two Mackerel, Mortar and Pestle, 1728. Oil on canvas, 80 × 63 cm (31½ × 24¾ in.). Thyssen-Bornemisza Foundation, Madrid.

26

These different images show almond-shaped eyes, a long nose, well defined lips with a hint of a slightly ironic smile, a searching gaze, which the spectacles of his later years did not hide, and an air of affable authority. He is described as being small in height, but strong and muscular, capable of losing his temper and even of reacting violently to things. When writing the notes for Chardin's eulogy which Haillet de Couronne was to deliver to the Académie of Rouen, Cochin mentioned a visit by the young painter to Crozat, Baron de Thiers, owner of a version of *The Washerwoman* (T.O.P. 81), a servant of whose Chardin is said to have thrown down a staircase.

Like many of his contemporaries, Chardin had a hearty appetite – witnessed by the menu of a meal which he had at Cochin's home with Jean Baptiste Marie Pierre, the painter, and Pierre Alexandre Wille, the engraver, on one of his days of Académie business: eels stewed in wine, a skate wing, mackerel, chicken, lamb, followed by plaice, shad, asparagus, artichokes, peas, cauliflower, cheese, a compote, a brioche, biscuits and pastries. Chardin was seventy-five years old at the time! He contributed the wine – twenty-four bottles of two different qualities.[28]

Many of his paintings of 1731 demonstrate Chardin's growing repertoire. Originally, a kitchen still life would show a skate hanging above a plucked chicken, a cauldron, a jug and some onions (T.O.P. 53). Now, in placing a glazed jug and a copper cauldron beneath a hanging skate, perhaps Chardin was trying to recreate on a modest scale the composition which had earned him so much praise. But there is nothing of violence or blood about this fish: it is an ordinary domestic scene, like those he had painted in the previous year. In the same vein, but more elaborate, are the two paintings of copper cauldrons in the Louvre which portray the traditional contrast between *The Fast-day Meal* and *The Meat-day Meal* (T.O.P. 54 and 55; see p. 157). His *Two Rabbits, Grey Partridge and Game-bag* (T.O.P. 59; see p. 22) dates from the same year, along with two further large overdoors commissioned by Rothenbourg: *Attributes of the Arts* and *Attributes of Science* (T.O.P. 56 and 57; see pp. 180 and 181). The first of these incorporates a bas-relief by François Duquesnoy, *Children Playing with a Goat* (see pp. 39 and 69), which Chardin used in several paintings.[29]

Thus, he gradually devised a formula, which he improved or varied using different utensils, vegetables or preparations for meals. He often reproduced exact copies of a particular kitchen table or a particular composition, either because he was satisfied with it or in response to a client's wishes. Chardin's own technical difficulties must also be taken into account – his slowness of execution, his inability to 'get away' from his model, his efforts to evolve a more satisfactory distribution of objects in space, and his lack of imagination.

These problems, and the repetitions which they brought about, do not just concern the still lifes with their trivial subject matter. They are found, with some variations, in the genre scenes which henceforth formed the main part of Chardin's work.

1731–1737: DECISIVE YEARS, AND THE START OF FIGURE PAINTING

In the early 1730s, years which saw his marriage and the birth of his two children, Chardin perfected his still life technique. At the same time, he got to

Charles Nicolas Cochin, *Portrait de Chardin* (Portrait of Chardin), 1755. Black lead and stump on vellum, diameter 11.5 cm (4⅝ in.). Louvre, Paris.

know and learnt to appreciate his talents, while building up a clientele of connoisseurs such as Rothenbourg and artists such as Jean Baptiste Van Loo and, before long, Aved. The existence of copies even before Chardin was received into the Académie, and particularly in the years after 1728, demonstrate this success. If he did repeat even his most humble compositions two or three times, it was because they were very successful and because several admirers wanted their own copy.[30] Elsewhere, although he did not repeat a composition exactly, he reused the same objects – a glazed jug, a copper cauldron, a cloth or a piece of linen, hanging herrings, a salmon steak, turnips, leeks, etc. – which gives the feeling of exact repetition, although the arrangement and use of space differ.

Should we believe Cochin when he says that these 'talents were not very lucrative' and that Chardin found it difficult to earn a living? This could be one of the reasons for the numerous copies of small kitchen still lifes which may have been easy to sell. Did Cochin not write, after Chardin's death, that 'up until 1737, he had never attempted pictures of people' and did Haillet de Couronne not specify, on the basis of this remark, that 'until about 1737, he was happy to paint inanimate objects'? This piece of information needs further explanation, as it introduces one of the many questions raised by the dating of the paintings.

Cochin relates the famous anecdote concerning Aved and the different genres of painting: 'M. Aved, portrait painter, was a very good friend of his. He often sought M. Chardin's opinions about things, which he respected. However, one day, M. Chardin's views were a little harsh and M. Aved said to him crossly, "you think that this is as easy to paint as stuffed tongues and saveloys".[31] M. Chardin was extremely annoyed with this retort. However, he restrained himself, saying nothing at the time. But the very next day, he began a painting which included a figure, namely that of a servant drawing water from a cistern. The result was extremely satisfactory and there followed a number of very attractive pictures, the subjects of which were improved by a more sophisticated choice of characters. These included his paintings of a governess and of a woman amusing herself in various ways.'

Mariette relates an episode – earlier than Cochin, since his notes are dated 1749[32] – which must have taken place between 1732 and 1733: 'At this time [i.e., Aved's comments on his saveloys], he resolved to abandon his first talent, but chance seemed to offer it to him again. He had the opportunity to paint the head of a young man blowing soap bubbles, of which there is a print. He drew it carefully from life and gave the young man a naive look; it was well spoken of – art masters praised the efforts he had made to reach this point, and the envious, in their over-attentiveness to this new genre, determined to embrace it. Some time later he painted the two kitchens, which M. Cochin[33] engraved, for the Chevalier Antoine de la Roque.' These two 'kitchens' show 'a girl drawing water at a tap' and 'a young woman washing', known as *Woman Drawing Water from a Cistern* or *The Copper Cistern*, and *The Washerwoman* (pp. 30 and 31).[34] Admittedly, Cochin considered these to be upgraded kitchen scenes, as he says that Chardin did not attempt any pictures of people before 1737.

Maurice Quentin de La Tour, *Portrait de Chardin* (Portrait of Chardin), 1760.
Pastel on paper, 53 × 45 cm (20⅞ × 17¾ in.).
Louvre, Paris.

The White Tablecloth, also known as *The Saveloy, c.* 1732. Oil on canvas, 96 × 124 cm (37¾ × 48⅞ in.). The Art Institute of Chicago.

The Washerwoman, c. 1733–34. Oil on canvas, 37.5 × 42.5 cm (14⅞ × 16¾ in.). Nationalmuseum, Stockholm.

Woman Drawing Water from a Copper Cistern, 1733. Oil on canvas, 38 × 43 cm (15 × 16⅞ in.). Nationalmuseum, Stockholm.

Saying Grace,
1740.
Oil on canvas,
49.5 × 39.5 cm
(19½ × 15⅝ in.).
Louvre, Paris.

But he ignored – or did he forget, some forty-five years later? – that *Lady Sealing a Letter* (T.O.P. 79; see p. 196) is dated either 1732 or 1733 and that between this time and 1737, the year when the Salon was re-established, Chardin had certainly painted three other paintings with figures (*The Chemist* [T.O.P. 99] in 1734, *A Lady Taking Tea* [see p. 200] in 1735 and *The House of Cards* [T.O.P. 102; see p. 201] shown at the Académie in 1735), and probably some others, starting with *Soap Bubbles* (T.O.P. 97; see pp. 124 and 194) which Mariette describes as his first attempt at a portrait.[35]

The Chemist (see p. 119) is dated 4 December 1734, the subject being a portrait of the painter Aved. This precise date should be seen as a homage from Chardin to his friend, who was responsible for his move from still life to figure painting. Aved had been received into the Académie the previous week, on 28 November, at one of the few sessions attended by Chardin, presenting portraits of the painters Pierre Jacques Cazes and Jean François de Troy. Among the sixteen pictures which Chardin had exhibited shortly before in the Place Dauphine was *Lady Sealing a Letter*, with 'children's games', 'live and dead animals', 'music trophies' and 'subjects in the style of Teniers', *The Washerwoman* and *Woman Drawing Water from a Cistern* (see pp. 30 and 31).

In April 1735, Chardin's wife, Marguerite Saintard, died. Shortly before her death, he had painted the wonderful *Lady Taking Tea* (see p. 200) which, by common consent, is a portrait of the twenty-six-year-old Marguerite, who may have also been his model for *Lady Sealing a Letter* (see p. 196) in 1733. On the back of the canvas is an inscription, apparently in the artist's hand, saying 'this picture was painted in February 1735'. It is tempting, as with Aved's portrait, to deduce that it was added after the picture was completed, in order to give the painting special significance – here making a straightforward declaration that this was a final eulogy. *Lady Taking Tea* was exhibited at the Salon in 1739 but was not engraved until about 1749 while its pendant,[36] *The House of Cards* (T.O.P. 102; see p. 201), was exhibited and engraved in 1737. I would see in this time difference – which is exceptional for pairs of pictures by Chardin – further evidence of the emotional significance which the painter attached to this portrait, one that he did not want to see too soon in the public domain.

Was Chardin, who did not date any other pictures that year, looking for activity as a reaction to his bereavement? He attended a session of the Académie a fortnight after his wife's funeral and, in the following months, he attended eight more – thus proving much more conscientious than in previous years. It must be pointed out that, although these sessions took place twice a month, few members would attend, since only those with the grade of officer had voting rights. This is no doubt the reason why, in June, just prior to its upcoming election of officers,[37] Chardin submitted four small pictures to the Académie which met the requirement of having been 'completed during that year or the previous one'. These were 'ordinary women doing housework' and 'a young boy playing with cards' which may be *House of Cards* (T.O.P. 102).

Although his submission did not achieve its objective – on 2 July it was Nicolas Lancret and Charles Parrocel who were appointed council members, while Chardin had to wait a further eight years – it does serve as a precise benchmark in his career. It was not until 1737 that a new stage was reached, when Chardin found himself 'officially' in the limelight.

1. In the notice which he wrote for *Abecedario* in 1749, Pierre Jean Mariette calls him 'Chardin (Jean Baptiste Siméon)'. On the back of Maurice Quentin de La Tour's portrait of Chardin, in the Louvre, the words 'Jean Baptiste Siméon Chardin, born in Paris' (etc.) appear in Chardin's hand. At least seven engravings made after his paintings and during his lifetime are signed 'J. B. S. Chardin' or 'J. B. Siméon Chardin'. This point intrigued historians and, in his catalogue of the 1979 exhibition, Pierre Rosenberg printed a notary's deed dated 4 March 1780, i.e., a few months after the painter's death, stating that 'it was in error and inadvertently if, in some titles and documents and particularly in his death certificate, he was called by his baptismal name, Jean Baptiste Siméon, Jean Bpte Simon, or other, instead of Jean Siméon'. The purpose of this deed was clearly to give Chardin's widow access to various pensions which may have been set up in the name of Jean Baptiste Siméon. This little mystery has a simple solution: the child's parents probably chose John the Baptist rather than John the Evangelist as his patron saint and celebrated his name day in June, not December.

2. Charles Nicolas Cochin the Younger (1715–90), famous illustrator and engraver, Secretary of the Académie in charge of the Arts, and Adviser from 1755 to 1770 to the Marquis de Marigny, who then held the post of Directeur des Bâtiments du Roi. All references in this regard are to C. Michel's *Charles Nicolas Cochin et l'art des Lumières*, École Française de Rome, 1993. In particular, Cochin was the author of *Essai sur la vie de M. Chardin*, a manuscript written in 1780 and kept at the Académie de Rouen, published by C. de Beaurepaire in *Précis Analytique des Travaux de l'Académie de Rouen*, vol. LXXVIII, 1875–76, pp. 417–41.

3. E. F. Gersaint, *Abrégé de la vie d'Antoine Watteau*, 1744.

4. This distinction was important in the eighteenth century and it was the subject of much theoretical debate and many dictionary definitions. Claude Henri Watelet defined nature, among other meanings, as 'that which is the opposite to what is called practical, i.e., what is done without a model and only out of habit'. (C. H. Watelet and P. H. Lévêque, *Encyclopédie méthodique*, Paris, vol. 3, 1791, entry on 'Nature'.)

5. In recounting this gap, Cochin notes, however, that although education is necessary for the artist, it has the effect of delaying study of the arts. This debate – which was partly the reason for the creation of the École des Élèves protégés in the 1750s to provide a better 'intellectual' education for young artists and to teach them history, mythology, the major works of literature and poetry, and about the recognized masterpieces of sculpture and painting – preoccupied academic teaching in the eighteenth century, resulting, after decades and successive directors, in various decisions about the cultural and practical training for young artists.

6. The date is not known, but it was certainly before 1720, as in April 1720, Noël Nicolas Coypel was a witness at the marriage of one of Chardin's sisters. It was probably the young artist who approached him.

7. Actually more of a wooden awning which Gersaint described as 'a ceiling [to] display outside'.

8. 'Notice historique…' *Journal de littérature, des sciences et des arts*, 1780.

9. Chardin also painted an oil sketch which he kept until his death and which was burnt at the Hôtel de Ville in 1871. As to the signboard itself, which was quite large (70 x 450 cm [27½ x 177 in.]), it did not remain long at the surgeon's. It belonged to Jean Philippe Le Bas, the engraver, and was described thus at his home in 1759: 'One sees people in a brawl, fighting with swords, a young man who has been injured and to whom the surgeon is applying a dressing and a priest attending to him in death. The police superintendent, the watchman, the crowd, and people at windows. So much activity makes this picture very animated. The mood differs throughout. The colour tone is good.' (*La Feuille nécessaire*.) This signboard was purchased at the Le Bas sale in 1783 by the sculptor Juste Sébastien Chardin, a nephew of the painter, after which all trace of it is lost and we only know of its composition thanks to an etching made after the sketch by Jules de Goncourt. If this sign is more or less contemporary with the *Gersaint Signboard* – which Chardin would have known – it is with Watteau's earlier drawings, such as *The Fabric Merchant's Shop* and, in particular, *The Barber's Shop* (Louvre, Department of Graphic Arts) that comparisons about composition should be made.

10. It is impossible to compare it in style or colouring with the surgeon's signboard, which we is lost. However, the preparatory drawings for *Servant Filling a Player's Glass* (T.O.P. 2a) and for *Man Wearing a Tricorne* seated on the right hand side, are not so stylistically different from *La Vinaigrette*, on the back of which a fragment of a male nude, similar to one of Cazes's nudes, gives us some chronological information. This drawing, like that of the servant pouring a drink, was purchased, more than likely directly from the artist, by Carl Gustaf Tessin, when he was in Paris during the 1740s. Count Tessin, who was Ambassador Extraordinary from the Court of Sweden in Paris from 1739 to 1742, only bought three drawings from Chardin, though he commissioned pictures both for himself and for the future queen, Louisa Ulrica. He may have considered Chardin to be a poor draughtsman and, also, there may not have been any others available in the studio (either because, as is most likely, Chardin had stopped drawing completely, or because he continued to use the few drawings which he had made several years previously).

11. D. Diderot, *Salon de 1765*, ed. Seznec and Adhémar, vol. II, 1960.

12. Reproduced by P. Rosenberg and I. Julia, 'Drawings by Pierre Jean Cazes', *Master Drawings*, vol. 23–24, no. 3, 1985–86.

13. See Oudry's lecture entitled *Discours sur la pratique de la peinture* given to the Académie in 1752 and published in *Cabinet de l'amateur* (1861–62, pp. 107–17), in which he discusses Largillierre's theories.

14. A survivor of the former guilds, the Académie de Saint-Luc trained artisans in all disciplines relating to the arts. This included cabinet-makers and gilders, as well as painters and sculptors, who went on to become masters. In permanent conflict with the Académie Royale which was established in 1648, the Académie de Saint-Luc was dissolved in 1776.

15. Was it at this time that he joined the team brought together by Jean Baptiste Van Loo to restore the frescoes of one of the galleries at Fontainebleau? Cochin logically places this episode in Chardin's early youth, while he was still a pupil at the Académie. Pierre Rosenberg dates it in the 1730s, which is hard to imagine as Chardin was by then a member of the Académie. This information is based on the knowledge which we have of a campaign to restore the François I gallery under the direction of J. B. Van Loo in 1733 (see *Les Gabriel* catalogue, Paris 1982, pp. 47–48). Cochin, writing his *Essai sur la vie de M. Chardin* in 1780, may have confused this with earlier restoration work at Fontainebleau in 1723–24 and 1727, dates which would be more logical for work done to earn a living, and for which Chardin would have been well paid on satisfying Van Loo, who became one of his earliest collectors.

16. The problem with Chardin's *singeries*, as with most of his compositions, is that he painted several versions (T.O.P. 23, 24, 93 and 94), most likely at different times in his life. Two of these were exhibited at the Salon in 1740, engraved by Pierre Louis Surugue in 1743 and accompanied by text explaining their significance. On the monkey painter's portfolio, there appears the date 1726. The versions in the Musée de Chartres, which are much smaller and which are by far the finest, came later.

17. These open-air exhibitions were organized, weather permitting, on Corpus Christi. Individuals were able to display their work there in an effort to become known.

18. T. E. Crow, *Painters and Public Life in Eighteenth-Century Paris*, Yale, 1985.

19. A propos the parallel which is generally drawn between the reception of Watteau and Chardin into the Académie, Christian Michel suggests that the anecdote relating to Watteau draws more from hagiography than biography. The first of his biographers to do this was Gersaint in 1744, i.e., *after* Chardin's reception, as related to us. On the other hand, neither Orlandi in 1719 nor La Roque, a close friend of Watteau's, in 1721, nor Jean de Jullienne, friend, collector and legatee of the painter, in 1726, mentions the episode. It is thus possible that Gersaint wanted to create a legend inspired by Chardin's reception

20. 'Éloge historique de M. Chardin', *Le Nécrologe des hommes illustres*, XV, 1780.

21. *Éloge de M. Chardin* read to the Académie de Rouen in 1780. Published in *Mémoires inédits sur la vie et les ouvrages…*, 1854, Part II, pp. 428–41.

22. In his *Réflexions sur la manière d'étudier les couleurs*, Oudry makes a long reference to the admiration of his master, Largillierre, for the Flemish school, particularly because of the training which favoured the study of nature and colour.

23. Watteau, accepted in 1712, was received in 1717 with his *Pilgrimage to the Island of Cythera* (Paris, Louvre).

24. At the same session the following were received: Dumont le Romain, history painter, with *Hercules*

and Omphale (Musée des Beaux-Arts, Tours); and Bonaventure de Bar with his *Country Fair* (Paris, Louvre; see p. 20) who was accepted and received at the same time as a 'painter with particular talent for figures like David Teniers and Philips Wouwermans', in effect an emulator of Watteau, painter of *fêtes galantes*. Among the members of the Académie present at the session, in addition to the 'grands anciens' such as Louis de Boullogne, Largillierre, Corneille van Clève, Guillaume Coustou, Noël Nicolas Coypel (who had employed Chardin), and Charles Antoine Coypel, there were also the young stars of painting, such as François Lemoyne, Jean François de Troy and some other participants from the competition organized the previous year by the Direction des Bâtiments (P. Rosenberg, 'Le Concours de 1727', *Revue de l'Art*, no. 37, 1977), as well as some still life painters such as Bouys, Delyen and Huilliot.

25. Cabinet des estampes, *Pièces de l'Académie*, Ya³ 55.

26. Among the paintings dated 1728, one version of *Cat with Salmon, Two Mackerel, Mortar and Pestle* (T.O.P. 29; see p. 26) and *Two Dead Rabbits with Game-bag, Powder Flask and Orange*, in the Staatliche Kunsthalle, Karlsruhe (T.O.P. 35; see p. 23), may have been among the pictures submitted by Chardin to the Académie. Note that these works, while not as large as *The Buffet* (194 x 129 cm [76⅜ x 50¾ in.]) are quite big (80 x 63 cm [31½ x 24¾ in.] and 93 x 74 cm [36⅝ x 29⅛ in.]), especially considering the small pictures painted in the previous years. This is a relatively consistent set of canvases whose style may be compared to those which are dated or which may be dated 1728: *Partridge with Fruit*, also in Karlsruhe (see p. 120), the lovely *Cat, Partridge, Dead Hare and Silver Tureen* (see p. 64) in the Metropolitan Museum, New York, and *Dead Hare with Gun, Game-bag and Powder Flask* (see p. 151) in the Musée de la Chasse, Paris, which measure about 75 x 95 cm (or 95 x 75 cm [29½ x 37⅜ in. or 37 ⅜ x 29 ½ in]).

27. Also dated 1730 is an ugly genre scene which is difficult to attribute to Chardin, given how awkward and even vulgar it is and how impossible it seems for it to precede *Woman Drawing Water from a Copper Cistern* in Stockholm by only three years. It is difficult to believe that Chardin could have painted this village scene (T.O.P. 50) in 1730, followed a few months later by masterpieces such as *The Meat-day Menu* and *The Fish-day Menu* (T.O.P. 54 and 55) and, particularly, his *Attributes of Science* and *Attributes of the Arts* (T.O.P. 56 and 57).

28. The caterer's account is published in F. Courboin's *L'Estampe française*, 1914.

29. He exhibited a reduced version the following year (T.O.P. 58) in the Place Dauphine, at the same time as the Rothenbourg overdoor; the bas-relief is mentioned in *Mercure de France* as being the work 'which brought most honour' to Chardin. 'The brush of the skilled painter was able to imitate [the bas-relief] so well that to the naked eye, however near one gets, one is deceived right up to the point that one absolutely has to put one's hand on the canvas and touch the picture in order to be disillusioned.' This criterion used to judge the success of a *trompe-l'oeil* comes up frequently in the writings of critics about various painters. With this bas-relief, Chardin seems to have wanted to enlarge his repertoire and prove that he could do as well as Desportes in this area. Jean Baptiste Van Loo, having seen the picture in the Place Dauphine, bought it from Chardin, paying the artist more than the asking price. It is difficult to believe, in these circumstances, that he would have employed him at a *later* date to restore the frescoes at Fontainebleau.

30. About 1730, there were no fewer than four versions of *Still Life with Loin of Lamb* (T.O.P. 52) or *with Ray* (T.O.P. 53). Around 1732, Chardin arranged a cabbage, hanging herrings and eggs in a vertical format (T.O.P. 65); a little later, he put various vegetables, a cauldron and a jug on a stone table, a composition which he was to repeat at least four times (T.O.P. 72); or again a cloth, a terrine and hanging meat (T.O.P. 73), with fish making up the second of a pair (T.O.P. 74), one version being dated 1734. Other paintings show an earthenware pot and eggs (T.O.P. 75) or a jug, cucumbers and fish (T.O.P. 83).

31. The reference is to *The White Tablecloth* (T.O.P. 78), which is now in the Art Institute of Chicago.

32. *Abecedario*, vol. I, pp. 357–58.

33. Charles Nicolas Cochin the Elder (1688–1754), father of Chardin's biographer and engraver of some of his compositions.

34. These panels, of which Chardin made at least two copies of each, are today in the Nationalmuseum, Stockholm, having been purchased by Tessin for the Court of Sweden at the La Roque sale in 1745. The first is dated 1733. They were probably exhibited in the Place Dauphine in 1734, where their spirit 'in the style of Teniers' was praised, and at the Académie the following year.

35. None of the three known versions of this subject, of the four which Chardin must have painted, is dated.

However, if we are to believe Mariette, the first was made in 1732 or 1733, which, stylistically, is quite plausible. In addition, it seems that the model of the young man is identical to that of the servant in *Lady Sealing a Letter*. Finally, P. Conisbee (*Soap Bubbles by Jean-Siméon Chardin*, 'Masterpiece in Focus', Los Angeles County Museum of Art, 1990), comparing the treatment of these canvases with that of *Still Life with Dead Game* (Dublin, National Gallery of Ireland), showed that the three known versions of *Soap Bubbles* must have been painted over a relatively short period, one or two years at the most.

36. See D. Carritt, 'Mr Fauquier's Chardins', *Burlington Magazine*, September 1974.

37. Grades were extremely important for members of the Académie and if Chardin, due to the genre – still life – for which he was received, could not hope to become a rector, director or teacher, he could, however, become a council member, the top officer grade, a title which conferred true academic status.

L'Enseigne d'un chirurgien
(The surgeon's signboard). Engraving by Jules de Goncourt after a lost painting by Chardin.

CHAPTER TWO

BECOMING FAMOUS

*Every exhibition of paintings
at the Salons held in the Louvre
was marked by new praise from the
public for M. Chardin's work.*

Mariette

On 18 August 1737, an exhibition of paintings, sculpture and engravings by Members of the Académie Royale opened in the Salon Carré of the Louvre, which gave its name to the exhibition. The Académie held its first public exhibition in 1667. Other Salons were to follow at irregular intervals and in various locations.[1] In 1699 and 1704, the exhibition was held at the Grande Galerie of the Louvre, accompanied by a catalogue listing the paintings and sculptures on display. In 1725, it took place in the Salon Carré. For financial reasons, it was only in 1737 that members of the Académie and those who had been accepted were once again able to show their work to the public on a regular basis.

The key role of the Salons in the eighteenth century has often been described.[2] Firstly, it was the only means which artists had to show their most recent work, and arrange its purchase by collectors, a prospect which was especially important in a time when official commissions were both rare and poorly paid. Restricted to members of the Académie, these exhibitions established a clear distinction between the artisans or master painters and sculptors of the Académie de Saint-Luc and those artists officially chosen by an elite body keen to exercize its prerogatives. This explains the many efforts made to organize exhibitions by the Académie de Saint-Luc in the years from 1751 to 1774, and, later, the organization of Salons such as that held in the Colisée in 1776, or the so-called Salon de la Correspondance in 1779 and 1787. Ultimately, the success of the Salons resulted in the emergence of a keen and controversial body of criticism, which was feared by the artists and greatly appreciated by amateurs, and whose most famous but not sole representative from 1759 was Diderot.[3]

The Salons were accompanied by a *livret*, a type of small catalogue produced by the Secretary of the Académie, entitled *Explication des peintures, sculptures et autres ouvrages de Messieurs de l'Académie royale* and published by Collombat. In 1737, 1738 and 1739, it was edited in a more or less topographical way, i.e., the works exhibited were listed wall by wall and pier by pier, giving details of the subject and the artist, as well as his academic grade (see table p. 40). In 1738, each canvas was given a number. From 1740 until the Revolution, the numbering was done by artist and according to the Académie's hierarchy: first came the works of professors, followed by those of the deputies and council members, then ordinary members who were listed by date of their reception and, last, members who had only been accepted. This layout, which had the advantage of clarity, prevents us from imagining how the pictures might have been hung. Hanging the exhibitions was the responsibility of a member of the Académie, who was known as the *tapissier* – François Albert Stiémart was the Académie's *tapissier* from 1737 to 1746 and Jacques André Portail assumed the role until 1755, when he was replaced by Chardin.

Page 36:
The Governess (detail).
National Gallery of Canada, Ottawa.

Children Playing with a Goat,
c. 1731. Oil on canvas,
23.5 × 40 cm (9¼ × 15¾ in.).
Private collection, Paris.

The catalogue is also useful for giving approximate dates for the works exhibited in a particular year, since members of the Académie were all keen to exhibit their latest work.[4] It also enables us to assess the importance of the buyers, as the artists prided themselves on exhibiting a painting or sculpture which already belonged to a famous *amateur* or, better still, which had been commissioned by the King or his Direction des Bâtiments.

At the Salon of 1737, Chardin exhibited eight paintings, including only one still life, a *Bronze Painted Bas-relief*, which is surprising since this genre was his official speciality. Did he decide to present himself as a painter of people and genre subjects for the reopening of the Salon?[5] In the still life category, he did not exhibit any paintings of animals or kitchens, but confined himself to this bas-relief. Perhaps this was the same one which, five years earlier, 'had brought him the highest honour' in Place Dauphine, and which had been purchased by Jean Baptiste Van Loo. At the same Salon, Desportes, then a council member of the Académie and something of a specialist in such *trompe-l'oeil* bas-reliefs,[6] exhibited a 'bas-relief in marble', two 'bronze painted bas-reliefs' and another on lapis lazuli with various vases, fruit and flowers. Was Chardin hoping to prove that his work was comparable to that of an acknowledged master of still life? This was probably the case, but at the same time he also wanted to show the public, as he had Aved, that he was capable of other things. What appears to have been an effort to move away from still life is all the more striking at this particular Salon at which other famous artists, such as Desportes and Oudry, were exhibiting paintings of this genre. The catalogue enables us to imagine the arrangement by Stiémart (see table p. 40), who tried 'to hang paintings by the same artist together' and to make stylish groupings.

Although criticism of the Salon had not yet found its voice, the report in *Mercure de France* lists the works exhibited by Chardin, noting that 'leading spectators and people of great distinction… were even more surprised as they

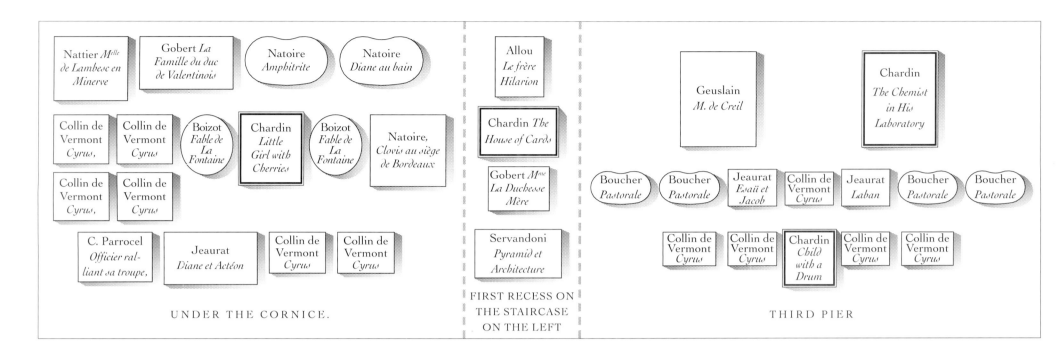

| UNDER THE CORNICE. | FIRST RECESS ON THE STAIRCASE ON THE LEFT | THIRD PIER |

Nattier *Melle de Lambesc en Minerve* — Gobert *La Famille du duc de Valentinois* — Natoire *Amphitrite* — Natoire *Diane au bain*

Collin de Vermont *Cyrus,* — Collin de Vermont *Cyrus* — Boizot *Fable de La Fontaine* — Chardin *Little Girl with Cherries* — Boizot *Fable de La Fontaine* — Natoire, *Clovis au siège de Bordeaux*

Collin de Vermont *Cyrus,* — Collin de Vermont *Cyrus*

C. Parrocel *Officier ralliant sa troupe,* — Jeaurat *Diane et Actéon* — Collin de Vermont *Cyrus* — Collin de Vermont *Cyrus*

Allou *Le frère Hilarion*

Chardin *The House of Cards*

Gobert *Mme La Duchesse Mère*

Servandoni *Pyramid et Architecture*

Geuslain *M. de Creil* — Chardin *The Chemist in His Laboratory*

Boucher *Pastorale* — Boucher *Pastorale* — Jeaurat *Esaü et Jacob* — Collin de Vermont *Cyrus* — Jeaurat *Laban* — Boucher *Pastorale* — Boucher *Pastorale*

Collin de Vermont *Cyrus* — Collin de Vermont *Cyrus* — Chardin *Child with a Drum* — Collin de Vermont *Cyrus* — Collin de Vermont *Cyrus*

Salon of 1737.
Partial reconstruction of how the paintings were hung on the 'large wall on the courtyard side' of the Salon Carré.

knew that M. Chardin excelled in painting dead and living animals in a manner both accurate and unique, but no one knew that his talent stretched so far… and the figures seen on this occasion… were greatly praised by the most critical connoisseurs'. This official recognition of his new talents clearly showed Chardin that he had chosen the right track, which he then pursued. He did not abandon still life completely, but during the fifteen years which followed, he exhibited only portraits and genre scenes at the Salon – though he might show the same work twice, or in the form of replicas.

As well as the risks which this change meant both to him and to the public, was there perhaps an economic factor involved – portraits and moral scenes being worth more than still lifes? Did Chardin think that these subjects, which were easier to engrave, would both hasten the establishment of his reputation through the circulation of engravings, and bring in additional income?

In November 1737, a few months after the Salon closed, Chardin was appointed guardian to his son, Jean Pierre, while his brother-in-law, Claude Saintard, became surrogate guardian. Three days later, an inventory of the goods of Marguerite Saintard was drawn up by Aved and the bailiff Grignard, in the house where she died and where Chardin continued to live, at the corner of the Rue Princesse and the Rue du Four. This two-year delay is possibly explained by the death of his daughter – in about 1737 – and by the prospect of remarrying, which would have encouraged Chardin to legalize the situation. It is also possible that he wanted to indicate that his financial situation was not very healthy, with regard to the Saintard family and the future coming of age of his son.

The personal property listed in the inventory is quite typical; in it, Pierre Rosenberg has identified some items as being those which are present in Chardin's paintings, namely: a copper cistern, a small red wooden table, two corner cupboards, a games table covered with green cloth, Turkish carpets and Aubusson tapestries, a pair of candle holders, a 'clock with an enamelled copper dial in a marquetry case', a rosewood smoker's box, a backgammon set complete with ivory pieces, etc.[7] More professional items include: 'frames and

Petite Fille aux cerises (Little Girl with Cherries) and *Le Jeune Soldat* (The Little Soldier), 1738. Engravings by Charles Nicolas Cochin after Chardin.

other utensils for the art of painting, …a box of colours, a palette and brushes', as well as two easels. Apart from a small sketch of a battle scene by Watteau, and three kitchen scenes by Chardin (valued at 30 *livres* for the three, like the Watteau), the paintings were anonymous works and copies after Joseph Christophe and Desportes. More surprising is the mention of two pictures 'of animals and fruit which are two copies after originals by the said M. Chardin', framed and valued at 30 *livres*. This suggests that in addition to making replicas himself, Chardin tolerated the fact that other people copied his work – unless these copies were in fact by him.[8]

Further proof of the success of the new subjects painted by Chardin was the publication in 1738 of the first engravings which he inspired: *Lady Sealing a Letter* announced in May and, in July, *The Little Soldier* and *Little Girl with Cherries* (T.O.P. 90, 91), a pair which he had exhibited the previous year. It became customary to make engravings of pictures exhibited at the Salon within the following year. In the case of *Lady Sealing a Letter*, however, Chardin exhibited the picture at the August 1738 Salon five years after it had been painted and a few months *after* it had been engraved by Étienne Fessard.[9] He exhibited eight other canvases at this Salon, which were all genre subjects or portraits.[10]

He continued with this repertoire, also dating 1738 two versions of *Girl Returning from the Market* (T.O.P. 115), *Woman Peeling Vegetables* (T.O.P. 116) and *The Governess* (T.O.P. 117), all works which he exhibited at the Salon the following year (see pp. 212, 42 and 43). Although *Woman Peeling Vegetables* deals with the same subject matter as *The Scullery Maid*, with *Girl Returning from the Market* and especially *The Governess*, whose engraving was announced in December 1740, Chardin marked a new stage in his portrayal of scenes from domestic life. The Chevalier de Neufville de Brunhaubois Montador wrote that *Cook Returning from the Butcher's and the Baker's* (*Girl Returning from the*

Woman Peeling Vegetables, 1738. Oil on canvas, 46.2 × 37.5 cm (18⅛ × 14⅞ in.). National Gallery of Art, Samuel H. Kress Collection, Washington.

The Governess, 1738.
Oil on canvas,
46 × 37.5 cm
(18⅛ × 14⅞ in.).
National Gallery
of Canada, Ottawa.

Market; see p. 212) 'is certainly the most accurate character' which he knew and that it was she who 'seems to have taken preference this year'.[11] He added that '*The Governess* who is making a little boy recite his lessons, while she brushes his hat before sending him to class, is also astonishingly natural and painted in the same style, i.e. in a rather sketchy way (the previous year, he said 'crude and rough'), which nevertheless results in marvellous compositions'. *Mercure de France* went further, saying that 'The young schoolboy scolded by his governess for having muddied his hat is the piece which has been most praised'. Three months later, when *Mercure de France* announced the sale of the engraving by François Bernard Lépicié, it again described the 'very simple' subject: 'It is of a woman sitting, properly attired, holding in one hand the dusty hat of a young schoolboy who is standing in front of her, and in the other a brush. The kindness, gentleness and restraint of the governess in correcting the young boy for his grubbiness, his untidiness and carelessness, and the young boy's attention, his shame and even his remorse are expressed with great naivety.' The success of this small scene led Chardin to develop further subjects of a similar nature in the years which followed: the equivalent of *The Governess*, with a little girl instead of a small boy, are *The Diligent Mother* (T.O.P. 118), and *The Morning Toilet* (T.O.P. 121), as well as, of course, *Saying Grace* (T.O.P. 119; see pp. 218, 47 and 32).

In September 1739, Chardin also exhibited at the Salon his *Lady Taking Tea* and *The Frivolous Amusement of a Young Man Blowing Soap Bubbles*, as well as *The House of Cards*. As in 1737, the catalogue suggests how paintings were placed in the Salon Carré. Thus, it appears that the six Chardins were all hung 'below the cornice on the quay side', in the second and third rows down, under major works by Charles Joseph Natoire, Oudry and Carle Van Loo. Again, it was a number of paintings by Oudry which served to punctuate the hanging, around which genre scenes by different artists were hung in pairs, such as *Lady Taking Tea* and *Soap Bubbles*, or flanking a larger picture, as with Étienne Jeaurat's *Young Boy Throwing Water out of a Window with a Syringe* and *Young Boy Throwing Cherry Stones out of a Window*, Christophe's *Children Playing on the Grass*, and Lancret's *Children Adorning Sheep with Garlands*.

Thus in choosing to show children and adolescents in their everyday occupations, Chardin was not painting anything exceptional. However, he did not give in to frivolous story-telling, but gave his models a gravity and a level of absorption which was not offered by Lancret or Jeaurat. That is what is exceptional about his painting and what caused him to be so admired, both in France and abroad. Mariette, remarking that 'foreigners have sought again with possibly even more zeal' Chardin's pictures, added that 'what has really made his reputation is the picture of the governess, which he thought he had painted for M. de Jullienne, who appeared to want it, but which was acquired by a banker by the name of Despeuchs and was sold for 1,800 *livres* to the Prince of Liechtenstein during his time as Ambassador to France.'

In 1740, Tessin, whose portrait by Aved was exhibited at the Salon, bought *The Dead Rabbit* (see p. 168) and commissioned *The Morning Toilet*. So it is hardly surprising that Chardin, who was very busy elsewhere, exhibited only five paintings at the Salon that year. Among these were *The Diligent Mother* and *Saying Grace*, in the same vein as the much appreciated *The Governess*.[12]

These two paintings were presented by Chardin to Louis XV in November 1740. The following month, *Mercure de France* published some verse addressed to Chardin by a professor at the Collège du Plessis 'about two pictures which he had painted for the King':

> D'une mère laborieuse
> Quel pinceau délicat pourrait comme le tien
> Tracer l'air imposant et l'austère maintien?
> ...C'est à peindre cet âge, orné de l'innocence,
> Que tu fais éclater tes plus vives beautés,
> Chardin, c'est à l'aimable enfance
> Que tu dois de ton art les traits les plus vantés.
> Près d'une sage gouvernante
> Ici la toile me présente
> Deux enfants, dont l'air seul annonce la candeur.
> Le dîner les attend; mais il faut au Seigneur
> Un petit mot préliminaire...
> Le connaisseur que ton ouvrage attire
> Sourit à ces enfants et, se laissant charmer,
> Sent encore bien plus qu'il ne peut exprimer.

(Of a diligent mother / What delicate touch could, like yours, / Trace the imposing look and austere bearing? / ...It is in painting this age, adorned with innocence, / That you make your most vivid beauties sparkle; / Chardin, it is to lovable childhood / That you owe the most vaunted features of your art. / Close to a wise governess / The canvas here presents to me / Two children, whose air alone proclaims sincerity. / Dinner awaits them; but the Lord is due / A small preliminary word... / The connoisseur whom your work attracts / Smiles at these children and, letting himself be charmed, / Feels far more than he can express.)

This recognition of Chardin's talent for painting children prompted Tessin to order one of these paintings from him. This was *The Morning Toilet* (see p. 47), which represented a new approach to the affectionate relationship of authority and harmless disobedience woven between a mother and her child. A very young woman adjusts her daughter's bonnet, before setting off to Mass; the child, who must be about six or seven years old, is looking in the mirror of the dressing table opposite her. In the foreground, on a stool, lie the mother's missal and muff. 'Nothing is simpler', as *Mercure de France* wrote, 'or more beautifully captured.... What is even more touching is the sense of the child's heart which this skilled painter has found a way of expressing in the look which the little girl gives in a mirror...' The anonymous author of a *Letter to M. de Poiresson Chamarande* which was published on the occasion of the Salon of 1741 praised this *Mother Adjusting her Small Daughter's Bonnet*, and remarked that Chardin always portrayed the middle classes and that he did this successfully. 'There is no woman from the third estate who does not recognize her face, the pattern of her domestic life, her round manners, her bearing, her daily occupations, her morale, the mood of her children, her furniture, her dress.'

Jacques André Joseph Aved, *Portrait de Tessin* (Portrait of Tessin), 1740. Oil on canvas, 149 × 116 cm (58⅝ × 45⅝ in.). Nationalmuseum, Stockholm.

45

The Abbé Desfontaines added more about the success of the picture and used the opportunity to praise Count Tessin 'who has exerted his exquisite taste and magnificent opulence for many years now and who has justly rewarded the talents of our top artists'.[13] And in December, *Mercure de France*, announcing the engraving of *The Morning Toilet* by Le Bas, used the opportunity to publish more verse addressed to Chardin by Charles Étienne Pesselier, the author of the engraving's legend; the verse rhymes the words verity, ability, naivety, simplicity and beauty, and finishes as follows:

Tu reçois du public un encens mérité,
Et, ce qui doit encore animer ton courage,
Tessin, dont le seul nom peut munir un ouvrage
Du sceau de l'immortalité
De ton heureux talent reconnaît la beauté.

(You receive from the public deserved acclaim, / And, what should raise your spirits even more, / Tessin, whose very name can give a work / The seal of immortality, / Acknowledges the beauty of your happy talent.)

The artist and his customer, Tessin, were thus united in a common eulogy. In January 1742, Tessin wrote to his wife Ulla, who had already left Paris: 'What madness of mine to include the other (verse) taken from *Mercure* last month, which Pesselier, the author of the charming comedy *Aesop on Parnassus*, composed about my Chardin painting…. And why do I blush about my Love for the Arts?'[14]

If *The Morning Toilet* received so much praise when it first appeared, this was certainly due to its complete success and to the reputation of the connoisseur who owned it; however, it was also because Chardin exhibited only two works at the Salon of 1741 – this one and *The Son of M. Le Noir Making a House of Cards* (see p. 202), which was probably a pendant for *The Schoolmistress* which he had exhibited the previous year. Jean Jacques Lenoir, a cabinet-maker and furniture dealer, seems to have been very close to Chardin, as he was a witness at his second marriage. Also, in 1743 the painter exhibited a *Portrait of Madame Le Noir Holding a Book* (see p. 206), which is known through its engraving, called *The Moment of Meditation* (T.O.P. 106a).

Then, except for copies of *Saying Grace* in 1744 and *The Diligent Mother*, Chardin ceased painting scenes of a woman with children and began to paint children or adolescents playing, before eventually coming back to small pictures depicting a woman alone at home. These were no longer paintings of humble figures such as a scullery maid, a vegetable peeler or a cook, but portraits of middle-class women going about their everyday business.

Chardin did not participate in the Salon of 1742, most likely for health reasons. From the minutes of the Académie meetings, it is clear that he was ill in January 1742. As was the practice, two members of the Académie, Charles Nicolas Cochin the Elder and Pierre Louis Surugue, were appointed to visit him. Chardin only returned to the Académie in June, to express his gratitude.

At the Salon of 1743, Chardin, submitted three paintings: *Portrait of Madame Le *** Holding a Book* and two pendants, *Game of Goose* and *Card Games*

The Morning Toilet, also
called *Le Négligé*, c. 1741.
Oil on canvas, 49 × 39 cm
(19¼ × 15⅝ in.).
Nationalmuseum,
Stockholm.

Le Jeu de l'oye (Game of Goose), 1745. Engraving by Pierre Louis Surugue after Chardin.

Les Tours de cartes (Card Games), 1745. Engraving by Pierre Louis Surugue after Chardin.

Le Bénédicité (Saying Grace), 1744. Engraving by François Bernard Lépicié after Chardin.

(see pp. 48 and 54), all three of which are known to us through their engravings, and *Card Games* through a worn and repainted version which is now in Dublin (T.O.P. 95).[15] A short time after the closure of the Salon, on 28 September, Chardin was appointed a Council Member of the Académie. Because of his speciality – still life and genre scenes – he could not achieve a higher grade, as priority was given to history painters and then portrait painters. This appointment did, however, enable him to participate more actively in the life of the Académie and to fulfil roles to which non-officer members had no access.

Chardin's mother died in November 1743. The inventory of her belongings was drawn up and, although it was some time before the inheritance was paid out, it did mean that he was able to rely on some financial support. This situation, in addition to his new title of Council Member, must have helped him take his decision in September 1744 to marry a thirty-seven-year-old widow, Françoise Marguerite Pouget (see p. 53), whose dowry included a house located at 13 Rue Princesse (he himself lived at 1 Rue Princesse), 2,000 *livres* in cash, personal property and silver, as well as various substantial funds. For his part, Chardin contributed 5,000 *livres* to the estate, as well as the goods listed in the inventory after Marguerite Saintard's death, and 4,000 *livres* which he had received in July from his mother's legacy. The contract, drawn up on 1 November, was signed by Chardin's two brothers, Juste and Noël Sébastien, as well as by the Lenoir couple. The marriage was celebrated at Saint-Sulpice on 26 November. The bride's witnesses were a relative, the banker Jean Daché, and Jean Jacques Lenoir, described as a merchant and burgher of Paris; the bridegroom's witnesses were his brother, Juste Chardin, cabinetmaker to the king, and Aved. In the same way that Chardin twice used his first wife as a model, he portrayed his second wife in some of his interior scenes, and notably in 1775 and 1776 painted her portrait in pastel (see p. 229), leaving us a fairly good idea of the appearance of this woman who seems to have actively participated in her husband's career.

The sale of the Chevalier Antoine La Roque's collections was held in May 1745. La Roque owned at least ten paintings by Chardin. Gersaint, who organized the sale, wrote to Tessin in June to tell him of the most important works which he had acquired for him – Flemish and Dutch paintings as well as two small and two large Chardins.[16] These were *The Embroiderer* and the young *Draughtsman*, *The Cistern* and *The Washerwoman*, bought by Tessin on behalf of Adolph Frederick of Sweden (see pp. 50, 51, 30 and 31). Consequently, Louisa Ulrica, who married Adolph Frederick in 1744, and who shared the liking of her brother, Frederick the Great, for contemporary French painting, in turn wanted to acquire work by Chardin. In October, Tessin wrote to Carl Frederik Scheffer, who had replaced him as ambassador of the Court of Sweden in Paris, that Louisa Ulrica 'would like to have two paintings by Chardin, the same size as the one he did for me (*The Morning Toilet*) which cost 600 francs. He may choose the subjects, but as he succeeded so well with governesses and children, the subjects of *Éducation douce* and *Éducation sévère* are proposed.[17] Their cost price, with frames, would come to 3,400 *livres*.' But in October, Charles Reinhold Berch, Secretary to the Ambassador of Sweden in Paris, wrote to Tessin that Chardin could not deliver the two pictures for a year. 'His slowness and the effort which he has to make are known to Your Excellency. The price of 25 *louis d'or* per picture is modest for him, as he has the misfortune of working so slowly', he wrote. A month later, Tessin wrote to Scheffer: 'Who says Princess, says impatient. She is asking me at every opportunity if I have not had a reply', and again in April 1746: 'You do not speak to me of Chardin – would you be so kind as to press him? I know his slowness and if one does not speak to him, he would do nothing. There are two pictures required, namely *Éducation douce* and *Éducation sévère*'. In June, Scheffer tried to justify the delays by 'François Boucher's libertinism which has to be witnessed to be believed,[18] and the slowness of Chardin from whose mouth the words must be heard, so as not to believe them to be an exaggeration'. Tessin replied that he had asked 'Her Highness if She would like the replicas which have been proposed, but she would rather wait and have original and unique pieces'. He continued, however, to press Chardin and Boucher, as the gallery which had been built to house the paintings at Drottningholm was ready.

The Salon opened on 25 August, the feast of Saint Louis and the King's feast day. Chardin exhibited a 'copy of *Saying Grace* with an addition' to make a pair with a Teniers, in the collection of M*** – presumably the version dated 1744, which, compared with the two versions in the Louvre, includes an addition in the form of a saucepan placed on the ground near a stove; 'another *Amusements of Private Life*, as well as a *Portrait of M.* *** *Wearing a Muff* and a *Portrait of M. Levret of the Académie royale de chirurgie*'.[19]

The Amusements of Private Life 'was admired by all connoisseurs at the exhibition in the Louvre', Scheffer wrote to Tessin in October 1746, for this was the first of the two pictures which Louisa Ulrica of Sweden had ordered from Chardin (see p. 52). The young woman in the picture, by her spinning wheel, with a book on her lap, is almost certainly Françoise Marguerite Pouget. La Font de Saint-Yenne 'admired the accuracy of his imitation, the finesse of his touch, whether it be the person, the ingenious operation of the spinning wheel or the furniture in the room'.[20] And, two years later, the author of *Observations sur les Arts* wrote of this painting: 'Has one seen anything more touching than this little picture which is as good as the best of the Flemish School and which would adorn the most interesting collections?'

The Embroiderer, 1733–34. Oil on canvas, 18 × 15.5 cm
(7⅛ × 6⅛ in.; reproduced actual size). Nationalmuseum, Stockholm.

Young Student Drawing, also known as *The Draughtsman*, *c.* 1733–34. Oil on canvas, 19.5 × 17.5 cm (7¾ × 7 in.; reproduced actual size). Nationalmuseum, Stockholm.

The Amusements of Private Life, 1746.
Oil on canvas,
42.5 × 35 cm
(16¾ × 13¾ in.).
Nationalmuseum,
Stockholm.

A letter from Chardin to Scheffer, after the exhibition of *The Amusements of Private Life*, sheds light on his method:[21] 'I would like to be able to respond to Count Tessin's anxiety to receive the two pictures which he desires from me. You may have the first of these which has been exhibited in the Louvre. As to its pendant, while it is at an advanced stage, I am unable to commit myself to giving it to you before Christmas. I am taking my time, because I have made a habit of not leaving my work until, to my eyes, it requires nothing further; and I will apply this even more rigorously in order to be able to uphold the favourable opinion of Count Tessin with which I am honoured. Also, as these two pictures will be lost to France and as one has a debt to the nation, I would like the Count to allow me time to have these engraved, which may take until the Spring. This favour would be even more pleasing for me as I have a certain debt to the public in recognition of the reception which they give my work.'

In February 1747, Scheffer wrote that Chardin 'has at last kept his word and has given me the two pictures which he promised, *The Amusements of Private Life* and *The Household Accounts*. The first has been engraved, but not the second – it came straight from the painter's hands, as it would have taken another three months if I had had to let it go through those of the engraver'. Despite the delays, and the impatience of the princess, Tessin wrote in receiving them that 'the pictures of Chardin are to be knelt in front of' and that two further paintings were desired, each with two figures, 'whatever the price may be'.

It must be that these two works occupied most of Chardin's productive time, for at the Salon in August 1747 he exhibited just one painting. He was aware of the criticism which could be made of him on this point and he used the catalogue to justify himself, thereby revealing a certain vanity. In effect, we are told that *The Attentive Nurse* (or *The Convalescent's Meal*) 'forms a pendant with another by the same artist, which is in the collection of the Prince of Liechtenstein, and which he was unable to show, as well as two others which had departed shortly beforehand for the Court of Sweden'.[22]

Chardin reoffended the following year, again showing only one piece at the Salon, namely *The Diligent Student* (T.O.P. 126; see p. 217), 'to serve as a pendant to those which had left for the Court of Sweden last year'. The statement is deliberately misleading, but there is some truth in it. It is true that he had sent pendants to Stockholm the previous year, and it is also true that Louisa Ulrica had ordered a new pair of pictures from him, but *The Diligent Student* is in no way the pendant of *The Amusements of Private Life* or *The Household Accounts*. On the other hand, the painter had begun, or was about to begin, another work to pair with *The Diligent Student*: *The Good Education* (T.O.P. 127; see p. 216), ordered in September 1747 and completed two years later.

Although *Mercure de France* bemoaned the fact that there was 'only one small picture by this fine painter this year', the Abbé Bridard de La Garde, author of *Lettre sur la peinture, sculpture et architecture*, praised it: 'in viewing the skill with which each of the subject's accessories is treated individually, the viewer feels himself caught up in details from which he cannot tear himself away'. There followed a criticism of the lack of relief in the figures: 'nevertheless, the public would be pleased to see a greater number of works by this author'. Baron Louis Guillaume Baillet de Saint-Julien added: 'why should we not reproach him for having given us, as he has, only one of his pictures?'[23]

Portrait de Françoise Marguerite Pouget, deuxième épouse de Chardin (Portrait of Françoise Marguerite Pouget, Chardin's second wife), 1755.
Engraving by Laurent Cars after Charles Nicolas Cochin.

1. In principle, these exhibitions were held every two years. They were held in the gallery of the Palais Royal, in the Hôtel de Richelieu and then in the Louvre.

2. See, among others, J. Locquin, *La Peinture d'histoire en France de 1747 à 1785*, Paris, 1925, Crow, *op. cit.*, 1985, and U. Van de Sandt, in the *Diderot et les Arts de Boucher à David* exhibition catalogue, Paris, 1984–85.

3. It must be remembered that the critical texts of Diderot, which were sent to Grimm in the form of manuscripts, were passed around among a restricted circle of French and foreign amateurs. Because of this, they were not generally known to the public or artists and it is unlikely that Chardin ever read them.

4. Things were different in 1737, as this was the first Salon which had been organized for twelve years. There had been an exhibition in 1725, without a catalogue, which is known only through its report in *Mercure de France*. Since then, artists had had no opportunity to exhibit their work. Some of them, like Chardin, Aved and Boucher, who had been elected to the Académie after 1725, had never had the opportunity to participate in a Salon. They therefore had to choose between the works which they felt most represented their talents, i.e., both relatively old and more recent works. This is why it is unwise to date anything which was shown at the Salon that year as being work executed in 1736 or 1737. This is true for all of the artists, but it complicates even more the chronology of Chardin's paintings, especially as he made copies and because the description in the catalogue does not tell us to which painting it refers. Also, Chardin was to exhibit the same picture twice, several years apart, so that the presence of a particular canvas at a particular Salon does not mean a great deal in terms of its execution.

5. The other pictures were: *Woman Drawing Water from a Copper Cistern*; *The Washerwoman*; *Young Man Playing with Cards* (*The House of Cards*, probably the Nuneham version [T.O.P. 102] or, as Pierre Rosenberg thinks, the version in Washington [T.O.P. 109]); the *Chemist in his Laboratory*; a *Small Child with the Attributes of Childhood* and its pendant, a *Small Girl Playing with her Lunch*, both of which are only known to us today through their engravings. Chardin also showed his *Girl with a Shuttlecock*, probably the version dated 1737 (T.O.P. 108) and which was therefore the only picture painted the year it was exhibited, the others dating back to between 1732 and 1735.

6. See M. Roland Michel, 'Mode ou imitation: sculpture et peinture en trompe-l'oeil au XVIIIe siècle', in *Clodion et la sculpture française de la fin du XVIIIe siècle* (Paris 1992 conference proceedings), 1993.

7. In the Chardin exhibition catalogue, 1979 (pp. 68–71).

8. By way of comparison, see the marriage contract of Largillierre in 1699 which included about fifty original portraits and about forty copies of portraits (published in the *Largillierre, Portrait Painter of the Eighteenth Century* exhibition catalogue, Montreal, 1981). But it is evident that the problem of portraits and their replicas is different to that of still life.

9. Carritt, *art. cit.*, 1974, even suggested that the picture may have been begun in 1732, because of the date on the print.

10. In addition to *Lady Sealing a Letter* were: *The Cellar Boy* and *The Scullery Maid*; *A Young Embroiderer* (a painting which is lost and for which there is no engraving), the pendant of which, apparently hanging on the opposite wall, was presumably *Young Draughtsman Sharpening his Pencil*. (The two versions of this painting are dated 1737. On this subject, see Carritt, *art. cit.*, 1974.) Also exhibited were two small paintings with similar themes, probably painted around 1733–34, *Embroiderer Choosing Wool from her Basket* and *A Young Schoolboy Drawing* (T.O.P. 84, 85), as well as two portraits with identical models: *The Son of M. Godefroy, Jeweller, Watching a Top Spinning*, which appears to have hung beside *Draughtsman Sharpening His Pencil*, and the *Portrait of a Small Daughter of M. Mahon, Merchant, Playing with her Doll* (known through its engraving, entitled *The Inclination of Her Age*). These two works certainly belonged at the time to Mr Godefroy and Mr Mahon who had ordered them from Chardin. Godefroy had Chardin paint portraits of both of his sons, probably at about the same time, and *Young Man with a Violin* (in the Louvre) seems to be the twenty-year-old Charles Théodose Godefroy, who was born in 1718. As far as *The Scullery Maid* and *The Cellar Boy* are concerned, Pierre Rosenberg has shown that the pictures which were exhibited at the Salon (T.O.P. 113, 114) were almost certainly not the ones which are now to be found in Glasgow, dated 1738 and 1735 (or 1736) respectively, but rather the versions engraved in 1740 by Cochin and purchased, no doubt during the Salon, by Count de Vence. The versions exhibited at the Salon of *The Embroiderer* and its pendant, *Young Student Drawing*, several versions of which are known to us as well as two sets of engravings, are no doubt those which Count Tessin had bought from Gersaint at the La Roque sale. These are now in the Nationalmuseum in Stockholm (T.O.P. 84, 85) and were engraved in about 1741 by Jacques Fabien Gautier-Dagoty.

11. *Description raisonnée des tableaux exposés au Louvre – Lettre à Madame la Marquise de S. P. R.* 1739 from Chevalier Jean Florent Joseph Neufville de Brunhaubois-Montador, to whom we are indebted for reports of the Salons of 1738 and 1739, which were written in the form of letters to a certain 'Marquise de S. P. R.'

12. The other works were *The Young Schoolmistress* (London, National Gallery), engraved the same year by Lépicié and put on the same level as the previous two by the Abbé Desfontaines (*Observations sur les écrits modernes*, 1740) as well as *Monkey as Painter* and *Monkey as Philosopher*. It is difficult to say which versions are involved and, admittedly, *Monkey as Antiquarian* can be identified with that in the Louvre (T.O.P. 23), the pendant of which was later lost.

13. *Observations sur les écrits modernes…*, 1741.

14. As has already been said, we are indebted to Tessin for our knowledge of Chardin's rare drawings. In addition to *The Morning Toilet*, he bought *Dead Rabbit and Cauldron* which was sent to Stockholm in 1741, at the same time as Oudry's portrait of his dog, Pähr, *The Birth of Venus* and *The Landscape of Tivoli* by Boucher, *Portrait of Marie Rosalie Van Loo* by Carle Van Loo, a miniature by Jean Baptiste Massé and drawings by Lancret and Edmé Bouchardon (all of these purchases are mentioned in a letter sent from Paris by Tessin to Hårleman in February 1740). On

Tessin, whose taste is responsible for the incomparable collection of eighteenth-century French paintings and drawings in the Nationalmuseum in Stockholm, see chiefly P. Bjurström, *Carl Gustaf Tessin och Konsten*, Stockholm, 1970; Carl Fredrik Scheffer, *Lettres Particulières à Carl Gustaf Tessin – 1744–1752*, critical edition by J. Heidner, Stockholm, 1982; *Tableaux de Paris et de la Cour de France 1739–1742*, unpublished letters of Count Carl Gustaf de Tessin, edited by G. von Proschwitz, Göteborg, 1983. In addition, in 1745 Tessin bought four Chardin paintings at the La Roque sale for the Swedish crown prince, Adolph Frederick, and acted as an intermediary for Princess Louisa Ulrica's commissions.

15. Pierre Rosenberg suggests a date of about 1734 for the pendants and 1740 for the portrait of Madame Lenoir (T.O.P. 106). But it seems that the little girl standing who is watching the card tricks is the same girl who appears in *Saying Grace*, and that the boy in *Game of Goose* is the same child being lectured to by *The Governess*, which would date the pictures more likely at 1739–40 (see p. 54). Certainly, when they were engraved the following year, the inscription indicates that they were in the collection of M. Despeuchs, who had for a short time been the owner of *The Governess* before the Prince of Liechtenstein bought it

Saying Grace (detail), 1740. Oil on canvas. Louvre, Paris.

Les Tours de cartes (Card Games; detail), 1744. Engraving after Chardin by Surugue.

The Governess (detail), 1738. Oil on canvas. National Gallery of Canada, Ottawa.

Le Jeu de l'oye (Game of Goose; detail), 1745. Engraving after Chardin by Surugue.

from him in 1739. One can therefore assume that this collector would have bought *Card Tricks* and its pendant in order to have paintings of children by Chardin.

16. J. Heidner, 'Edmé-François Gersaint – Nine Letters to Count Carl Gustaf Tessin, 1743–48', Archives de l'Art Français, new period, vol. XXVI, 1984.

17. These subjects, which were very much the taste of the time, had been treated by Charles Antoine Coypel; the engravings by Louis Desplaces after his paintings are entitled *Éducation douce et insinuante donnée par une Sainte* and *Éducation sèche et rebutante donnée par une prude*.

18. At the same time as she commissioned work from Chardin, Louisa Ulrica had asked Tessin to have Boucher paint four pictures illustrating the times of the day.

19. One of the two portraits 'as large as life' is unknown to us. The second, the portrait of André Levret, a specialist in childbirth, recently reappeared, and it provides a good example of what Chardin was trying to do. La Font de Saint-Yenne said that they were 'the first of their kind which he had seen'; as Chardin had exhibited *The Chemist* eight years earlier and the *Portrait of Madame Lenoir* only three years previously, it must be deduced that this time real portraits not 'genre portraits' were involved, comparable to those of Louis Tocqué – who in 1746 had exhibited a *Portrait of Madame Terisse Wearing a Muff* – Aved, Robert Tournières and even La Tour or Jean-Baptiste Perronneau who had recently been accepted. Furthermore, La Font de Saint-Yenne in praising them wrote that 'the public would be very sorry to see [Chardin] abandon, or even neglect, an original talent and an inventive brush to bring himself through complacency to a genre which has become too common and without the spur of necessity'; i.e., to abandon genre painting in favour of the more lucrative portraiture.

20. *Réflexions sur quelques causes de l'état présent de la peinture en France*, 1747. We know nothing of La Font de Saint-Yenne, other than that he is the author of two pieces of criticism on the Salon of 1746, as well as of *Sentiments sur quelques ouvrages de peinture du Salon de 1753* and an essay on architecture, *L'Ombre du grand Colbert*. His *Réflexions* constitutes one of the first significant documents about the relationship between criticism and artists and it was the subject of much debate.

21. Published by Heidner, *op. cit.*, 1984.

22. Was it Chardin or the Prince of Liechtenstein who wanted to paint a pendant for *Girl Returning from the Market*, which had been purchased by the Prince in Paris between 1739 and 1741, along with *Woman Peeling Vegetables* and *The Governess*? *The Attentive Nurse* should still have been completed in 1747, between the completion of *The Household Accounts* and the opening of the Salon, almost ten years after its 'pendant'; the picture was sent to Vienna immediately, even before it could be engraved – the only known instance among Chardin's genre scenes.

23. *Réflexions sur quelques circonstances présentes…*

Gabriel de Saint-Aubin.
Drawing in the catalogue of
the Salon of 1761.

CHAPTER THREE

THE 1750s: A NEW DIRECTION

*He was not content
merely to imitate nature,
but wanted to achieve greater truth
in his tones and his effects.*

Cochin

In 1749, Chardin completed a second commission for Princess Louisa Ulrica. The pictures remained in Paris for a short time, giving him time to make second versions. No Salon was held that year and Chardin did not exhibit at the next one in 1750. The reason for this may have been a commission which he received through Charles Antoine Coypel, First Painter to the King, from Le Normant de Tournehem who was the King's Directeur des Bâtiments, for *The Bird Organ* (T.O.P. 133). This painting was exhibited at the Salon of 1751 as *Lady Varying her Amusements*, without the owner's name, which is surprising given that it was a royal commission of which the artist would rightly have been very proud. In September 1751, Coypel made a payment of 1,500 *livres* – the highest price ever paid to Chardin – stating to Tournehem that the painting 'had been completed and was very satisfactory'. In January 1751, the artist gave his bill to the Marquis de Vandières, who had succeeded his uncle at the Direction des Bâtiments, and the account was settled in February.[1]

In June 1752, Coypel ordered frames for six paintings in the King's collection at the Palais du Luxembourg, including 'a painting by M. Chardin of a woman playing a bird organ to her canary'.[2] A year later, on 2 August, Lépicié, Secretary of the Académie, asked Vandières on behalf of Chardin for permission to dedicate a print to him 'and for permission to mention that the said picture is in your collection'.

In announcing Laurent Cars's print after *The Bird Organ*, *Mercure de France* praised Chardin's talent: 'The painter's compositions, although simple and reflecting the standards of the time, do not claim to be heroic. But the aptness of choice and the charm of the images present a lively criticism of the Flemish painters in general. In effect, groups of smokers, brawling fist fights and man's basic physical needs, i.e., nature at her most abject, are the subjects more commonly treated by artists such as the Brouwers, the Ostades and the Teniers. M. Chardin has always kept his distance from these degrading images of humanity. In truth, he has always taken a small but interesting scene as his subject, at least in his choice of figures, which have never been at all ugly or coarse. Here we see a young woman with a touching face, whose simple pose is fulsome, while at the same time demonstrating her propriety. She is seated by the tools of her profession, but has ceased her work and replaced these tools with a bird organ. Her gaze is fixed with attentive pleasure on the canary whose cage is in the corner of the picture. The room is decorated in a manner appropriate to the character and status of the woman portrayed. There are some paintings, and one of these, which appears in full, represents an ingenious allegory by the recently deceased M. Coypel [Charles Antoine Coypel had died on 14 June 1752]. It is in compositions like those of M. Chardin that it is possible to deal with the activities of daily life. It should be admired and envied. Also, it can be said, without exaggerating, that the model whom M. Chardin chose on this

occasion portrays a person who is devoted to her honest work, who is full of gentleness, who knows how to occupy herself.'

The length of this text, as well as its laudatory tone, are clearly related to the fact that the painting belonged to the King's new Directeur des Bâtiments. Again, one might ask how it was that a picture, which had been commissioned by the King and which had been framed for hanging in his collection, managed to end up in Vandières's private collection!

Reading *Mercure de France*, it is clear that his contemporaries recognized that by including Coypel's *Thalia Chased away by Painting* (see p. 224) in the background of the picture, along with his *Children's Games*,[3] Chardin was paying explicit homage to the First Painter who had ordered *The Bird Organ* from him. The depiction of the subject and Chardin's style in relation to Flemish genre scenes, however partial it was, gives a better understanding of what the public and connoisseurs liked about the artist's work.

This is undoubtedly why Chardin made at least one other version, with different details (in the Frick Collection, New York) and also one repainted copy (T.O.P. 133). When *The Bird Organ* (see p. 59) was exhibited at the Salon of 1751, we read, in *Jugements sur les principaux ouvrages exposés au Louvre* that no one possessed like Chardin 'the art of portraying nature so accurately'. This was followed by a positive critique of *The Bird Organ* which ends as follows: 'after this praise prompted by the truth, he will allow me to tell him that nature, in showering him with its favours, *has been working for an ungrateful person*. The public is angry that it has only ever seen one painting by such a gifted hand. I am told that he is at present completing another, and I am struck by the remarkable nature of its subject. On a canvas in front of him on an easel, he is painting a little genie, representing Nature, who is bringing him brushes; he takes them, but at the same time, Fortune is taking some of them away. And while he looks at Idleness who is smiling at him with an air of indolence, the other brush falls from his hand. With M. Chardin's talent, how happy the amateurs would be if he was as hard-working and prolific as M. Oudry!'[4]

However, if we only regard the dates of the administrative correspondence, it was certainly the genre painter of *The Bird Organ*, whom, in July 1752, Lépicié proposed to Vandières for a pension, as being 'commendable both for his talents and for his integrity'. On 1 September, Vandières proposed to the King that the pensions which had been made available on the deaths of Jean François de Troy, Charles Parrocel and Charles Antoine Coypel, be reallocated to La Tour, Hyacinthe Collin de Vermont and Chardin. On 7 September he wrote to Chardin: 'H. M. has granted you, in the distribution of his favours for the Arts, a pension of five hundred *livres*. It is my pleasure to inform you that I remain at your disposal for any occasions which may arise and which could involve me in the future.'[5]

This official recognition of Chardin's talents, through a commission and a pension, was accompanied by a radical turnaround in his output. From then on he exhibited several paintings at each Salon.[6] From 1753 until 1771 he mainly showed still lifes, as his inspiration for genre scenes and portraits seems to have dried up and he only exhibited copies and old versions which he had already shown. In 1753, he exhibited 'a draughtsman copying M. Pigalle's Mercury and a young girl reciting her Catechism. These two paintings in the

L'Aveugle (The Blind Man), 1761.
Engraving by Pierre Louis Surugue after Chardin.

60

L'Etude du dessein
(The Drawing Lesson), 1757.
Engraving by Jean Philippe
Le Bas after Chardin.

collection of M. de La Live are copies after the originals which are part of the King of Sweden's collection. The Draughtsman is being exhibited for the second time with changes.' At the same Salon, there was a 'small picture of a blind man', and there are good reasons to believe that this was painted between 1735 and 1740 (T.O.P. 89), as well as 'a philosopher reading' which is none other than his 1734 portrait of Aved.[7] Oudry, who remained Chardin's biggest rival, showed twelve of his paintings (recent works which had not yet been sold), six others belonging to various connoisseurs including Ange Laurent La Live de Jully, and five drawings. Chardin could certainly never have competed against such an output, but their methods of painting were compared by some critics. Abbé Garrigues de Froment wrote 'if one had to compare M. Chardin's method of painting animals with that of M. Oudry, I would have reason to believe that M. Chardin's style is more noble and more picturesque, while M. Oudry's is looser, but more studied and more affectionate.... A parallel (between these two skilled artists) would take me far; I will shorten it; the loss of either artist would be equally damaging for the Académie'.[8]

It was certainly this brilliance which won him critical and public acclaim that led Chardin – whose son, Jean-Pierre, won the Académie's first prize in painting in 1754[9] – to concentrate more and more on still life. In 1755 the two paintings he exhibited were both still lifes: one was a bas-relief after Duquesnoy and Baillet de Saint-Julien stressed its 'perfect illusion', and the other 'his picture of animals which lacks, as they say, only the words'.[10] Elsewhere, the critic asks Chardin 'what magic, what unknown art is it that only you have which can do such enchanting things [with your brushes]? Everything is pleasing about the decoration of your paintings, their subjects and their execution.'[11]

Before the Salon opened, at the proposal of Charles Nicolas Cochin, who was the new Permanent Secretary of the Académie in charge of the arts, Chardin had been appointed Treasurer of the Académie. The Académie's finances were at their lowest ever, partly following the death of the concierge who had been misappropriating profits from the sale of the Salon catalogues. Chardin had already been asked, along with other members of the Académie, to approve the accounts in 1747 and 1754. His integrity was well known and he was unanimously appointed Treasurer in April to 'safeguard our funds for the future'.[12]

In August 1755, Portail, the draughtsman, who was in charge of hanging the Salon, had an accident and Chardin, swiftly appointed to replace him, from then on became the Salon's 'tapissier', responsible for hanging the Salons. In March 1757, Cochin nominated him for an apartment in the Louvre[13] which had a kitchen, a cellar, a dining room, a studio on the third floor with a storage area, a drawing room overlooking the Rue des Orties, a bedroom on the second floor overlooking the street, another bedroom on the Rue des Orties side, another on the fourth floor and a bedroom overlooking 'the gallery' (of the Louvre) and a room for the cook.

In August 1757, Jean Pierre Chardin, who had come of age, was nominated by Carle Van Loo, then director of the École royale des Élèves protégés, for a visit to Italy. He therefore asked his father for the proceeds of his trust fund, but seems to have been forced by his father to renounce his inheritance from his mother.[14] This unpleasant episode did not stop Chardin from exhibiting at the Salon a few days later six paintings including four still lifes, as well as the version of *The Scullery Maid* (see p. 211) which belonged to the Comte de Vence and which had already been shown in 1738 (T.O.P. 114). Later, Diderot, describing a genre scene by Jean Jacques Bachelier, wrote: 'yes, of course, Chardin is allowed to show a kitchen with a servant leaning over a barrel, washing dishes (this was certainly *The Scullery Maid*); but it must be noted how true to life the action of the servant is, how accurately the top of her face is drawn and how the folds of her petticoat imply everything which is beneath. One cannot fail to notice the astonishing accuracy of all the household utensils, as well as the colour and the harmony of the entire composition. There is no background, no interesting ideas, no original subject or astonishing execution. It would be better to join the two, the touching thought and the happy execution. If his technique were not so sublime, Chardin's ideal would be miserable. Take careful note of this, M. Bachelier.'

Also exhibited at the Salon of 1757 was 'the medallion portrait of M. Louis, Professor and *Censeur Royal* of Surgery'. This is known to us only through its engraving made by Simon Miger eight years later, which depicts Louis in profile in an oval medallion held by a bow. The silence of the critics about this work seems to bear witness to Chardin's semi-success in this genre;

Portrait d'Antoine Louis (Portrait of Antoine Louis), 1766. Engraving by Simon Miger after Chardin.

in fact, the praise which he received was for his colouring, his accuracy and for the comparisons which were henceforth made between him and Jean-Baptiste Greuze. However, *The Kitchen Table* and *The Pantry Table* (see pp. 171 and 172) which belonged to La Live de Jully, were not given favourable descriptions. And the painting of *Game with Game-bag and Powder Flask* is similar to the paintings of the 1730s, although it cannot be confirmed.

This full-scale return to still lifes is hardly surprising as, from then on, Jeaurat, Greuze and soon Lépicié were painting the sort of genre subjects which Chardin had made popular, and there was also a 'market' to be exploited in this area. Desportes had died in 1743 and Largillierre in 1746. The latter was certainly more of a portrait painter than a still life painter,[15] but Oudry had delivered two lectures praising his style of painting and, at his sale in 1765, there were several pictures – mainly overdoors – of flowers, fruits and animals. Oudry himself, Chardin's main rival in this field, died in 1755 after having painted several still lifes with game during the 1750s, the composition of which was not very different to what Chardin was doing at the time (see right). Chardin had no longer anything to prove, only needing to confirm his superiority in the so-called lower genres. It was no accident if, from then on, the critics put Chardin and Vernet on the same level, both genre painters.[16] Nor was it any accident that from then on Chardin received royal favours as much as, if not more, than history painters.

ARTISTS WHO ADMIRED CHARDIN'S WORK

In the 1750s, the perfection of Chardin's painting was recognized, as much by informed collectors such as La Live de Jully, the Comte de Vence and Marquis de Marigny, as by contemporary artists. Of the nine paintings which he exhibited in 1759, two belonged to the engraver Laurent Cars, two to Louis François Trouard, the architect, and two to Jacques Augustin Silvestre, whose sale after his death included sixteen Chardins. Several artists collected Chardin's work, starting with Jean Baptiste Van Loo, who had owned a bas-relief after Duquesnoy since 1732.

Aved probably begin to acquire works by Chardin around this time. Among the nine paintings listed in the inventory at the sale after his death in 1766,[17] P. Rosenberg identifies four as being paintings from the years 1728–30. However, this information should not be taken too literally, as Aved had always acted as a dealer and the works in question may have been purchased by him long after their completion. Nevertheless, given the nature of his relationship with Chardin, we can imagine that from an early stage he was interested in paintings of 'saveloys and forked tongues'. He owned various still lifes of fruit and animals, *The Hound* and a painting of some flowers in a vase (most likely the one which is now in Edinburgh). At the Jean-Baptiste de Troy sale in 1764, there were four Chardin still lifes, including *The Copper Cistern*, two pendants of kitchen table scenes and a composition of game. Artists who owned works by Chardin included miniature painters such as Jacques Charlier, portrait painters such as Aved, and history painters, such as Michel François Dandré Bardon, as well as Guillaume Taraval, Lépicié, Hubert Robert and Jean Antoine Peters. Draughtsmen and engravers such as Cochin, Cars and Wille all liked and sought out his work. Some were only interested in

Jean Baptiste Oudry, *Pheasant, Hare and Red Partridge*, 1753. Oil on canvas, 97 × 64 cm (38⅛ × 25¼ in.).

63

Cat, Partridge, Dead Hare and Silver Tureen, c. 1728. Oil on canvas, 73 × 105 cm (28¾ × 41⅜ in.). The Metropolitan Museum of Art, New York.

still life, such as Peters, Taraval, Lépicié and Louis Joseph Le Lorrain. Some, such as Dandré Bardon, owned genre and still life paintings. Others owned only paintings of people, such as Largillierre who owned 'a woman at her toilet' and Hubert Robert. The case of Jacques Augustin Silvestre, drawing master to the royal children, is unique: at his sale in 1810, some one hundred and fifty paintings from three different schools were listed, along with thousands of drawings. Prints took up three hundred and fifty pages of the catalogue alone, and there were also bronzes, marble and porcelain, as well as geometry and optical instruments. The editor, Regnault Delalande explained that 'this collection, which he had inherited from his ancestors (Israël, Louis, Charles, François and Charles Nicolas) and to which he had added considerably, was his only pleasure'. It is likely that it was he who had purchased the sixteen Chardins, from the 1750s onwards. His taste was eclectic, as he owned the pastel portraits of *Chardin with Spectacles* and *Madame Chardin*, his wife, *The Cistern*, *Girl Returning from the Market* and *The Scullery Maid* in pendants, as well as the small panels of *The Embroiderer* and *The Draughtsman*, three sets of still lifes in pendants and, finally, 'three paintings of fish, fruit, household utensils and other inanimate objects'.

In the inventory after Jean-Baptiste Pigalle's death in 1785, in addition to two hunting scenes, two overdoors of fruit and lunch, and, of course, *Attributes of the Arts* around a plaster of *Mercury* (T.O.P. 180; see p. 179), there was a 'self-portrait in pastel of M. Chardin', the presence of which is explained by the mutual admiration and friendship between the painter and sculptor. In the inventory after the death of the sculptor Robert Le Lorrain in 1743, there were 'two small canvases by Chardin' and anonymous paintings of fruit, portraits of children and returning from the hunt.[18] Other famous sculptors, such as François Lemoyne and Jean Jacques Caffieri, also owned still lifes and genre scenes by Chardin: Lemoyne owned eight canvases, including *The Draughtsman*, *The Embroiderer*, *Monkey as Painter*, *Monkey as Antiquarian* and 'studies grouped around a plaster cast of Mercury belonging to M. Pygalle'; Caffieri had four different still lifes and a *House of Cards*. Le Bas had engraved four of Chardin's compositions, but prior to that he 'had become a friend of this great man early on. One day when he found himself in (Chardin's) studio in front of a dead hare which he had just painted, he said "I would very much like to have this painting; but I have no money". "That can be arranged", said Chardin, "you have a jacket which I like very much". "Done", said Le Bas and took off his jacket immediately, put on his coat without the jacket and took the picture.'[19] This painting may well be identified as the 'cat looking at a dead hare with fruit on a stone ledge' in the Le Bas sale of 1783 (T.O.P. 39; see p. 64). Le Bas also owned the *Surgeon's Signboard* which he tried to sell in Sweden in 1746, through the draughtsman, Jean Éric Rehn, who had been his pupil in Paris. It was Rehn who in 1754 had made a drawing of *The Household Accounts* after the painting in Stockholm, so that Le Bas could engrave it. This anecdote is reminiscent of Watteau exchanging a painting for a wig which he liked. If it is well founded, does it explain the presence of so many Chardin canvases in the collections of artists who would have had them at a good price?

It would not be surprising to see some of Chardin's work in Cochin's collection, even if Cochin owned only a modest number of paintings. He owned grisailles after Gerard Van Opstal which Chardin had exhibited at the Salon of 1769, as well as a small round painting which measured twenty-five centimetres in diameter 'of books and papers on a table'. Conversely, Chardin owned two drawings by Cochin, including the very important *Allegory of the Death of the Dauphin*. He also owned a painting by Vernet of 'the view from the dwelling place of a great lord over the Bosphorus and several women from the harem bathing in front of His Highness', sold in 1780 when he died.[20] The goldsmiths Charles Roettiers and François Thomas Germain also owned work by Chardin. Roettiers owned *Cut Melon* and *Jar of Apricots* (see p. 80) and another painting of fruit. His liking for still life is witnessed by the big painting by Oudry which he lent to the Salon in 1753, 'representing a pheasant with a hare, a ham pie, bread, colza, etc'. Why not imagine that the two oval paintings by Chardin may have been hung, a few years later, on either side of this Oudry? The Salon of 1753 included Chardin's *Partridge and Fruit*, which belonged to the goldsmith François Thomas Germain who does not seem to have collected very much at all, although in the inventory after the death of his mother in 1758 there were paintings by Van Loo and Oudry.[21] In addition, he had rooms at the Louvre, close to Chardin's, which were sumptuously decorated with models by his father and also by Claude Ballin, which Chardin could have seen there.

Among architects who collected work by Chardin were Pierre Boscry, owner of *The Philosopher*, who had ten Chardins: four still lifes, as well as *Soap Bubbles* and *Game of Knucklebones*, *The Draughtsman* and *The Embroiderer*, and a small copper point of *Lady Sealing a Letter*. Trouard, who was the King's Contrôleur des Bâtiments, owned six Chardins, all pendants: two of dead game, two kitchen scenes and *Soap Bubbles* paired with *House of Cards*. These collections show that the leading connoisseurs of painting did not hesitate to collect copies or second versions. It may be that they were less expensive, or perhaps they were easier to purchase than the originals, which were already scattered in different collections, but one has the feeling that their quality was not considered inferior and that possession of a version of a work, the other version of which was owned by the Queen of Sweden or which was at Versailles, was a compliment to the taste of its owner.

It was not only artists who collected replicas by Chardin. Margravine Caroline Louise of Baden, a pupil of Jean-Étienne Liotard, who had purchased two still lifes with game dating from 1728–30 through her architect, Pierre Louis Philippe La Guépière and her advisor, Fleischmann, wanted to acquire others without having to pay too much. She therefore wrote to Fleischmann, who lived in Paris: 'I would be delighted to learn from you what the Abbé Trublet paid to M. Chardin for two small paintings, one of which was of a glass of water with cherries and I am not sure what other fruits. You will be surprised that I know these paintings – it is because I saw them praised in a small periodical about the fine arts'. Fleischmann replied that 'the pictures which Chardin painted for the Abbé Trublet are no longer in the possession of the latter; they were included in the exhibition in the Louvre and since then Chardin has withdrawn them and is keeping them himself. As this skilled painter has been a friend of mine for more than ten years, you may count, Madame, on having copies by him which will cost you barely more than what the Abbé Trublet paid for his, although he asked me to excuse him and not to disclose the price which he had paid.'[22]

COLLECTORS AND AMATEURS

The taste of the Margravine of Baden, or of artists who sought work by Chardin, is further witnessed by the names of owners listed in the Salon catalogues which clearly show that, from 1757, Chardin had already sold some of the paintings which he was exhibiting to famous collectors, including La Live de Jully, the Chevalier de Damery, the Comte de Saint-Florentin and the Abbé Pommyer. The Abbé, advisor to the parliament, friend and model of the pastel portraitist La Tour, was also a friend of Cochin and Chardin, who supported his nomination to the Académie in 1767 as an honorary free associate. There was also the Comte de Vence, the Comte de Luc, marshal and brigadier of the king's armies, whose portrait was exhibited by Aved in 1753. In addition, on Chardin's death, there remained only eight genre scenes and portraits in his studio, all of which were second versions, and six or seven still lifes. On 6 March 1780, Madame Chardin sold her husband's paintings. These were six genre scenes presented in pendants: *The Governess* and *The Diligent Mother*, *House of Cards* and *Game of Goose*, 'two paintings of monkeys', as well as *The Washerwoman*.

Other collectors, who let their Chardins be exhibited at the Salon, and who would have been rightly proud to see their names in the catalogue, are less well known: M. de Chasse, Fortier the notary and the Abbé Trublet, who would have been better known in intellectual than artistic circles (and who, incidentally, was disliked by Voltaire and by Diderot, who called him 'the unpleasant Trublet'), M. de Bombarde, a friend of the Comte de Caylus, whom Cochin mentions ironically in his *Mémoires* as an important, rich and very decent man, but very mediocre, one of these would-be connoisseurs who exist all over the world, giving their opinion on everything. As for René Nicolas de Maupeou, his status was certainly more glorious than his collection, but for Chardin it was a form of endorsement to let it be known that one of his paintings belonged to the Chancellor of France.

In addition to these amateurs, we recall those early collectors such as La Roque, whose sale after his death in 1745 included no fewer than ten Chardins. One notes his predilection for small paintings, perhaps from necessity as much as taste, as Gersaint, the author of this catalogue, says that he was 'embarrassed and constricted by the arrangements of the places where he lived'. The subjects of the many Dutch paintings in his collection helps us understand what La Roque liked about Chardin's work: Herman Saftleven's barn with all its kitchen implements, Willem Kalf's four small panels of fish, vegetables and kitchen utensils, an old woman sitting in an armchair by Gerrit Dou, as well as a 'painting by a Dutch master of a young man drawing, whose pose is very natural'. *The Embroiderer* and *The Draughtsman* are followed in the catalogue by two small Ostades which are the same size, of the upper bodies of a *Sailor* and a *Peasant*. Chevalier Despuech bought two Chardins at this sale, panels of 'kitchen utensils', before acquiring *Card Games*, *Game of Goose* and *The Governess* at the time when they were painted. Madame de Pompadour owned *The Scullery Maid* and *The Cellar Boy*, which, after her death, passed into the collection of her brother, the Marquis de Marigny, where they joined *The Bird Organ*.

Ange Laurent de La Live de Jully, head of protocol at Versailles, *associé libre* of the Académie Royale de Peinture and a distinguished harpist, collected painting, sculpture and shells. In 1764 he published a *Catalogue historique du cabinet de peinture et sculpture françoise de M. de Lalive*, in which he justified his taste for contemporary art. In 1769, through Pierre Rémy, he held a sale of his paintings from three schools, his sculptures, furniture and miscellaneous objects.[23] Most of his acquisitions had been made between 1752 and 1762 and he loaned copies of *The Drawing Lesson* and *The Good Education* to the Salon of 1753, as well as *The Kitchen Table* and *The Pantry Table* to the Salon of 1757. He also owned paintings of animals by Desportes, a *Bacchanal* by Oudry painted in 1730 imitating a bronze bas-relief by Duquesnoy, two *trompe-l'oeil* paintings, a fire screen and two still lifes by Roland Delaporte, and flowers and a grisaille of children's games by Jean Louis Prévost.

There were also paintings by Chardin in the collections of the following: Baron Crozat de Thiers; Vassal de Saint-Hubert and Leroy de Senneville, both connoisseurs of modern painting, who had collected the early paintings of Jean-Honoré Fragonard; collectors of drawings such as Dezallier d'Argenville and Blondel d'Azaincourt; Baron de Saint-Julien who commissioned *The Swing* from Fragonard; and his work was also to be found in the two sales of the Prince of Conti, in 1777 and 1779. The catalogue of the first sale in 1777, which is illustrated with a drawing by Gabriel de Saint-Aubin (see p. 69), includes a bas-relief and a still life of a partridge and fruit. The second catalogue, also illustrated with drawings,[24] includes *Young Student Drawing* and *The Embroiderer*. The Boyer de Fons Colombe, Nicolas Beaujon and Charles Alexandre de Calonne collections and sales should also be mentioned, as well as those in London belonging to Geminiani, Major, Prince Victor Amédée de Carignan and also Dr William Hunter who bought *Lady Taking Tea*, *The Scullery Maid* and *The Cellar Boy*, which are today in the Hunterian Museum and Art Gallery at the University of Glasgow. In Saint-Aubin's book of drawings made between 1760 and 1764, which is in the Art Institute of Chicago,[25] three pages testify to the success of Chardin's models (see p. 70). The first shows, on the left hand side of the page, *Girl Returning from the Market*, drawn in detail. The right hand side is devoted to a caricature drawing of the head and the silhouette of a man, possibly a singer. On the following page, Saint Aubin has sketched the wall of a drawing room with its fireplace, panelling, an armchair, and the outline of a table leg. On the right of the chimney, two paintings are hanging on the wall, in rococo frames. The first reproduces *The Scullery Maid* and the second is of Watteau's *Antiope Sleeping*. The juxtaposition of these two paintings has not so far enabled us to identify the collection to which they may have belonged – perhaps it was simply Saint-Aubin's imagination, as was frequently the case. The third sketch is on the back of the cover. On the left hand side there is an oval still life, in a frame topped with a bow, in which one can see a tumbler, a bottle and fruit or biscuits, making up a composition rather similar to that of a rectangular painting of a *Seville Orange, Silver Tumbler, Apples, Pear and Two Bottles* (T.O.P. 130). Underneath the frame, the draughtsman has written a list of food, no doubt with a kitchen recipe in mind.

Huit Enfants jouant avec une chèvre
(Eight Children Playing with a Goat).
Drawing by Gabriel de Saint-Aubin
in the catalogue of the first sale
of the Prince de Conti, 1777.

Ecole Françoise. 119

lant; il eſt peint ſur toile de 13
pouces de haut, ſur 12 pouces de
large.

727 Une Sainte Famille, très belle
esquiſſe terminée, ſur bois : hauteur
12 pouces, largeur 9 pouces.

728 Une autre eſquiſſe ; ſon ſujet eſt
Bacchus & Ariane : hauteur 19 pouces, largeur 13 pouces, ſous verre,
& bordure.

729 Minerve qui préſide aux Arts,
exercés par des Amours ; eſquiſſe ſur
bois : hauteur 19 pouces, largeur
22.

Simon Chardin.

730 Un jeu d'enfants, bas-relief,
imitant le bronze, d'après les Quef-
noy ; ſur bois : hauteur 8 pouces,
largeur 14 pouces.

731 Une perdrix & des fruits.

Jean Marie Vien.

732 Une jeune femme aſſiſe dans ſon
appartement ; elle tient de la main
gauche un pigeon blanc, près d'elle
eſt une caſſolette ; de l'autre côté
une table, ſur laquelle eſt une ca-
raffe remplie de fleurs.

K ij

Le Dessinateur (The Draughtsman)
and *L'Ouvrière en tapisserie*
(The Embroiderer).
Drawings by Gabriel de Saint-Aubin
in the catalogue of the second sale
of the Prince de Conti, 1779.

M. CHARDIN.

90. Deux petits Tableaux pendants. L'un
repréſente un jeune homme aſſis à terre dans
un attelier, & deſſinant d'après une figure
d'Académie : l'autre repréſente une jeune fille
aſſiſe ſur une chaiſe, & occupée à faire de la
tapiſſerie ; elle a devant elle un panier d'oſier
où ſont ſes pelotons.

Les Amateurs connoiſſent la vérité & le mérite des

Gabriel de Saint-Aubin, drawings, 1760–64.
Black chalk, ink and wash.
The Art Institute of Chicago, gift of Herman Waldeck.

Basket of Plums, Bottle, Glass of Water and Two Cucumbers, c. 1727. Oil on canvas, 45 × 50 cm (17¾ × 19⅝ in.). The Frick Collection, New York.

It was at the beginning of the 1760s that the painter's fame began to relate directly to the market value of his work and that his prices were openly discussed. Thus, in 1759, Fleischmann proposed to the Margravine of Baden repetitions of two of the Abbé Trublet's paintings 'which will scarcely cost you more than the price which the Abbé paid for his'. Caroline Louise of Baden replied 'I do not know this artist's work, but I have heard much praise of him and also that he is terribly expensive'. This is certainly why Jean Georges Wille was able to boast in 1760 of having 'bought two small works by M. Chardin; on one there is an upturned cauldron, onions and other items; on the second, a cauldron, a casserole and other items; they are both very well executed and cost 36 *livres*; this is good value, and it was friendship that gave them to me.'

This was good value compared with the prices for small Dutch paintings and similar subjects. At the Aved sale in 1766, *Flowers in a Porcelain Vase* was sold for 12 *livres*; a kitchen table with cucumbers and mackerel fetched 9 *livres*; a pair of hunting trophies, 45 *livres*, and *Duck with a Seville Orange* 45 *livres*. Only *The Water Spaniel* fetched 120 *livres*, which is low compared with Flemish and Dutch paintings. A landscape by Paul Bril sold for 1,520 *livres*, two paintings by Cornelis van Poelenburg fetched 3,400 and 600 *livres* respectively and paintings by Teniers, Van Ostade, Bartolomeus Breenberg, Wouwermans, Nicolas Berghem and Caspar Netscher were sold for 1,500 to 3,000 *livres*. This did not stop Diderot from thinking that 'the combination of so many qualities already gives these works such value' and from asking 'who will pay for Chardin's pictures, once this exceptional man is no longer with us?'[26]

1. The signed document is in the Custodia collection of the Institut Néerlandais in Paris.

2. Letter of 2 June 1752 from the Abbé Joly to a clerk at the Direction des Bâtiments, published by M. Furcy-Raynaud, about the frames ordered from the framer and woodcarver Maurissant (*Correspondance de M. de Marigny avec Coypel, Lépicié and Cochin*, vol. I, 1903, p. 9).

3. Like *The Bird Organ*, this was engraved by Lépicié and it was also in the Marigny collection and at his sale.

4. No trace has ever been found of any such allegorical painting. Regarding the reference to Oudry, this painter did exhibit eighteen paintings at the Salon of 1751, five of which were of fables by La Fontaine, as well as a 'bas-relief after a plaster by François Flamant', which had been a favourite subject of Chardin's and also Desportes, twenty years earlier. Perhaps his comparison made Chardin think again, as well as similar comments, such as those of the Abbé Bridard de La Garde who wrote in 1748 in *Lettre sur la Peinture* that 'the talent which he has for rendering so well moments from private life should not cause him to stop painting fruit and animals, at which he also excels'.

5. We will come back to the problem of the generous pensions granted by the king to Chardin, largely at the request of Cochin who had always given him great support, although he was only a genre painter. In *Cochin et l'Art des Lumières* (*op. cit.* 1993), Christian Michel studied in detail the pensions granted by his intermediary and gives a table on p. 503 which shows the extent to which Chardin was well treated.

6. From 1751 on, the Salon finally adhered to the biennial cycle, which had only applied in theory up until then.

7. Huquier the Younger, who clearly did not visit the Salon of 1738, wrote (in *Lettre sur l'exposition des tableaux au Louvre*): 'This year M. Chardin has given us something new and even astonishing, not for those who know his merits, but for the general public. It is a large painting of a philosopher reading...' There followed five still lifes of animals, game and fruit, belonging to various amateurs, including Germain the goldsmith, and Aved. In *Sentiments d'un Amateur*, 1753, the Abbé Garrigues mentions these 'pictures of fruit and animals which this artist has exhibited for a second time, as they date back further than the Philosopher'.

8. Chardin and Jeaurat were also compared, certainly on the basis of *Woman Preparing Salad* or *Two Savoyardes* exhibited by Jeaurat. In his *Ode à Milord Telliab*, Baillet de Saint-Julien wrote 'in the future it will be said that Chardin is the La Fontaine of painting and Jeaurat the Richer'.

9. The subject proposed to candidates for the painting prize was *Mathatias Killing a Jew Worshipping Idols*; malicious gossip held that without such a famous father, the young man would not have won the prize. Cochin wrote that 'he won the prize for painting. In truth, he got it cheap, that is for a picture which was too weak. This was not unjust, because the competition was even weaker than him. It would certainly have been better not to have awarded a first prize at all this year. It is forgivable for a father to be blind to his son's talents and, also, it was not easy to refuse to please an artist who is held in such high esteem and who is as loved as M. Chardin the Elder'.

10. *Lettre à un partisan du bon goût.*

11. *Caractère des peintres français.*

12. Chardin was the Académie's Treasurer until 1774, and he carried out this role extremely conscientiously and to general satisfaction. The job included various different tasks, two examples of which follow. In 1758, he became responsible for taking subscriptions for the engravings after Joseph Vernet's *Ports of France* series. At the end of 1759 Count Caylus paid him two hundred livres for the *Têtes d'expression* prize; in January 1760 he made the arrangements for the prize and in June, along with Jean Bernard Restout, Noël Hallé, Joseph Marie Vien and Cochin, he witnessed the signature which made this prize official and for which he received a further 113 *livres*.

'13. These rooms had been reserved for artisans up until then.

14. Details of this are given on p. 392 of the 1979 Chardin exhibition catalogue. On 11 August, Jean-Pierre Chardin asked for the money owing to him from his mother's legacy. The arguments given by his father are quite interesting: 'with regard to all of the expenses and payments that the said M. Chardin the Elder was absolutely obliged to make in relation to the said M. Chardin the Younger during the course of the said guardianship up until the present time, for his maintenance and subsistence, fees for his studies, drawing and painting, for his education in general and for all that it takes to make a young man capable of making an honest and adequate living for his family, the said M. Chardin the Younger accepts that all that which was spent on him over the some twenty-two and a half years of his guardianship, greatly exceeds any sum which could be owing to him in the said inheritance and estate, even if he settled for return of the dowry of one thousand *livres* and interest'. But on 12 August, i.e. the following day, Jean Pierre Chardin presented himself to the Police Superintendent 'who informed us that after the death of the Saintard woman, his mother, an inventory was drawn up, and that as he was on the point of departing for Rome to continue his studies, the said M. Chardin, his father, married for a second time, explained to him that his education had cost him a considerable amount and that he was therefore to renounce his claim on his mother's legacy; that having been to the notary where the said M. Chardin had explained to him that he had to sign an essential deed ... that he had completely refused to sign; but following reproaches from the said M. Chardin his father, who had made him understand that it was he who was lacking in respect in doubting his good faith and that moreover he would constrain him by law, that he had decided to sign a deed which, having been read to him, led him to understand that it was a pure and simple renunciation of his inheritance from his mother; such that, in relation to this, he had taken advice, etc.'

15. G. de Lastic, 'Nicolas de Largillierre, Peintre de Natures Mortes', *Revue du Louvre*, 1968, no. 4–5, pp. 233–40.

16. Like still life and scenes of daily life, landscapes belonged to 'genre painting' which was considered inferior in the Académie's hierarchy of genres.

17. G. Wildenstein, *Le Peintre Aved*, Paris, 1922.

18. M. Beaulieu, *Robert Le Lorrain*, Paris, 1982.

19. R. Hecquet, hand-written text in *l'Oeuvre de Le Bas* in the print collection of the Bibliothèque nationale, *Ee 11a* (vol. 2).20. L. Lagrange, *J. Vernet et la Peinture au XVIIIe siècle*, Paris, 1864, p. 472.

21. See C. Perrin, *François Thomas Germain, Orfèvre des Rois*, 1993.

22. Details of this correspondence are given on p. 393 of the 1979 Chardin exhibition catalogue.

23. C. Bailey, *Introductory Essay to a facsimile reprint of the Catalogue historique and the Catalogue raisonné des tableaux*, New York, 1982.

24. Both are kept in the print collection of the Bibliothèque nationale.

25. Gift of Herman Waldeck, 46.383.

26. *Salons* of 1761 and 1765, ed. Seznec and Adhémar, vol. I, 1957.

CHAPTER FOUR

THE 1760s: OFFICIAL COMMISSIONS AND A SELECT CLIENTELE

I have been told that Greuze was visiting the Salon and that when he saw the painting by Chardin which I have just described, he looked at it and passed by, heaving a great sigh. This praise is shorter and more valuable than anything I could say.

Diderot

By 1760, Chardin was a very famous painter. His work, whether genre scenes, portraits or still lifes, received unanimous praise and Diderot became his champion – although his writings about the Salons were privately subscribed. His work became known through engravings and he was unable to satisfy the demand from the public and from collectors. He received a pension and had lodgings at the Louvre – both exceptional for a genre painter.

From 1755, he was officially in charge of hanging paintings at the Salons, which had previously been the responsibility of Jacques André Portail. Portail's death gave Cochin a pretext for proposing in June 1761 to the Marquis de Marigny (Vandières's new title) that the arrangements of the Salon be henceforth the responsibility of the Académie's treasurer: 'The Salon could be better hung and more to the Académie's satisfaction, as he would be more available to attend on account of his residency in Paris. His rank within the Académie would help him win over minds, while respecting the seniority rights, which the artists guard jealously, and giving due regard to the aesthetic.... If, therefore, Monsieur, you confirm your arrangements, I would ask you kindly to give your instructions in this regard to M. *Chardin*'. It is easy to deduce from these words that during the three previous Salons, Chardin had won respect for his work as the *'tapissier'*, and that his apartment in the Louvre enabled him to supervise hangings at the Salon Carré easily.

At the Salon of 1761, Chardin exhibited five paintings, of which four were still lifes including the famous *Basket of Wild Strawberries* (T.O.P 165; see p. 78) and *Cut Melon* of 1760 (T.O.P. 157), with its pendant executed four years before, namely *Jar of Apricots* (T.O.P. 156; see page 80). The fifth painting was a different sized version of *Saying Grace*[1] (see page 55). Interestingly, at least to modern-day eyes, no critic mentioned the still lifes; instead, it is *Saying Grace* that was spoken of. The *Journal encyclopédique* was delighted to find 'the same fund of naïveté, the same truth of expression, but differently expressed'. *Mercure de France* commented on the double genius of the Dutch for fidelity to nature and of the Italians for the quality of the brushwork. The Abbé de La Porte wrote: 'in this piece, we find this celebrated and rare imitator of nature, who never had a guide to imitate and who himself is inimitable with his truly original style of rendering objects of this kind, which is due to his fine brushwork, the accuracy of his expression and all the interest which these inspire.'[2] Diderot, on this subject, had not quite fully absorbed Chardin's painting at this point. Like all of the others, he raises the point of Chardin's imitation of nature, the 'execution which is rough and uneven'; he criticizes Chardin's supposed ease, his negligence, his lack of achievement, while all the time praising the painting and saying that *The Buffet* (see p. 19), which he had seen at the Académie, proved that the painter was a great master of colour, thus sharing Largillierre's opinion of thirty years earlier. Diderot made the most of the

Page 74:
Basket of Plums with a Glass of Water,
Two Cherries, a Nut and Three Green Almonds (detail).
Musée des Beaux-Arts, Rennes.

years which followed, taking opinions, mixing with artists, 'borrowing the eyes' of Cochin, learning to look at paintings and to understand them so that, from one Salon to the next, his assessment of Chardin becomes increasingly enthusiastic.

CHARDIN AS 'TAPISSIER'

Without wishing to diminish the critical merits of Diderot, it must be said that he was clearly influenced by Chardin's reputation and by the unanimous praise which he received, and also by the official recognition of his talents. In 1763, when Carle Van Loo was appointed First Painter to the King, Cochin suggested that his previous allowance of one thousand *livres* be divided into two funds: one to pay Joseph Marie Vien for his high standard of teaching and the other to recompense Chardin for his work as *tapissier*. In February 1763, he wrote to Marigny: 'The Académie would like the organization of the Salon to be entrusted to one of its Members who is based in Paris. You have kindly agreed that this person be M. *Chardin*, who is delighted with this as he regards this expression of confidence in him as a mark of your personal esteem. When I had the pleasure of asking you on his behalf, I believed that there was some fee or income attached to this service.... M. *Chardin* has no opinion on the matter and is carrying out his duty with as much pleasure as if he were in receipt of a fee. He seems to be particularly concerned – and is even over-anxious every time – to know if you are satisfied with his work. But I feel I must consider this on his behalf, and inform you of this, particularly since I can see that the work is taking him much more time than it took M. *Portail*, who, having spent the few days required for the general organization, was able to escape to Versailles, whereas M. *Chardin* is obliged to be available at all times for the duration of the Salon.' A few days later, Cochin stressed: 'I still feel it only fair that M. *Chardin*, in working for the Salon which takes up a lot of his time, should be compensated by an increase in his allowance. A fee of five hundred *livres*, as I initially had the honour of proposing to you, would be acceptable to all concerned. However, since his work has only been every two years up until now, it would be quite appropriate to grant him an increase of two hundred and fifty *livres*.' In May 1763, Marigny wrote to Cochin informing him that the allowance which up until then had been enjoyed by Van Loo would now be divided among Dumont le Romain, Vien and Chardin, to whom 'the king is granting two hundred *livres* per annum in recognition of the work and trouble taken during the exhibition of paintings at the Louvre. I am extremely pleased to inform them directly of the favour which the king has bestowed upon them.[3]

The work involved was quite considerable and Chardin's work was very satisfactory, if we are to believe the Abbé de La Porte, who wrote in 1763 that 'we owe him a good deal of praise for the order which he has been entrusted to give to so many different masterpieces. It is generally agreed that, both at first glance and after more detailed examination, the paintings in this marvellous collection have never before been so well hung, both in terms of the beauty of the whole exhibition and in terms of the individual setting for each piece.'[4] This success was undoubtedly due to the criteria which Chardin used when hanging paintings. He did not hesitate to sacrifice, or at least to relegate to a less visible corner, those paintings which he felt were weakest, even if he advocated

Basket of Wild Strawberries, c. 1760. Oil on canvas, 38 × 46 cm (15 × 18⅛ in.). Private collection, Paris.

78

leniency! It was thus that in 1761 Jacques Charles Oudry, unhappy about how his work had been displayed, wrote to Chardin complaining of the 'judgment of the Académie's stewards in terms which were insulting to the Académie and to M. Chardin'. Faced with such arrogance, the Académie suspended Oudry temporarily and removed his two paintings from the Salon – his *Return from the Hunt* and *Wild Cat Caught in a Trap*. Three weeks later, Oudry apologized and was readmitted to the Académie, but the Salon had finished and the public was therefore unable to view his work.[5] On the other hand, in 1769 when Jean Baptiste Perronneau exhibited his *Portrait of Mademoiselle Desfriches*, he wrote to Aignan Thomas Desfriches that the pastel 'had been even better placed than in the first days. M. Chardin told me that he would send it back to you'.[6] Chardin therefore had real power in his role as *tapissier*. He could bring attention to an artist's work: in 1765, for example, when the Salon opened a month after the death of Carle Van Loo, Chardin hung his portrait by Louis Michel Van Loo 'on the wall with the best lighting. Above it hung paintings of Susanna, Augustus and the Three Graces; on each side hung three sketches; beneath it were angels who seemed to be bringing St Gregory and the painter up to heaven; further down, a little distance away, were the Vestal and the supplicating Arts. Chardin had mounted a mausoleum to his colleague.'

The importance of Chardin's role as *tapissier* is further witnessed by a note from Friedrich Melchior Grimm in Diderot's review of the Salon of 1765: 'The Salon's *tapissier* is the person whom the Académie chooses to arrange and hang its paintings. This is important work. Some artists may be favoured, at the expense of others. Not every day is equally favourable. Not all of the neighbouring pictures are equally desirable. There are paintings which kill their neighbours mercilessly. Thus, the *tapissier*'s taste and any malice which he may have could play cruel tricks on his colleagues.' On the subject of such 'tricks', we can quote the example of La Tour, who in 1759 'had painted several pastels which remained in his possession, because they were refused the place which he sought', and the hanging in 1765 of a sketch by Greuze, 'cruelly satirizing' two sketches by Hallé which Chardin had placed next to it. The same year, Chardin seemed to be in top form, if we are to believe Diderot, and he hung another drawing by Greuze, *The Nursemaids*, below a family portrait by Roslin. 'It is as if he had written underneath one of the paintings: Model of discord, and underneath the other: Model of harmony.' Elsewhere, a man of letters asked Étienne Falconet, the sculptor, why Taraval's *Head of a Beggar* 'was hidden away in an obscure corner where no one could see it'. Falconet replied that 'it was because Chardin, who did not recognize a good head, had organized the Salon that year'. Diderot advised Bachelier, who was exhibiting some oil pastels, 'M. Bachelier, leave your secret there and go to thank M. Chardin who hid your picture so well that I am the only person who saw it.'

However, Chardin seems to have been most formidable in establishing parallels. In 1769, Diderot wrote again that 'Chardin as *tapissier* is a first-class monkey, who delights in mischief. It is true that his mischief benefits both the artists and the public. He puts things within the reach of the public, enlightening them by making comparisons; and he helps the artists by establishing a truly perilous struggle among them. This year he played a rotten trick on

Jar of Apricots, 1756. Oil on oval
canvas, 57 × 51 cm
(22½ × 20⅛ in.).
Art Gallery of Ontario, Toronto.

Greuze. In hanging *Young Child Playing with a Black Dog* between *Young Girl Praying to Love* and *Young Girl Blowing a Kiss* he has used one painting by the artist to kill two others. It is a good lesson, but a cruel one. In showing us two paintings by Philippe Jacques de Loutherbourg below two by Casanove, he has certainly not insulted the former; by hanging pastels by La Tour and Perronneau opposite each other, he ensured the latter's rejection by the Salon.' As early as 1765, criticizing Michel Ange Challe's *Hector and Paris*, Diderot added: 'as if the faults of this composition are not clear enough on their own, imagine that the mischievous Chardin hung on the same side, at the same height, two paintings by Vernet and five of his own paintings – all masterpieces of accuracy, colour and harmony. M. Chardin, it is not done to play such tricks on a colleague: you do not need such foils to advance yourself.' Again in 1765, Loutherbourg exhibited a night scene 'which we could have compared with one by Vernet, had the *tapissier* so wished; but instead he hung one of the paintings at one end of the Salon, and the other at the other end. He was anxious that these two pieces would not kill each other'. Or did he simply fear that the public would no longer treat Vernet as the best living landscape painter, when they saw Loutherbourg's talent? At the same exhibition, Vernet's work was hung opposite work by Jean Baptiste Le Prince. 'Chardin seems to have been saying [to Le Prince]: Young man, look well and you will learn to make your backgrounds more fluid and your skies not so heavy, and how to give strength to your touch, to make it lighter and more sensitive to its effect.' Other work exhibited by Loutherbourg did not receive as much praise from Diderot, who once again refers to Chardin's judgment: 'A painter who is jealous of his reputation would not have shown this piece; a painter jealous of a colleague's reputation would have brought it to light. I am pleased to see that Chardin thinks and feels well.' The same applies to another landscape by this artist 'as dry, dull, cold and foul as the first one. Chardin stuck it into the same corner. M. Chardin, you have my praise.' When De Machy showed his *Peristyle of the Louvre* at the Salon of 1767, Diderot praised its composition and certain details which were particularly apposite; 'but this painting, maliciously placed beside Robert's *Gallery of Antiquities*, shows the enormous difference between something which is good and something which is excellent. It is our friend Chardin who is making these parallels at the expense of the artists involved; this does not matter to him, as long as the public is able to use their eyes and that excellence is appreciated. Many thanks, M. Chardin, without you I might have admired Machy's colonnade, had Robert's *Gallery* not been beside it.' In this particular case, however, it is not unthinkable that Chardin wanted to hang one beside the other, as pendants so to speak, two paintings of similar size and subject matter, thinking that this would favour harmony on the wall and help compare the merits of both artists. But elsewhere Diderot wrote: 'Chardin must be a friend of Robert: he has brought together as many paintings as possible which he considers important: he has spread the others around. He has killed Machy with the hand of Robert.'

The task of hanging the Salons was quite difficult. Account had to be taken of the size of the canvases, their visibility and their political importance – a work ordered by the king would have to be appropriately acknowledged, as would a portrait of a famous person. To this Chardin clearly added the

Roland Delaporte, *Les Apprêts d'un déjeuner rustique*
(Preparations for a Country Lunch).
Oil on canvas, 92 × 73 cm (36¼ × 28¾ in.).
Louvre, Paris.

criterion of quality; however, it is not certain that his 'malice' was called into play quite so systematically as Diderot maintains. At any rate, his hangings were considered by his contemporaries to express his knowledge of painting.

Chardin's function as *tapissier* did not prevent him from exhibiting about ten paintings at the Salon of 1763, all of which appear to have been still lifes,[7] including his famous *Jar of Olives* (see p. 83) which belonged to the Abbé Pommyer. The painting was hung in the staircase leading to the Salon Carré and is described in detail by Diderot: 'The artist has placed an old Chinese porcelain vessel on a table, with two biscuits, a jar full of olives, a shallow container of fruit, two glasses half filled with wine, a Seville orange and a pie. When looking at paintings by other artists, I feel that I need new eyes; when looking at paintings by Chardin, I have only to use those which nature gave me and use them well. If I were to steer my child towards painting, this is the painting which I would buy. "Make me a copy of this", I would say "and then copy it again." But perhaps nature is not more difficult to copy. For this porcelain vessel is made of real porcelain, these olives are really separated from the eye by the water in which they are floating; one only has to reach out and take these biscuits and eat them; cut open this orange and squeeze it, take this glass of wine and drink it, or pick up this fruit and peel it, or cut this pie with a knife. This is the true harmony of colour and its reflections. Oh Chardin! It is not just white, red or black which you grind on your palette: it is the very substance of your subjects. It is the air and the light which you put on the tip of your brush and attach to the canvas.' A little later, Diderot continues: 'I have been told that Greuze was visiting the Salon and that when he saw the painting by Chardin which I have just described, he looked at it and passed by, heaving a great sigh. This praise is shorter and more valuable than anything I could say.' Elie Fréron simply wrote that 'the pictures which Chardin exhibited this year are the finest of his which have ever been seen'.[8]

At this Salon of 1763, Roland Delaporte – whom Diderot was to compare harshly with Chardin on several occasions – exhibited for the first time, having been accepted into the Académie, *Preparations for a Country Lunch*, five paintings of flowers and fruit, his famous *Orange Tree* (in the Staatliche Kunsthalle, Karlsruhe; see p. 258) and a bas-relief. Delaporte belonged to that new generation of still-life painters whom Diderot described as being 'Chardin victims' and whose work clearly showed the latter's influence.

In October 1764, Cochin showed Marigny an ambitious plan to decorate the gallery of the Château de Choisy. The idea was to commission the leading history painters of the time to illustrate the peaceful acts of the great Roman emperors and, at the same time, to compare these with Louis XV. Thus, Carle Van Loo was commissioned to paint *Augustus Closing the Temple of Janus*, Noël Hallé to paint *Trajan Administering Justice* and Vien *Marcus Aurelius Comforting the People*. Cochin also proposed a series of overdoors: two allegories by Louis Lagrenée, four seascapes by Vernet, as well as others depicting the arts and flowers. Overdoors depicting historical subjects would be paid 1,500 *livres*, Vernet's landscapes 1,000 *livres*, 800 *livres* for allegories of the arts, and 600 *livres* for the flowers which Bachelier would be asked to paint.

The day after he had shown these plans to Marigny, Cochin proposed Chardin to him: 'You are aware of the degree of illusion and beauty which he

Jar of Olives, 1760. Oil on canvas, 71 × 98 cm (28 × 38⅝ in.). Louvre, Paris.

brings to the imitation of things which he undertakes and which he copies from life. His talents could therefore be used by asking him to make two or three of these paintings. In one, he could bring together the different attributes of the sciences, such as globes, air pumps, microscopes, telescopes, graphometers, etc. In a second, he could bring together attributes of the arts, such as a compass, a square, ruler, rolls of drawings and prints, a palette and brushes, a mallet and various sculpture tools, and so on. If these were for the room where three paintings are required, a third could depict the attributes of music – various string and wind instruments, scores, etc. I feel that these paintings would give a great deal of pleasure by the accuracy which seduces everyone and the art of rendering this, which has made M. Chardin the greatest painter ever in this genre.'[9]

We do not know if this precise list of objects to be portrayed came from Chardin himself or from Cochin, who had proposed the subjects for the history paintings at Choisy and who was very aware of Chardin's capabilities. Either way, despite his slowness, Chardin produced the three large overdoors, *Attributes of the Sciences*, the *Arts* and *Music*, one year later, 'for the rooms at Choisy'. The first of these paintings has disappeared, but its composition is known to us through a small drawing by Saint-Aubin and particularly through its description by Diderot which mentions, among other things, a globe and a telescope. *Attributes of the Arts* (T.O.P. 177; see page 182) contains rolls of drawings, a compass, rulers, set-squares, a palette and brushes, a mallet and various sculpture tools. *Attributes of Music* contains both string and wind instruments as well as scores, etc. In November, Cochin wrote to Marigny that 'M. Chardin's paintings are extremely beautiful and fulfil their role at Choisy perfectly, where I saw them. I feel that eight hundred *livres* for each of these was a very good price.'[10]

These large canvases, so brilliantly and knowledgeably composed, won praise for Chardin which was always along the same lines. Mathon de la Cour provides a good example: 'There is always a perfect imitation of nature, an admirable art of rendering the transparency of a substance and the softness of feathers. M. Chardin excels in this genre. His paintings often deceive the eye; and although this quality does not make him the top painter of all, he is still very great.'[11] However, it is Diderot to whom we should turn, as the Salon of 1765 provided him with the chance not only to marvel at the paintings exhibited by Chardin, but also to explain Chardin's artistic ideas (this was the occasion of his famous words on the difficult and often fruitless apprenticeship of painting), to speak of artists whom he liked or criticized and also to explain how Chardin organized the hangings of his contemporaries' work. The introduction sets the tone with a few pages devoted to 'the great magician' and to his 'silent compositions': 'How eloquently they speak to the artist! Everything they say to him about the imitation of nature, and the science of colour and harmony! How the air circulates around these objects! The light of the sun does not treat any better the disparate nature of the objects which it illuminates. You know neither friendly colours nor hostile colours.' Diderot then describes in greater or lesser detail the paintings exhibited, 'all equally perfect'. He begins with *Attributes of the Sciences*: 'This is nature herself, in terms of the accuracy of the shapes and the colours; the objects are quite separate from one another, advancing and receding as if they were real; there can be nothing more harmonious; there is no confusion, despite the number of objects and the small space which they are in.' The three paintings of *Refreshments* follow: two of them, which are now lost, bring together various objects in a sort of niche described by Diderot thus: 'Imagine a square structure of grey stone, a sort of window with a sill and a cornice. As nobly and elegantly as possible, add in a garland of vine leaves along the length of the cornice, tumbling down on both sides.' Within this window various refreshments were placed, such as wine, coffee, bread, eggs, radishes or fruit, lemonade, barley water and biscuits. 'So many objects!' Diderot exclaims. 'Such diversity of form and colour! And yet such harmony! Such peace!'

The third painting must have hung between the first two. This was *Dead Duck with a Pie, Porcelain Bowl and Jar of Olives* (T.O.P. 174; see p. 88), a large oval canvas, dated 1764, taller and narrower than the two rectangular paintings on either side of it. Diderot wrote 'if a connoisseur could only have one Chardin, then this is the one he should have. The artist is getting old. He has some paintings which are as good, but none better.' After a brief description of the painting, he added: 'here we see that there are hardly any unattractive objects in nature and that the aim is to render these'.

Diderot's praises applied also to *Basket of Grapes* (T.O.P. 172; see page 87) and to its pendant, *Basket of Plums* (T.O.P. 173; see p. 86), which made Chardin 'the Salon's best master of colour'. Diderot concluded with a definition of Chardin's painting which he refined further at the following Salon: 'Chardin's technique is quite individual. It is an uneven style in that close up one does not know what it is, and as one moves away, the subject reveals itself, eventually becoming nature herself. Sometimes it pleases as much close up as from a distance.'[12]

Following this success and particularly the success of his *Attributes* painted for the Château de Choisy, Chardin – who in January 1765 had been elected a member of the Académie de Rouen, having been nominated by Cochin and Jean Baptiste Descamps – was approached with another official commission. This was for the planned refurbishment of the Château de Bellevue. In July 1766, Cochin suggested the following names to Marigny: Lagrenée for two overdoors and a painting for the king's bedroom, Taraval for the overdoors in the dining room and Fragonard and Jean Bernard Restout for the games room. 'The music room seems to me to require something which reflects its purpose. This is why I feel it would be well decorated with two overdoors by M. *Chardin*. This artist achieves a unique degree of perfection in his field.'

Marigny would have liked Hubert Robert to contribute to the decoration, but Cochin objected that the scale of the figures in his compositions was not comparable with the others, particularly Chardin. Moreover, Cochin added with a certain hypocrisy, 'I preferred to employ [with Chardin] talent which is both certain and recognized, and which relates better to the intended use of this room.'

At the same time, Chardin was busy completing a different, no less prestigious, commission: this was his *Attributes of the Arts and Their Rewards* (see p. 179) which Catherine the Great had commissioned for the meeting room of the

Basket of Plums with Nuts, Currants and Cherries, c. 1765. Oil on canvas, 32 × 42 cm (12⅝ × 16½ in.). The Chrysler Museum, Norfolk, Virginia.

Basket of Grapes with Three Apples, a Pear and Two Marzipans. Oil on canvas, 21 × 40 cm (8¼ × 15¾ in.). Musée des Beaux-Arts, Angers.

*Dead Duck with a Pie, Porcelain Bowl and
Jar of Olives*, 1764. Oil on canvas,
150.5 × 95.2 cm (59¼ × 37½ in.).
Museum of Fine Arts, James Philip Gray
Collection, Springfield, Massachusetts.

Academy of Arts in St Petersburg. Although this may have been suggested to the Empress by Diderot, nonetheless it was Chardin who arranged the books, plans, rolls and portfolios of drawings and a palette with brushes around Pigalle's *Mercury* (see p. 184) on a large canvas. The sash of the Order of St Michael, on the left of the ledge in the foreground, symbolizes the 'rewards granted to the arts', as Pigalle had received the royal decoration in 1765 after completing his monument to Louis XV in Rheims. This painting, which is now in the Hermitage (T.O.P. 180), is dated 1766, along with a second version which was doubtless made for Pigalle, as it was included in the sale after his death in 1785. We can therefore understand why Chardin waited until the following year to paint, or at least complete, the two canvases which had been commissioned for Bellevue, namely *Attributes of Civil Music* and *Attributes of Battle Music* (T.O.P. 181 and 182). These two paintings, for which Chardin was paid 2,000 *livres*, a sum listed in his records for December 1767, are remarkably well balanced. They contrast not only civil music and battle music, but also popular music with music which emphasizes glory. In one, we see a violin, a flute, a drum, a tambourine, a hurdy-gurdy and a hunting horn; in the other, there are a trumpet, a drum, kettledrums, an oboe and cymbals, arranged around bound volumes, on embroidered fabric which appears to be the coat of a knight of the Order of the Holy Ghost; on the left-hand side, partly covering the drum, is some red fabric with a gold fringe which is probably a regiment's ensign. For Diderot it had 'an incredible strength of colour, a general harmony, a touching and true effect, beautiful masses, a magic of execution that makes one despair, a *ragoût* both in the selection and in the arrangement'.

It was about the time that he was finishing these paintings that Chardin's son, Jean Pierre, died. In Venice, where he had accompanied the Marquis de Paulmy in June 1767, it seems that he committed suicide by drowning in a canal. This tragic event was never mentioned by his father's contemporaries before the latter's death. Cochin was alone in writing in 1780 that the artist 'had experienced sorrow which had left him very sensitive: this was the death of his son. He had brought him up studying painting and…he had never neglected to encourage him to study the classics. [Jean Pierre Chardin] had spirit and reason, but had an unusual nature which was harmful to himself.'

It is to the success of the paintings for Bellevue that we can attribute the increase in Chardin's allowance the following year, after Restout's death. Henceforth he received a further 300 *livres*, which brought the allowance to 1,000 *livres*, the equivalent of what Carle Van Loo received as First Painter, and considerably more than the amount received by Hallé, Jeaurat, Vien, Louis Michel Van Loo, Aved and Louis Lagrenée, all of whom were history painters.[13]

At the Salon of 1769, Chardin exhibited two small paintings of fruit (T.O.P. 186 and 187; see p. 175) and a third version of *Attributes of the Arts and Their Rewards*, which belonged to the Abbé Pommyer, a version of *Girl Returning from the Market* and *Head of a Wild Boar* (see p. 91). He also showed ' under the same number two paintings of bas-reliefs' which, thanks to Saint-Aubin, we know were of *Bacchante Milking a Goat Held by a Child* (see p. 112) and *Satyr Holding a Goat Suckling a Little Satyr* (see p. 113), both dated 1769 (T.O.P. 188 and 189); these paintings were not hung until the day after the

Salon opened. Perhaps Chardin had not quite completed them in time for the hanging, but had nevertheless reserved a place for them![14]

'His two bas-reliefs are admirable', wrote Daudé de Jossan, the critic, 'and I have more faith in these miracles than in Zeuxis's grapes.'[15] This power of illusion is taken up satirically by Cochin.[16] 'Have you not seen these two paintings of bas-reliefs either? You must have thought that they were sculptures. Me, I was not fooled but you passed in front of them like someone who does not know anything about sculpture and you should admit that you know as little about painting.' This imitation of nature was also noted in Chardin's still lifes of fruit and animals and, above all, in his *Attributes of the Arts* where a critic noted that 'the sash seems to project out of the canvas'.[17] 'Who would not be pleased to complete a history painting as true and as decisive as this Mercury and these Attributes of the Arts…which maintain their effect at every moment of the day right up until evening', wrote Daudé de Jossan. *L'Avant-Coureur* added that 'this picture is remarkable for its vigorous and transparent colouring and for the intelligence of its chiaroscuro which makes one wonder if that which is depicted is not the real thing'.

Diderot, when discussing the paintings exhibited, wrote that he enjoyed repeating himself where praise was involved. Chardin 'is the great master of harmony, this thing which is so rare, which everyone speaks of and which very few know.… It is between nature and art.' The bas-reliefs had reproduced mediocre sculptures beautifully and 'I admire them greatly. One sees here that it is possible to be harmonious and colourist in the objects which least require it. They are white and yet there is neither black nor white; no two tones are similar and yet there is perfect harmony.'

The return of the bas-relief after a break of about forty years was a major artistic event. The 'old magician from whom age has not yet taken the wand'[18] understood it and he would try it again during the following decade, apparently renouncing fruit and animals and throwing himself, at the age of seventy and despite his health problems, into new experiments.

1. Reproduced by G. de Saint-Aubin in his catalogue. See E. Dacier, *Catalogue de ventes et livrets de Salons, illustrés par Saint-Aubin*, Paris, 1909–21, vol. I.

2. *Observation d'une société d'amateurs*, 1761.

3. These letters are all published by Furcy-Raynaud, *op. cit.*, 1904.

4. 'Description des tableaux…', *Mercure de France*, September 1763.

5. *Procès-verbaux de l'Académie*, 5 and 26 September 1761.

6. Quoted by J. Seznec and J. Adhémar in *Diderot, Salon de 1769*, 1963.

7. A painting of *'Fruit'* and 'another of a Bouquet' belonged to the Comte de Saint-Florentin: Pierre Rosenberg thinks that these can be identified as *Grapes and Pomegranates* and *The Brioche* in the Louvre (T.O.P. 166, 167), which are indeed dated 1763. But the word 'bouquet' seems difficult to apply to the orange blossom in *The Brioche*, a theme which was frequently the subject of still lifes at the time, and one is therefore tempted to think of a vase of flowers, such as the one exhibited at the previous Salon or the painting in Edinburgh (T.O.P. 139). Silvestre again lent two paintings, which were certainly pendants, namely *'Fruit'* and *'Leftovers of a Lunch'*. These are probably *Basket of Plums with Nuts, Currants and Cherries* (see page 86) and *Basket of Grapes with Three Apples, a Pear and Two Marzipans* (T.O.P. 172, 173; see page 87). The other works are described with even less precision.

8. *L'Année littéraire*, 4 October 1763, vol. VI.

9. M. Furcy-Raynaud, *op. cit.*, 1904, pp. 324–34.

10. At the same Salon of 1765, Van Loo, Hallé, Vien and Lagrenée exhibited paintings which they had completed for Choisy (Hallé and Lagrenée respectively replacing Jean Baptiste Deshayes and Boucher who had originally been approached by Cochin); Bachelier exhibited two overdoors of flowers in vases. In addition to the three *Attributes*, Chardin exhibited three paintings of *Refreshments*, including an oval (T.O.P. 174) and 'several paintings under the same number, one of which was of a basket of grapes'. This last painting, dated 1764, is in the Musée d'Angers (T.O.P. 172) and another version dated 1765 is in the Musée d'Amiens (T.O.P. 172A).

11. *Letters to M***…*, 1765.

12. This image had already been used twelve years earlier by Baillet de Saint-Julien (in his *Ode to Milord Telliab*, of 1753): 'The eye…would in vain, by its attention and many researches, learn the secret [of your paintings]: it is confounded, lost in your touch; drained of its efforts and without being any wiser, it moves further away, then closer and eventually only leaves promising to return.'

13. It should be pointed out that the Direction des Bâtiments for a long time delayed the payments for royal commissions. Chardin's bill for his paintings in Choisy and Bellevue was not settled in full until 1771. But he sold paintings and drew on his pensions, and also had the rent for the house in the Rue Princesse. In 1768 this was occupied by François Vernet, brother of Joseph, who paid him rent for fifteen months.

14. The date 1769 is also marked on a still life with mackerel hanging over a table on which there is a cabbage, radishes, onions, cheese in a round wooden box, a silver cruet, two brioches and some earthenware pots (San Francisco, Collection of Mrs Phoebe Cowles – see p. 176). This contrast between a kitchen table and pantry table seems to have been Chardin's last attempt at this sort of representation, but he does not appear to have exhibited it at the Salon.

15. *Sentiments sur les tableaux…*, 1769.

16. *Réponse de M. Jérôme à M. Raphaël.*

17. *Lettre sur l'exposition…*, 1769.

18. D. Diderot, *Salon de 1769*, ed. Seznec and Adhémar, vol. III, 1963.

Gabriel de Saint-Aubin,
drawings in the catalogue of the Salon of 1769.

CHAPTER FIVE

THE EVENING
OF A BEAUTIFUL DAY

*It may truthfully be said
that never have we seen an old man
sustain his talents for so long.*

Cochin

For the last time in his career, Chardin submitted to the Salon of 1769 a truly broad sample of his work: still lifes of fruit and game, bas-reliefs, a genre scene and a large decorative canvas. This selection of his work received unanimous praise. Perhaps this was why Cochin, on being relieved of his administrative duties when Jean Baptiste Marie Pierre was appointed First Painter to the King, asked Marigny for one last favour for Chardin. On Boucher's death, Cochin asked on 6 June 1770 that the Académie's allowance of 1,200 *livres* which Boucher had received be used to pay 500 *livres* to Vernet and Alexandre Roslin 'and that the remaining two hundred *livres* be paid to M. *Chardin* as an increase. He is now in his seventies and, at his age, it is comforting to be looked after by one's superiors, particularly as he is still very capable. This is likely to be the last favour which I shall ask of you in relation to the artists who are both my colleagues and my friends.'

On 21 July, Marigny informed Chardin that the King had granted him an increase of 400 *livres*, which brought the total amount of allowances received by Chardin since 1752 to 1,400 *livres*, the highest amount ever received by a painter.[1] Chardin thanked Marigny for this increase. It seems that it was Madame Chardin who put pen to paper[2] and Chardin explained himself as being 'confined to the house by infirmities which have overwhelmed [him and] deprived him of the pleasure of going to visit you to give you [his] humble thanks, [he] hopes to have a little extra time to complete his duty', and repeated his excuses 'given the current circumstances'.[3]

Chardin's only known work of 1770 is a large painting of *Autumn* after a sculpted bas-relief which Edmé Bouchardon had designed for the fountain in the Rue de Grenelle (T.O.P. 190; see p. 95). He had already used the central part of this, the City of Paris, in his overdoor of *Attributes of the Arts* (see p. 182) painted for the Château de Choisy. Although he showed this at the Salon of 1771, it was his 'three studies of heads, in pastel' which caused surprise. The septuagenarian artist who, as we saw at the beginning, was a poor draughtsman, appears to have tackled pastel for the first time. Increasingly, he used this technique only for portraits of individuals – which he executed with unbelievable skill although he had painted very few of them and none for a long time. We are torn between fascination and questions about this move suddenly to abandon painting still life and genre scenes in favour of portraiture and to begin to use pastel where previously he had painted in oil. It has been said that Chardin was suffering from a sort of allergy to the pigments used in oil paint, on the basis of a letter which the painter sent, a year before his death, to the king's new Directeur des Bâtiments, the Comte d'Angiviller. 'My weaknesses prevent me from painting in oil and I have fallen back on pastel, which has allowed me to pick a few more flowers, if I dare to count on the public's indulgence.'[4] Cochin, meanwhile, wrote in 1780 that 'several years before the end, he fell prey to a number of disabilities which led him to abandon or at least to

Autumn, 1770. Oil on canvas, 51 × 82.5 cm (20⅛ × 32½ in.). Pushkin Museum, Moscow.

Head of an Old Man,
1771. Pastel,
45 × 37 cm
(17¾ × 14⅝ in.).
J. Horvitz collection,
United States.

96

paint less frequently in oil. This was the time when he began to paint in pastel, a field of painting which he had not tried before. He did not use it for his usual subjects, but used it to paint life-size studies of heads.' It is indeed likely that he had health problems, but it is also possible that a final burst of pride pushed Chardin to prove his mastery of what for him was a new genre. Some forty years earlier he had shown that he was not limited to still life, but that he knew how to paint a figure; he also proved that he could equal Desportes in bas-reliefs. He was therefore keen to try a new technique, a new genre. This may be because since 1745 La Tour had brought renewed acclaim to pastel, or because in 1769 Lépicié had exhibited several heads of old men, but particularly because at the Salon of 1771, still life was largely the field of the new generation – the field of Nicolas Desportes, Roland Delaporte and Anne Vallayer-Coster.

The three pastels exhibited included his *Self-portrait with Spectacles* and *Head of an Old Man* (T.O.P. 191 and 192; see pp. 96 and 228). Oddly enough, if the critics noticed this new medium, they do not seem to have grasped the boldness of the execution at which we marvel today, putting both his pastels and his bas-reliefs at the level of mere truthfulness to life. 'The admirable Chardin has exhibited several pastels, including a self-portrait, which are as true as all of his work: bas-reliefs, etc., etc. This is the father of effects whom the young should consult often.'[5] The author of these lines immediately moves on to the *Military Trophy* by Anne Vallayer-Coster, the subject of which may well have derived from previous models by Chardin. Diderot emphasizes the illusion of his bas-relief, adding that he had 'seen more than one person fooled. It seems to me that one could say that Nature has taken M. Chardin and M. Buffon into her confidence.' On the subject of the three studies of heads, he wrote that 'it is still the same sure and free hand, the same eyes accustomed to looking at nature, and to seeing it well and to extracting the magic of its effects'. However, in *L'Année littéraire*, Fréron stressed that 'it is a completely new genre for him and yet he has excelled in his efforts'. On the subject of the pastels, Cochin wrote that 'He made several of different individuals, young people, old people and others. He was very successful due to his skill and his broad and easy manner, in appearance at least, for in fact it is the fruit of a great deal of reflection and he was a hard man to satisfy. These works show that he had a feeling for greatness and that he could have been a history painter had he so desired.' Once again, Chardin was praised in the same way, but no specific attention was paid to his new talent. Chardin took no notice and continued.[6] Although he had been ill at the beginning of 1772,[7] he spent a great deal of time dealing with the sorry state of the finances of the Académie's school and it seems that he devoted less and less time to his painting. In 1774, he resigned his post as Treasurer[8] and in May 1775 he requested and received an additional payment of 600 *livres*.

Although the critics were silent in 1773, Cochin did comment on the pastels which he showed in 1775, this time with the praise which they deserved: 'These works have all the ease and lightness which an artist in the prime of his life could give. The freshness of the tones of the woman's head, compared with the strong tones of the man, are a true and complete contrast in taste, to which must be added that the execution is magical, proud and truly bold.'[9] However,

Diderot has Jacques Philippe de Saint-Quentin say that 'the colour is a little mannered. Overall, I prefer his genre paintings.'[10]

Chardin continued his series of paintings after the bas-reliefs on the fountain in the Rue de Grenelle with *Winter* (T.O.P. 197) executed in 1776, apparently his last painting. In the same year, he made a second version of the portrait of Madame Chardin (in the Art Institute of Chicago) and a pastel copy of a portrait of Rembrandt's mother (T.O.P. 196; see page 227). Although he exhibited these works at the Salon, it is more than likely that they were intended for his own use or for his family and that he had no intention of selling them.[11] Quite naturally Chardin kept his own portrait and those of his wife and his sister-in-law, Madame Daché, in his own collection. The second *Self-portrait with Spectacles* was to be presented by Chardin to one of his pupils, Mademoiselle de La Marsaulaye. *Head of an Old Man* and *Portrait of the Painter Bachelier* (see p. 226) were clearly studies, intended for his own use – perhaps, in the case of the latter, commissioned by the sitter. In his portrait, Bachelier is wearing a 'Spanish' costume, similar to that seen in Fragonard's fantasy portraits in the 1770s, which, like Chardin's work, show Rembrandt's influence.

In 1777, Chardin exhibited his bas-relief of *Winter* and, one is tempted to say as usual, 'three studies of heads in pastel under the same number', which included his portraits of a *Young Girl* and a *Young Boy* (T.O.P. 198 and 199; see pp. 100 and 101). Both the performance of the ageing artist and their intrinsic quality was praised: 'M. Chardin reminds me of those athletes who, reeling after a terrible contest, summon all their strength to go on, only to expire in the arena.'[12] Chardin did not reserve his energy only for his work – he used it harshly on occasions which seemed to him to be unjust. His friend, Cochin, who had always supported him, had just left his post as Secretary of the Académie in 1777. This provided Pierre, First Painter to the King, who had never got on with Cochin, with an opportunity to humiliate Cochin by putting him at the bottom of the hierarchy of councillors, without taking his seniority into account. An indignant Chardin wrote a letter to the Comte d'Angiviller which deserves to be quoted, as it explains the way in which bonds were woven between the artists.[13] Pierre is supposed to have said 'it was those for whom M. Cochin had arranged favours from the King who started that hare… Everyone received allowances. I cannot apply this remark to myself without being wounded by it. Does he think that M. Cochin arranged the support of his superiors for me? I dared to believe that I owed these favours to my services and a little to the talent which God gave me. It is dreadful to abuse an old man to whom the King has made a pensioner of the Invalides.'

Chardin reluctantly gave in to d'Angiviller's reply, which supported Pierre, while expressing the esteem in which Chardin was held by artists and even by the First Painter himself! This was small consolation for the old artist whose health was deteriorating and whose output was decreasing. Although his pastels were well received, particularly by artists such as Silvestre who added Chardin's *Self-portrait with Spectacles* and his *Madame Chardin* to his collection, they were not really aimed at the collecting public.[14] However, Chardin was not in financial need, as the inventory after his death would show. He had sold the house in the Rue Princesse in 1773 for 1,800 *livres* in the form of a life annuity and he also received an allowance which was more than adequate. But the delays in payment and the form which these sometimes took made his income unpredictable.[15] This is doubtless the reason why in June 1778 he expressed his desire to d'Angiviller to have some form of annuity. He highlighted the disastrous financial situation of the Académie when he took up his post as Treasurer in 1755: 'On the other hand, when I retired from this post at the end of 1774, all debts paid and, despite the many extraordinary and considerable expenses which the Académie found itself obliged to meet, I left it with some thirty thousand *livres* either in cash, or in sums which could be easily recovered. In this respect, my only merit was the precision and the care which I took in fulfilling my obligations, but I can also say that I never had anything less than true satisfaction from seeing order re-established in our finances…. It is quite usual, sir, that a person who has carried out a role honourably for twenty years, in any institution, continues to receive a fee – what is known as a pension. In 1775, when I left my post, you were certainly kind enough to allow me to benefit from the kindnesses of His Majesty, by giving me an additional payment *despite the difficulty of the times*. Because of these same difficult times, I had to be satisfied with this, but you led me to believe *that I would receive further kindnesses from the King, should there be some means available*…. Such means would allow me to enjoy the continuation of my income, and could be taken from the surplus of funds available at the Académie…. To finish, if I might be so bold, having spoken not only of the interests of the Treasurer, but also those of the painter, I would like to take the liberty of pointing out to the Protector of the Arts that this favour would benefit an artist who is concerned only with truth, the favours of His Majesty having helped him sustain his painting with honour, but who has unfortunately proved that the long and arduous study which nature demands does not lead to fortune.' This letter is dated 21 June 1778, and is followed by a postscript: 'Alas, you are not yet finished, sir. My wife, who also wishes to be involved in this matter, maintains that it is not sufficient to have passed on my letter, but that she would also like to speak on her own account as follows: "You would not", she says to me, "have prejudiced your request, had you mentioned the trouble and the care which I have taken in running your affairs, and I am not satisfied with the sterile compliments which the Académie has paid to me in the past: if compensation is due, the Lady Treasurer has a right to it. She only desires a promissory note instructing the new Treasurer to pay sums owing dating back to 1755."'[16]

The Comte d'Angiviller's reply shows surprise at this request: 'I thought I had made clear on this occasion the favours which you have successively obtained and I have found that for a very long time you have enjoyed rooms and an allowance which was quite quickly increased to fourteen hundred *livres* (independently of the two hundred *livres* granted for your work hanging the paintings), while the top-ranked officers of the Académie received only five, six or eight hundred *livres*. I could not avoid seeing this as the expected compensation for your services as Treasurer; for although your works prove the care which have earned you a deserved reputation in your genre of painting, you will no doubt recognize that the same justice is due to your peers who have worked in genres which are equally if not more difficult.'[17]

Although Chardin's arguments and his wife's indignation did not have the expected results, their efforts do, however, seem to have been justified.[18]

Portrait of a Young Girl,
1776. Pastel,
45 × 37.5 cm
(17¾ × 14⅞ in.).
Private collection.

Portrait of a Young Boy, 1776.
Pastel, 45 × 37.5 cm
(17¾ × 14⅞ in.).
Private collection.

However, final recognition of his talents came on the occasion of the Salon of 1779 when Chardin once again showed 'several studies of heads in pastel under the same number'. One of these, a *Jacquet* or young boy, was noticed by Madame Adélaïde (according to Cochin) or by Madame Victoire (according to Haillet de Couronne). Chardin said that he would be very happy to present the picture to the princess if the work pleased her, and she in turn gave him a gold snuffbox as a token of her gratitude. Among the other pastels, there is every reason to believe there was his final, moving *Self-portrait* (not dated; T.O.P. 201; see p. 225). In it we see Chardin, as eight years previously, wearing a sort of turban tied with a blue ribbon; again he has a scarf around his neck and his spectacles on his nose. The face has thinned and the flesh is sunken, but the eyelids frame a look which is still as sharp as ever. On an easel in front of him, attached to a frame, is a piece of blue-tinted paper and he is holding a pastel crayon. This ruthless portrait stirs our emotions; but the critics, who mentioned only *Jacquet*, cruelly said that 'his prime was past', giving the impression to the public that Chardin should have faded away quietly.

Admittedly, the *Journal de littérature* wrote: 'it is very interesting to see M. Chardin prove once more the passion of his art at eighty years of age and to give our young pupils some excellent lessons in effect, in true colours, harmony and three-dimensional composition. This good colourist will certainly never teach them to render flesh as shiny as porcelain figures.' *Le Miracle de nos jours* devoted some verse to him, laudatory to begin with, but quite harsh at the end:

> O surprise! O fait incroyable!
> Du temps qui le respecte il a détruit les lois.
> Le sentiment, pour lui toujours inaltérable,
> Brille, respire encore, et parle sous ses doigts.
> Une tête jeune et nouvelle,
> (Ah! sans doute en dépit de ses quatre-vingts ans)
> Rendit tout caduque autour d'elle;
> Et le dernier Salon couronna ses talents.
> Le bruit des applaudissements
> A dû le rajeunir en charmant ses oreilles:
> Que ne fut-il forcé
> D'employer plus de veilles!
> Que ne fut-il encouragé,
> Il aurait produit des merveilles.

Oh, surprise! Oh, incredible deed! / He has destroyed the laws of Time who honours him. / Feeling, always unchangeable for him, / Shines out, breathes again, and speaks beneath his fingers. / A new young head / (Ah! doubtless despite its eighty years) / Renders everything about it null and void; / And the last Salon crowned his talents. / The noise of the applause / Should have rejuvenated him by charming his ears: / If only he had been forced / To spend more sleepless nights! / If only he had been encouraged, / He would have produced marvels.

The author of *Encore un Rêve* wrote more severely that Chardin 'having grown old in harness, still tries, with a trembling hand, to paint the young. M. Chardin has done enough for the glory of the French School; he enjoys quite a good reputation, and he should not try to improve it.'[19]

A short time later, at the beginning of October 1779, Chardin was unable to attend the Académie and, during the same month, Pierre informed d'Angiviller that 'M. Chardin is not fully well, but not so much as to give cause for concern.' However, he added, in a note in the margin, that 'this had changed greatly', since he had written the letter. By May, Cochin had written to Descamps, 'M. Chardin is quite well except for his legs which become swollen during the day and which go down again at night and which, in addition, are affected by a little erysipelas.' On 30 September, he wrote that 'M. Chardin is not at all well, his swollen legs are making him suffer and, together with his other infirmities, this adds to his distress. He seems to have lost his cheerfulness and his appetite.'[20] On 6 November, Lagrenée and Cochin were nominated by the Académie to visit the 'dangerously ill' painter and on 16 November, Doyen wrote to his friend Desfriches: 'M. Chardin has received the sacraments; he is declining and this is causing a good deal of worry; he has his full senses, the swelling in his legs has moved on to other parts of his body; it is not clear what the result will be.'

Cochin wrote: 'M. Chardin had been suffering from a gallstone for a very long time. However, it had not yet fully formed and manifested itself in the form of small flakes. He also suffered from other infirmities. In these last days his legs became very swollen; dropsy finally reached his chest and he died…'

On 6 December 1779, Chardin died at his rooms in the Louvre. He was buried the following day. In *Mémoires secrets*, the entry for 21 December reads: 'His end was like the evening of a beautiful day. Like Rousseau, he believed that a dying man should never seek to frighten onlookers with a sad and disgusting manner; during his final illness, he went on having himself shaved as usual.'

On 18 December, the inventory of his possessions was drawn up.[21] The paintings and prints were valued by Vernet and Cochin. Among Chardin's own works were six pastels, one of which was a replica of *Jacquet* estimated at 300 *livres*, the others being put at between 6 and 96 *livres*, eight different still lifes which were given quite a low value of 6 to 24 *livres*, a bas-relief valued at 500 *livres*, twelve sketches which together were estimated at 24 *livres* and the sketch for the surgeon's signboard which was valued at 6 *livres*.[22]

Shortly afterwards, Haillet de Couronne, who was to give Chardin's eulogy at the Académie de Rouen, asked Cochin to give him details. In a letter to Descamps, dated July 1780, Cochin wrote: 'I think that M. de *Couronne* may be a little worried by their quantity and apparent insignificance, but what could one find of great note in the life of an artist who lived quietly and simply in carrying out his art?' Three weeks later, Cochin wrote again to Descamps to add a few more details and the dates which he had not given in his first text. He added: 'I am currently working on a few detailed notes on certain facts. But as they are not the sort of thing to be made public, it will not be necessary for M. de *Couronne* to have these before reading his eulogy – on the contrary it will relieve him of the temptation to let anything slip out.'[23]

1. Only sculptors received higher allowances. Bouchardon received 3,400 *livres*, Pigalle 2,350 *livres*. In the case of Pigalle, 1,600 *livres* were paid in the form of an indemnity for the loss of his studio in 1756 (Michel, *op. cit.*, p. 516).

2. See P. Rosenberg, Chardin exhibition catalogue, 1979, p. 400.

3. It was said that this increase was one of Cochin's last interventions before he lost his official post. However, in 1772, when he learnt that the king's Direction des Bâtiments still owed Chardin 8,830 *livres*, 2,800 of which were outstanding for the paintings commissioned for Choisy and Bellevue, Cochin wrote a note saying: 'I still feel a secret remorse for having acquired the five paintings mentioned above from M. *Chardin* at such a good price when I was in charge of purchases for the Arts; a man of his merits should have been treated more generously. Is there a way that the Director could see his way to making good my mistake? Perhaps he could grant M. *Chardin* a bonus, given the delay which he has tolerated and the nature of the terms under which he agrees to be paid' (quoted in the 1979 Chardin exhibition catalogue, p. 400). Cochin proposed increasing the sum from 8,830 to 10,000 *livres*, and this was granted.

4. Letter of 28 June 1778 in which Chardin asked for a pension.

5. *Plainte de M. Badigeon*, 1771.

6. In 1773, he again exhibited heads in pastel, as well as a version of *Woman Drawing Water from a Copper Cistern*. In 1775, a further 'three studies of heads in pastel', including his *Self-portrait with Eye-shade* and his *Portrait of Madame Chardin* (T.O.P. 194 and 195; see pp. 8 and 229).

7. In January 1772 Cochin wrote to Descamps that Chardin 'sent him many compliments and is still cruelly incapacitated' (C. Michel, 'Lettres Adressées par Charles-Nicolas Cochin Fils à Jean Baptiste Descamps, 1759–90', *Archives de l'Art Français*, new per., vol. XXVIII, 1986).

8. P. Rosenberg, Chardin exhibition catalogue, 1979, p. 401.

9. *Observations sur les ouvrages exposés au Salon du Louvre* or *Lettre de M. le comte de …*

10. The Salon of 1775 is written in the form of a dialogue between Diderot and the painter Jacques Philippe de Saint-Quentin, who represents the 'anti-Académie' trend.

11. The inventory after Chardin's death lists what appear to be six heads in pastel: 'a small study of a head, a beggar – the little Jacquet, a replica – the head of an old man – portrait with spectacles, a replica – two studies, a little boy and a little girl'. The last two of these were given a total value of 300 *livres*, while the little Jacquet and the old man were valued at 96 *livres* and the self-portrait at 72 *livres*.

12. *La Prêtresse*, 1777.

13. Letter quoted in full by P. Rosenberg, Chardin exhibition catalogue, 1979, p. 75. See also Michel, *op. cit.*, 1993.

14. Could the fantasy portrait said to be of *Bachelier* in the Vassal de Saint-Hubert sale in fact represent a member of the family or one of the collector's relatives?

15. The payments for his work at Choisy and Bellevue, for example, were made by means of an allowance of 4 per cent on *Aides et Gabelles* (types of taxes).

16. Regarding this postscript and the vehemence of Madame Chardin, it must be said that she was very ill at the beginning of 1778, as witnessed by two letters from Cochin to Descamps (Michel, 1986, letters XXXIV and XXXV); it may be that she was worrying about her financial future, because of her husband's chronic ill-health.

17. This remark highlights once again the different treatment given to each genre, but it expresses politely what Pierre had planned to write to Chardin: 'Although your works prove the efforts which have won you a reputation in a genre, you must feel that we owe the same justice to your peers, and you must admit that for equal work your studies have never incurred such high costs or such considerable amounts of time as those of your colleagues who have painted in the higher genres. One might even be grateful to them for their unselfishness, because if the incomes expected by them were related to their efforts, the administration would not be in a position to satisfy them' (letters quoted in full by P. Rosenberg, 1979, pp. 404–5). Should we recall here Chardin's beginnings and Cochin's phrase about the study of the classics delaying study of the arts? This translates exactly into the 'considerable loss of time' incurred by history painters. This is why Chardin who was 'angry that he had not learnt Latin and its literature in his youth, for which he was only able to compensate with reading, never neglected to encourage his son to study the classics. He had hoped that his son might be able to acquire some distinction in his art'.

18. In December 1778, the Direction des Bâtiments owed Chardin four years of allowances in arrears, i.e., 5,600 *livres*, and in January of the following year we find a reference to the 3,800 *livres* owing to him for paintings (presumably those which he did for Choisy and Bellevue). These documents are in the Archives Nationales, series 0¹ and they are quoted by P. Rosenberg, 1979, p. 405.

19. *Le Journal de Paris* summarizes what most of the critics said about Chardin without excepting those who were particularly hard on him. It lists two or three who reported, despite everything, what the public still admired in him: in addition, an article drawn from a previous issue of the *Journal* said that 'this old man, an octogenarian, who like the old *Entelle*, always goes down and shows himself in the lists and who, not having let a single exhibition pass without showing his paintings, teaches the young their lessons, has given us this year several studies in pastel where we recognize the touch of sentiment which never dies.' In addition it quotes *La Lunette*: 'M. Chardin has distinguished himself again with his Heads of Old Men and above all with his *Jacquet* [it had been purchased by Madame Victoire de France]. One could say that painting caresses him and has done for thirty years'. Finally, *Le Visionnaire* wrote: 'We saw several heads in pastel. At the sight of these works, the God of taste witnessed a living joy. It has been over forty years, he said, since I have seen this Artist's work here and it is always

crowned by deserved success. Always a bold and learned colour, a deep knowledge of the harmony of a painting, a generous and easy manner and, a warmth of execution which is rare in youth. Look at this head of a young boy – do you know any paintings where the colour is fresher or sparkles so?'

20. These two texts are reproduced by C. Michel, 1986, letters LVI and LIX.

21. Most of this inventory is reproduced by G. Wildenstein in *Chardin*, 1933, p. 144 ff.

22. In addition *Saying Grace* was valued at 48 *livres*, *Soap Bubbles* at half that, *Game of Goose* at 48 *livres* and *Card Games* at 30 *livres*; a *Washerwoman*, who is probably the woman at the copper cistern, was valued at 36 *livres*; *Child with a Spinning Top*, a replica of the portrait of the young Godefroy boy, and *The Governess* were valued at 24 *livres* each; and a *Boy Grinding Colours* and *Two Children*, life-size, were valued at 6 *livres* each. There were also some paintings by La Hyre, Silvestre and Jouvenet, engravings, a plaster horse by Pigalle and, also by Pigalle, a *Mercury* and a *Child*, as well as drawings by Cochin, one of which, an *Allegory of the Death of the Dauphin*, was valued at 120 *livres*, while the total sum of Chardin's possessions was valued at relatively low prices. The inventory also listed the furniture, the possessions, jewelry and silverware, as well as the contents of Chardin's wardrobe which comprised seven complete outfits including one made of velvet, and another decorated with silver braid, as well as a list of the documents relating to his annuities and pensions. In total, and excluding his painter's pension which has already been discussed, Chardin and his wife enjoyed an annual income of a little over 6,000 *livres*, which was very decent. A few months later, on 6 March 1780, when Madame Chardin put her husband's paintings up for sale, there remained only seven genre subjects in pendants: *The Governess* and *The Diligent Mother*; *Card Games* and the *Game of Goose*, 'two paintings of monkeys', and *The Washerwoman*.

23. C. Michel, 1986, letters LXIII and LXIV.

PART II

THE GREAT
MAGICIAN

CHAPTER ONE

THE PAINTER
AND THE CRITICS

*Here you are again, you great magician,
with your silent compositions. How eloquently
they speak to the artist! Everything they
say to him about the imitation of nature,
the science of colour and harmony!*

Diderot

For some forty years, Chardin's work was greeted with almost unanimous praise from the critics. Reviews of his work were sometimes repeated verbatim, which was not that unusual at a time when this very specialized literary genre was just being established. The reviews show that there were already several ways of discussing painting. One of these was purely descriptive ('in this painting, one sees…'), and another more of an aesthetic and conceptual discourse. The two methods were sometimes used together by the same writer. At the Salon of 1765, for example, Diderot began his critique of Chardin with the famous words: 'There you are, you great magician, with your silent compositions. How eloquently they speak to the artist'. This was followed by a digression on genre painting, and then a precise description of the contents of the various attributes of the arts, the sciences and music, and the baskets of fruit. He even wrote: 'I will say just one thing to you on the subject of Chardin and it is this: choose his setting, place the objects into this setting as I will show you, and rest assured that you will have seen his paintings.'

TRUTH AND MAGIC

Over the years, in critiques and eulogies, the characteristics of Chardin's painting were defined. The main criterion was Chardin's imitation of nature, the magic of his brush in capturing reality: 'natural' and 'imitation' being the key words. In 1738, the Chevalier de Neufville de Brunhaubois Montador stressed 'the striking naturalness of his figures' which were filled with 'nature and spirit'. The following year, he again admired the 'astonishingly natural' *Governess* (see p. 43). La Font de Saint-Yenne acknowledged Chardin's 'talent for rendering with a truth which is his alone' certain moments in life and he pointed to 'the truthfulness of imitation' in Chardin's *Amusements of Private Life*. Meanwhile the Abbé Le Blanc 'admired both the care with which he studied Nature and the happy talent which he has for rendering it'.

Described in 1748 as a 'great imitator of nature', whose 'truthfulness of (taste) charms us', Chardin 'renders nature with the utmost precision and truth'. In the same way that Bernard Le Bovier de Fontenelle described a philosopher, 'he bases nature on fact'. And what is more, he knows better than anyone how to render the finest touches 'with a truth of illusion that always seems new'.[1]

While Fréron wrote that the 'strength and the truth with which he renders nature in all of the subjects which he represents is incalculable', and the critic Abbé Bridard de la Garde went into raptures about his 'Luncheon which portrays the exact nature of the objects which he imitated', Diderot was not to be outdone in praising his powers of verisimilitude. At the very first Salon which he reported on in 1759, he exclaimed 'it is always nature and the truth'. Two years later, he again praised the 'imitation which is so faithful to nature', while pointing out that it concerned 'basic, ordinary and domestic nature',

Page 106:
The Attributes of the Arts (detail).
Louvre, Paris.

Page 108:
The Schoolmistress (detail).
National Gallery, London.

110

which was a way of paying homage to the talent of a painter who transcends his subject through his depiction of it. In 1763, he went further, in an effort to explain how the painting was more than simply realism: 'this is nature itself … the objects are quite separate from the canvas and are so true that they deceive the eyes'. Diderot repeated this description word for word in 1765 when describing *Attributes of the Sciences*.

In 1767, Diderot wrote of his paintings of musical instruments that Chardin 'compares his painting to Nature and that he deems his work to be poor if he has not maintained her presence'. This gives us a better understanding both of what the encyclopaedist liked about the artist's work and also what the imitation of nature meant to him. In 1769, Diderot continued this line of thought when discussing *Attributes of the Arts* ('everyone sees nature, but Chardin sees it well and exhausts himself in rendering it as he sees it'; see p. 179) and *Girl Returning from the Market* ('Chardin is such a rigorous imitator of nature, such a harsh judge of himself…'; see p. 212). Of the bas-reliefs which Chardin exhibited in 1769 (see pp. 112 and 113) he was driven to write: 'it seems to me that one could say of M. Chardin and M. Buffon that Nature has taken them into her confidence.'

In these various comments on a painter whose work he greatly admired, we see that for Diderot the relationship between Chardin's painting and nature was manifested in different ways. He wrote of 'nature as he has seen her at home and against which he compares his picture until there is no difference between the object represented and his model': at the same time he wrote that Loutherbourg, whom he admired, had seen nature in the work of Teniers and Wouwermans. It is true that when Diderot wrote his *Salons*, Chardin was mainly exhibiting still lifes. Thus, his judgments in relation to nature, a painting's illusion and imitation differ greatly from those of critics who were commenting on Chardin's genre scenes and how he recreated reality in these. There is also the nature which Chardin 'exhausted himself in rendering as he sees it'. Here Diderot introduced a further aspect to his analysis of the artist's pictorial plan and how he was received by connoisseurs. This was no longer concerned, as in the much quoted stories of Zeuxis, with deceiving the viewer which any skilled painter is capable of doing. In 1769 when he exhibited two bas-reliefs after Van Opstal, Diderot, who 'admired them greatly', emphasized the harmony and the mastery of colour. 'It is [Chardin] who sees the light ripple and the reflections on the surface of a body; it is he who seizes these and who renders their incomparable results, with what I do not know.' The same year, Diderot related an anecdote about Chardin being 'such a rigorous imitator of nature' that he did not finish a still life when the rabbits for it began to rot, as he despaired 'of achieving the harmony which he had in mind, with any others'. Although this relates to a technical problem, i.e. Chardin's slowness, above all it demonstrates the importance of the general harmony of a painting, which would be based on a set idea in his mind. The composition was built up through a general harmony of tone, which Chardin would sketch out and then work on gradually. However, *at the same time* he needed to keep the model in front of him in order to achieve final harmony and he was unable to paint from memory or to capture an exact colour or value without referring to this model.

Bacchante Milking a Goat Held by a Child, 1769. Oil on canvas, 53 × 91 cm (20⅞ × 35⅞ in.). Private collection, Switzerland.

Satyr Holding a Goat Suckling a Little Satyr, 1769. Oil on canvas, 53 × 91 cm (20⅞ × 35⅞ in.). Private collection, Switzerland.

Four years later, writing about Chardin's *Dead Duck with a Pie, Porcelain Bowl and Jar of Olives* (see p. 88), Diderot noted: 'Here one sees that there are no unattractive objects in nature and that the aim is to render them.' Render them, but not duplicate them – this is the ambiguity of the commentaries on imitation and illusion. A perfect example is the bas-relief imitating a bronze exhibited in 1755, in which the 'illusion is [so] perfect that it fades only slightly when it is touched.' On the subject of a still life with a pie, Daudé de Jossan had his M. Raphaël write 'this is the beauty of nature, which deceives the eye of the connoisseur and the tooth of the gourmand....My mouth was watering.'[2] The *Réponse de M. Jérôme*, written by Cochin, points to the limits of this illusion with humour as Jérôme replies to Raphaël that if this picture 'is deceptive, one should not be distracted so by greediness'. He reproaches him for not having noticed the bas-reliefs: 'you simply took them to be sculptures. I myself was not fooled because I touch everything', and he concludes that Raphaël knew as little about sculpture as he did about painting! These fictitious characters invented by Daudé de Jossan and Cochin were intended as parodies of the public's reaction. They clearly show that the wind had changed in the way that painting was perceived. Henceforth, painting was defined by its intrinsic qualities and no longer by how perfect an illusion it was of reality. If the food and drink painted by Chardin whetted the appetite, everyone knew that it was futile to try to take it and 'were it not for such a sublime technique, then Chardin's ideal would be miserable'.[3]

For his contemporaries, what made Chardin's art so unique was his own special way of portraying his subjects. Still in 1769, when writing about *Attributes of the Arts and Their Rewards* (see p. 179), the chronicler of *L'Avant-Coureur* noted that 'this painting is remarkable for its vigorous and transparent colouring and an intelligent use of chiaroscuro which makes one wonder if that which is represented is not the actual object itself'.[4] The 'magic' of the imitation and appreciation of an admirable technique of achieving this are clearly evident here. This is 'the object itself', but it is primarily a work of art, which Chardin achieves largely through his talents as a colourist. Fréron showed clearly how one enables the other, when he wrote that 'these are not the colours seen on an artist's palette; these are real tones and tints; in fact, they are nature herself and all of her harmony'. Fréron went on to praise 'the [incalculable] strength and truth with which he renders nature in all of the objects which he attempts to represent, as well as the amazing understanding of colour and the effects of directly reflected light'.[5] In 1763, Diderot wrote of the same paintings that 'he is the one who understands the harmony of colours and reflections'.

As early as 1757, when comparing the talents of Greuze and Chardin as colourists, Antoine Renou remarked how Chardin's subjects 'are mirrored in each other and the result is a transparency of colour which enlivens everything touched by his brush', referring to 'the magic of his tones'. Diderot took up this idea in 1761, speaking of the 'magic of colours' which, from the early years, characterized Chardin's work. This term was not used by chance, as 'the *magic* of painting is based on the magic of light, that is on the countless effects which produce colours and which change these constantly before our eyes', and 'it is the vigour of the colouring, the quality of harmony and the agreement of

Opposite:
The Attributes of the Arts and Their Rewards (detail). Hermitage, St Petersburg.

neighbouring tones which ensure that the colour I have mentioned is exactly the right colour for the place to which it has been assigned and that at this moment it adds to or completes the *magical* illusion which gives relief to an object painted on a flat surface and makes it stand out from the background against which it appears to be set.'[6]

In *Essais sur la peinture*, almost certainly written in 1765–66, Diderot again devotes a long passage to colour in painting, which naturally refers to Chardin, in particular when he defines the great colourist as 'he who has taken the tone of nature and well lit objects and who has known how to make his painting match this.'[7] Later, stressing how much more difficult it is to paint flesh than birds, fruit or flowers, he indirectly praises La Tour, and adds: 'This Chardin, why are his imitations of inanimate beings taken for nature herself? It is because he paints flesh when it suits him.'

CHARDIN'S TOUCH AND HIS BRUSH

This praise for truth, imitation and colour raises a major question at a time when the debate was predominantly about technique: how did Chardin work, what was his method of painting, how did he use his palette and how did he obtain his unique effects? Diderot, who appreciated his theories about painting, claimed that 'it is said that he has a technique all his own and that he uses his thumb as much as his brush. I do not know what it is; what is certain is that I have never known anyone who has actually seen him paint.'[8] However, from the beginning, it was noted that 'his taste in painting is unique; there are no set lines or smooth strokes. On the contrary, it is rough and coarse. It seems that his brushstrokes are laboured, but nevertheless his figures have a striking truth.'[9] These terms are not purely descriptive, as they use the terminology of the studio. Do his 'smooth strokes' mean that the colours were imperceptibly mixed, so that one could not discern how one blends into the other? Watelet explained that it was achieved 'by running the brush from one to the other, until [the two colours] offer no hard edge where they meet, nothing to disturb the scene by changing the harmony. The gradually weakening light, the interposition of the air and, above all, the reflections, perform in front of our eyes this blending into the colours of nature.'[10] Where Chardin is concerned, it is the 'sketchy touch', as opposed to the blended touch, that differentiates him from the northern painters so often referred to when discussing Chardin.

In 1753 Cochin, remarking on 'the breadth and the boldness of his brush', noted that his paintings 'have the touch of a great master'.[11] This praise compares with the thoughts which the same works inspired in Baron Louis Guillaume Baillet de Saint-Julien, who was one of the most important critics of the Salons from 1748 to 1755. 'Deceived by their pleasant lightness and the apparent ease which reigns, the eye searches in vain to learn their secret. It fails, losing itself in your touch.'[12] This term was not used lightly, as it concerned a 'way of indicating certain accidents, certain circumstances of the visible appearance of objects in the arts of drawing and painting and circumstances which are caused by their nature, by their positions and by their movements'.[13]

In his essay on the Salon of 1753, Jacques Lacombe tried to take this analysis of touch and tone in Chardin's paintings a step further: 'This is a work whose full effect requires a certain distance; close up, a sort of haze seems to envelop all the objects in the painting. This method is similar to mezzotint, which, as we know, is made up of small flecks which are polished to a greater or lesser extent in order to create shading and light.'[14] On the other hand, in his *Sentiments d'un Amateur* about the same Salon, the Abbé Garrigues de Froment criticizes the contrast of 'lights which are too white and which do not have enough colour with shadows which have precisely the right amount of vigour' in *The Good Education* (see p. 216). 'There is also a sort of fog which does not lift, either up close or from a distance and which I feel I am correct in regarding as the effect of a touch which is too soft and too undecided.' He went on to compare this with the brushwork in *The Philosopher* (see p. 119) which was also exhibited that year, but which had been painted twenty years earlier. According to Garrigues de Froment, this painting was far superior to the work which Chardin was producing at the time and which he felt was too finished, smooth and polished.

However, about fifteen years later, Daudé de Jossan saw Chardin's still lifes as 'an excellent source of principles for all the genres: generous and without affectation in his highlights, his effects and his touch, he gives each object its proper local colour, using a combination of a thousand other tones which are his alone; he then gives each object the distance it needs from other objects and the result is a firm and luminous tone'.[15]

Diderot himself also appears to have been intrigued by Chardin's pictorial cuisine and by the technical processes involved in his work. In 1759, he remarked that Chardin 'gives such breadth to his little figures that it is as if they were cubits tall', adding that 'the generosity of his execution is independent of the size of the canvas and its subjects'. Two years later, Diderot mentions his 'rough, almost harsh execution' and in 1763, he wrote his famous passage on the 'thick layers of colour applied one on top of the other, their effect seeping through from the bottom layer to the top. Sometimes it is as if a mist had descended over the canvas and sometimes as if a light foam had been thrown over it. Rubens, Berghem, Greuze and Loutherbourg would explain this to you better than I; all could make your eyes aware of the effect.'[16]

Elsewhere, in a digression about the paintings exhibited by Jean Baptiste Deshayes the same year, Diderot tried to define the technical skill of the painter as 'the art of keeping a certain amount of dissonance, of evading the difficulties that art cannot overcome…. Hence the need for a careful choice of subjects and colours…. Some elements win, others lose and the real magic is in examining nature very closely and then making everything win and lose proportionally.' Diderot resumed these reflections on Chardin's vigorous brushwork and technique in 1765: 'Chardin's technique is quite individual. It is an uneven style in that close up one does not know what it is, and as one moves away, the subject reveals itself, eventually becoming nature herself. Sometimes it pleases as much close up as from a distance.' In 1767, Diderot wrote again of Chardin's 'incredible strength of colour, general harmony, a touching and true effect, beautiful masses, a magic of execution that makes one despair and a true mix of composition and arrangement.'[17]

CHARDIN AND FLEMISH PAINTERS

Publications on Chardin's painting make frequent references to Flemish and Dutch painting, as did Chardin's contemporaries. The comparison arises because Chardin painted still lifes, which was largely a Dutch tradition, and scenes of everyday life which reminded contemporary connoisseurs of the many small paintings by Gerrit Dou, Gerard Ter Borch and others which were the delight of French collectors.[18]

It is Rembrandt whose name is most frequently mentioned, even at the beginning of Chardin's career. Already at the Salon of 1737 it was said of his *Woman Drawing Water from a Copper Cistern* and its pendant (see pp. 30 and 31) that 'the author had a manner of his own, which was original and Rembrandtesque'.[19] However, it was with his *Philosopher* (see p. 119) exhibited for the second time in 1753 that this comparison was generally made. Among those who compared Chardin to Rembrandt were Pierre Estève, who wrote about the Salons of 1753 and 1755, describing 'the large portrait of the chemist, that one could take to be a Rembrandt'.[20] Huquier the Younger wrote that 'in terms of effect, [*The Philosopher*] could be paired with a Rembrandt, but the precision and finesse of the drawing make it superior'.[21] Still on the subject of this painting, Baron Melchior von Grimm wrote to Diderot, 'to me this painting seemed very beautiful and worthy of Rembrandt, although it has hardly been mentioned'. The composition of *The Philosopher* is similar to some of Rembrandt's portraits, but obviously this criterion alone would not suffice were it not for the rather mysterious subject of this *Chemist* or *Philosopher* absorbed in his reading or thoughts, whose clothes are trimmed with fur and who is seen at an angle which casts a shadow over his face, the light falling onto his fur hat, one of his cheeks, his arm and his right hand. This reference is further explained by the rough highlights in red, the contrasts of light and the touch which is reminiscent of Rembrandt's *Portrait of Hendrickje Stoffels* (Berlin-Dahlem), or of his *St Paul the Apostle* (in the National Gallery of Art, Washington), in which the Apostle is against a stone wall, lost in thought, in front of his books and holding a pen in his hand.

Rembrandt is not the only artist to whom reference was made. At the Salon of 1769, Diderot wrote: 'Take your time in front of a beautiful Teniers, or a beautiful Chardin; absorb the effect into your imagination; then relate everything which you see to the subject and rest assured that you have found the secret of rare satisfaction.' Here, the comparison applies to the perfection of the painting itself, rather than to a genre or style (did Diderot not say that he would give ten Watteaus for a painting by Teniers?). Meanwhile, the announcement in *Mercure de France* in 1739 of the engravings of *The Cistern* and *The Washerwoman* spoke of their 'lovely composition, in the style of Teniers, and capable of evoking the same in the enlightened public who had seen them' (at the last Salon). Mariette, in turn, wrote that 'he had captured the bearing and features very well and there was no lack of expression. This is what has contributed most to making his paintings fashionable and to winning them a place alongside Teniers and the other Flemish painters who have worked in almost the same genre as him, although there is some distance between their work and his.'[22]

Rembrandt, *St Paul the Apostle, c.* 1657.
Oil on canvas, 128 × 101 cm (50⅜ × 39¾ in.). National Gallery of Art, Washington.

*Portrait of the Painter Joseph
Aved*, also known as
Le Souffleur (The Prompter),
The Chemist and *The
Philosopher*, 1734.
Oil on canvas, 138 × 105 cm
(54⅜ × 41⅜ in.).
Louvre, Paris.

*Dead Partridge with
Bowl of Plums and
Basket of Pears,
c.* 1728. Oil on
canvas, 92 × 74 cm
(36¼ × 29⅛ in.).
Staatliche Kunsthalle,
Karlsruhe.

120

In 1748, Saint-Yves wrote that Chardin's severest critics 'did not hesitate to call him the French Teniers. I would go even further: I find his drawing more correct and his expression finer and more delicate.'[23] Of his *Blind Man Begging*, Fréron wrote that 'the rival of Teniers, or rather Nature, the inimitable M. *Chardin is always content to seize*, as he excels in representing, *the simplicity and the truth of ordinary life*'. There is a good deal to say about such 'ordinary life', as seen by Teniers and Chardin, but again, it is a case of showing that this essentially French painter could be compared with the northern painters in terms of the subjects which they painted. Thus, his *Amusements of Private Life* (see p. 52) 'would stand up to comparison with the best of the Flemish School'.[24] On two occasions, in 1753 and in 1761, the Abbé Le Blanc repeated that Chardin 'renders the smallest details [of Nature] with all the patience of the Flemish painters', although his brush had the energy and strength 'of the good Italian masters'.[25]

If these references to Flemish and Dutch painting became a *leitmotif* throughout Chardin's career, it is important to establish what this concerned – whether it was his manner or materials, his technique or his subjects, or a mix of all of these aspects. One recalls Largillierre's remark when Chardin was introduced to the Académie: 'You have some very good pictures there. They must be the work of some good Flemish painter. The Flemish school is excellent for colour.' Almost forty years later when discussing paintings of flowers and fruit exhibited by Roland Delaporte at the Salon of 1771, Diderot described 'the magic, the magic of the air that the Dutch render so well and which Chardin made us notice so much in their work'. With the exception of these two comments, which allude to the painting of still life, all of the other texts relate to genre scenes, which made Grimm say that Chardin 'excelled in small simple subjects in the Flemish style'.

It is not at all surprising that such references would be made to a school which was famous for its still life and genre painting. As for still life, it was more concerned with formal subjects than with a style of painting. Certainly the kitchen utensils in paintings by Kalf or Van den Bos did influence how Chardin painted his kettles, his bowls and his pots. It may also have been from Kalf that he borrowed his fruit reflected in a glass, or the use of sideboards along which objects are judiciously spaced, while a tablecloth hangs off the table or the handle of a knife lies across at a diagonal. Also, there are formal analogies between certain compositions with game, such as the admirable *Dead Partridge with a Bowl of Plums and Basket of Pears* (T.O.P. 37; see p. 120) and some of Jan Weenix's compositions, such as *Still life with Hanging Fowl, Monkey and Fruit*, in the Hermitage Museum.

Where genre subjects are concerned, the relationship with Dutch painting is obvious, although contrary to what Chardin's contemporaries say, it is not the names of Teniers and Van Ostade which come to mind, but rather those of Dou, Ter Borch, Pieter de Hooch, Willem van Mieris and Caspar Netscher. This is the case in scenes where Chardin shows a mother tending carefully to her child – *The Governess*, *The Diligent Mother* and *The Morning Toilet* – which recall the manner in which Pieter de Hooch treated this type of subject: a woman peeling apples and handing a piece of peel to a little girl (in the Wallace Collection, London; see p. 125), or another woman in a bedroom where a little

Nicolas de Largillierre, *Perdrix rouge dans une niche* (Red Partridge in a Niche). Oil on canvas, 71.5 × 58.5 cm (28¼ × 23⅛ in.). Musée du Petit Palais, Paris.

Jan Weenix, *Still Life*, 1688.
Oil on canvas, 86 × 68 cm (33⅞ × 26¾ in.).
Hermitage, St Petersburg.

Gerard Ter Borch,
The Reading Lesson. Oil on wood, 27 × 25.3 cm
(10⅝ × 10 in.). Louvre, Paris.

Gerard Ter Borch, *The Letter*, c. 1660.
Oil on canvas, 81.9 × 68 cm (32¼ × 26¾ in.).
The Royal Collection
© 1996 Her Majesty Queen Elizabeth II.

girl has opened the door (in the Staatliche Kunsthalle, Karlsruhe; see p. 125) or sitting beside a crib undoing her bodice (Berlin-Dahlem). In his scenes of everyday life, de Hooch paid attention to depicting people's surroundings and their environment, which acquired a further dimension by opening onto other rooms or to the outside of the house. His delightful painting of a woman buttering a slice of bread for her son while he says grace (in the J. Paul Getty Museum, Malibu; see p. 125) recalls Chardin's treatment of similar scenes.

Netscher, who continued with the models of his master, de Hooch, clearly influenced Chardin's choice of themes. Although *The Little Physicist* – a child blowing soap bubbles out of a window – was not engraved by Wille until 1761, when it belonged to the collection of Chevalier de Damery, it had been in France before. Aved, Chardin's lifelong friend, owned two paintings by Netscher,[26] one of which was also of a young boy blowing soap bubbles. Ter Borch's *Woman Reading a Letter* (see p. 122) or *Woman Writing a Letter* (in Mauritshuis, The Hague) could well have been Chardin's inspiration for *Lady Sealing a Letter*. Ter Borch's *Reading Lesson* (in the Louvre) immediately evokes Chardin's *Young Schoolmistress* (see p. 123) which appears to be almost a transposition.

Mieris, who is so well represented in the private and royal collections of the time is, of course, referred to – Wille engraved his *Dutch Woman Knitting* or *The Distracted Observer*, again dealing with the subject of soap bubbles. But we should above all look to Gerrit Dou. Dou's name was already mentioned in connection with Chardin from the eighteenth century. Wille had engraved Dou's *Dutch Cook* (see p. 125) and his *Dutch Household* which belonged to the King (both now in the Louvre), the portrait of his mother, known as *La Dévideuse;* and the Duc de Choiseul owned his famous *Chopped Onions*. This painter, who specialized in subjects of middle-class life, often depicted the domestic occupations of women and young girls.[27] However, although paintings such as *The Scullery Maid*, *The Cellar Boy* and *Woman Peeling Vegetables* (see pp. 210, 211 and 42) are likely to have been based on Dutch models, such as *Old Woman Peeling Apples* in the kitchen of an inn, as painted by Dou and Nicolas Maes, the figures in Chardin's paintings were not conventional types, but real subjects from everyday life, in which he painted people to whom he gave individual lives, thoughts and a 'sentiment' which we are invited to share.

One final category shows the role of the northern models: this was bas-reliefs, which were either separate subjects, or which were part of various compositions. Whether in Van Loo's *Children Playing with a Goat* (see p. 39), the *Attributes of the Arts* commissioned by Rothenbourg (see p. 181) or *Soap Bubbles* (see p. 193), the model is a famous bas-relief by Duquesnoy showing children playing with a goat, which was a recurring theme in French still-life painting between 1725 and 1750.[28] This was directly inspired by a pictorial convention that was common in the Netherlands during the seventeenth century and at the beginning of the eighteenth century. Mieris was certainly at the forefront here, with his numerous depictions of popular trades showing two people in a window of which this bas-relief decorates the sill (see pp. 125 and 126).[29] This is also the type of scene painted by Matthijs Naiveu in his *Soap Bubbles* (in the Museum of Fine Arts, Boston – see p. 126), where the protagonists are two very young children who are sumptuously dressed.

The Schoolmistress, 1738–39. Oil on canvas, 61.5 × 66.5 cm (24¼ × 26¼ in.). The National Gallery, London.

Soap Bubbles, c. 1732–33. Oil on canvas, 60 × 73 cm (23⅝ × 28¾ in.). Los Angeles County Museum of Art, Ahmanson Foundation Fund.

Willem van Mieris, *Soap Bubbles*
Oil on wood, 32 × 26.5 cm
(12⅝ × 10½ in.). Louvre, Paris.

Matthijs Naiveu, *Soap Bubbles*,
49.6 × 41.5 cm (19½ × 16⅜ in.).
The Museum of Fine Arts, Boston.

Previous page, from left to right
and from top to bottom:

Pieter de Hooch, *Woman Peeling an Apple*.
67.1 × 54.7 cm (26⅜ × 21½ in.).
The Wallace Collection, London.

Pieter de Hooch, *Woman Buttering Bread for a Child*.
Oil on canvas, 68.3 × 53 cm (26⅞ × 20⅞ in.).
The J. Paul Getty Museum, Malibu.

Gerrit Dou, *Woman Pouring Water into a Bowl*,
also known as *The Dutch Cook*. Oil on wood,
36 × 27.4 cm (14⅛ × 10¾ in.). Louvre, Paris.

Pieter de Hooch, *In the Bedroom*
Oil on canvas, 51.8 × 60.6 cm (20½ × 23⅞ in.).
Staatliche Kunsthalle, Karlsruhe.

Willem van Mieris, *The Vegetable Seller*.
Oil on wood, 39 × 32.1 cm (15⅜ × 12⅝ in.).
The Wallace Collection, London.

The window which they are leaning out of is framed with sculpted foliage and two *putti*, while below is Duquesnoy's bas-relief. The same bas-relief also appears below the window in Dou's *Trumpet Player* and its pendant *Girl at the Window* (Waddesdon Manor, Buckinghamshire), as well as Dou's self-portrait playing a violin, which was engraved by Pierre Charles Ingouf in 1776. In the case of the *Trumpet Player* it seems that the feast in the background had moral overtones and that in this case the children with the goat represent luxury. But I do not think that Chardin, when painting a boy blowing soap bubbles watched by a small child (see pp. 124 and 194), had in mind an allegory of the vanity or of the fragility of the human condition, or that he gave any undue significance to the bas-relief which is clearly visible in the engraving, where the honeysuckle around the window could be reminiscent of Van Mieris's *Soap Bubbles*.[30]

1. La Font de Saint-Yenne, *Sentiments sur quelques ouvrages*, 1754.

2. Daudé de Jossan, *Lettre de M. Raphaël à M. Jérôme*, 1769.

3. D. Diderot, *Salon* of 1765, ed. Seznec and Adhémar, vol. II, 1960.

4. 11 November 1769.

5. *L'Année littéraire*, 31 August 1757 and 4 October 1763.

6. C. H. Watelet, *Encyclopédie méthodique*, vol. 2, 1788, entry on 'Magie' (magic).

7. D. Diderot, *Essais sur la peinture*, ed. G. May, 1984.

8. *Salon* of 1767, ed. Seznec and Adhémar, vol. III, 1963, p. 128.

9. J. F. de Neufville de Brunhaubois Montador, *Lettre à la marquise de S. P. R.*, 1738.

10. C. H. Watelet, *Encyclopédie méthodique*, vol. 2, 1788, entry on 'Fondre' (blending).

11. *Lettre à un amateur en réponse aux critiques…*

12. *La Peinture – Ode à Milord Telliab*, 1753. Baillet de Saint-Julien repeated his commentaries almost word for word in 1755 in his *Caractères des peintres actuellement vivants*.

13. C. H. Watelet, *Encyclopédie méthodique*, vol. 4, 1791, entry on 'Touche' (touch). Four pages are devoted to this term.

14. *Le Salon en vers et en prose…*, 1753.

15. *Sentiments sur les tableaux exposés au Louvre…*, 1769.

16. *Salon* of 1763, ed. Seznec and Adhémar, vol. I, 1957, p. 223.

17. *Salon* of 1767, ed. Seznec and Adhémar, vol. III, 1963, p. 128.

18. For some of these collections, see the introductions in the catalogue of the *L'Age d'or flamand et hollandais* exhibition, Dijon, 1993.

19. Rembrandt's fame in France during Chardin's lifetime is witnessed by the large number of his works in French collections, although many of the paintings originally attributed to him are no longer thought to be his. In 1751, Helle and Glomy published a *Catalogue raisonné de toutes les pièces qui forment l'œuvre de Rembrandt*. This remarkable work, compiled by Gersaint, with notes on Rembrandt's students, Jan Lievens, Van Vliet and Ferdinand Bol in particular, was preceded by a 'Summary of the life of Rembrandt', complete with engravings, which gave an overall impression of his work and a clear picture of how the connoisseurs of Chardin's time regarded his work. Helle and Glomy wrote that his engravings were an 'inexhaustible source of the intelligent use of chiaroscuro, an area in which it is difficult to succeed, as is evident by the few painters who excel at it. Rembrandt was one such painter. He excelled at drawing and concentrated on painting beautiful nature, as depicted in Classical antiquity and in the works of the great Italian masters. However, he made little effort to distance himself from the natural coarseness of his country and his compositions are of peasant taste and very often quite base….The main feature of Rembrandt's compositions was the effects of an accidental light, usually coming from above, which produced strong shadows, with extremely sharp highlights; however, these shadows were not at all harsh and the half-tones which blend them into the light mean that the subject itself appears in astonishing relief.'

20. *Lettre à un ami sur l'exposition des tableaux…*

21. *Lettre sur l'exposition des tableaux au Louvre*, 1753.

22. *Abecedario pittorico*, notes written in 1749.

23. *Observations sur les arts… par une société d'amateurs*, 1748.

24. *Ibid.*

25. In *Observations sur les ouvrages…*, 1753, and 'Beaux-Arts – Explication des peintures…', *Mercure de France*, October 1761.

26. These were included in the sale of 14 November 1766, numbers 85 and 86.

27. These paintings sometimes had a hidden meaning, which seems to have been quickly forgotten. In *The Golden Age – Dutch Paintings of the 17th century*, Bernard Haak points out that at the start of the eighteenth century, when Houbrakken criticized Dou for painting so many dull scenes from domestic life, their double meaning had already been misunderstood or forgotten, and this misunderstanding was even more widespread in Chardin's time. In addition, the catalogues of the famous collections sold in France in the second half of the eighteenth century, where many of these works are mentioned, are purely descriptive and do not refer to any hidden meanings.

28. See M. Roland Michel, 1993.

29. *The Vegetable Seller* (in the Wallace Collection, London), *The Grocer's Shop* (in the Mauritshuis, the Hague) and its pendant *The Cook* and also *The Game Seller* (both in the Louvre). The latter belonged to Louis XV, as did *Soap Bubbles* by the same artist (in the Louvre) which shows a young boy at a window blowing his bubble towards a young girl seen in the background.

30. The engraved version of *Bubbles* or to quote the title of the print, *Soap Bottles*, which is lost, had as its pendant *Game of Knucklebones* (in the Baltimore Museum of Art), a painting also engraved by Fillœul and of which there is only one known version. Choiseul owned a painting by Van der Werff, which came from the Gaignat collection, of *Young Girls Playing Knucklebones*, engraved by Massard in 1771 for the Choiseul Collection. The scene is very different to Chardin's painting of the same subject, as it contains two young girls, one of whom is holding the knucklebones in her hand and who is not throwing them. It is worth noting that they are in front of a window underneath which is a bas-relief of cupids; between them is a small boy whom the Choiseul sale catalogue describes as 'treated in half-tones', which is precisely the case of the small child beside the young man in Chardin's *Soap Bubbles*. But perhaps this is merely coincidence…

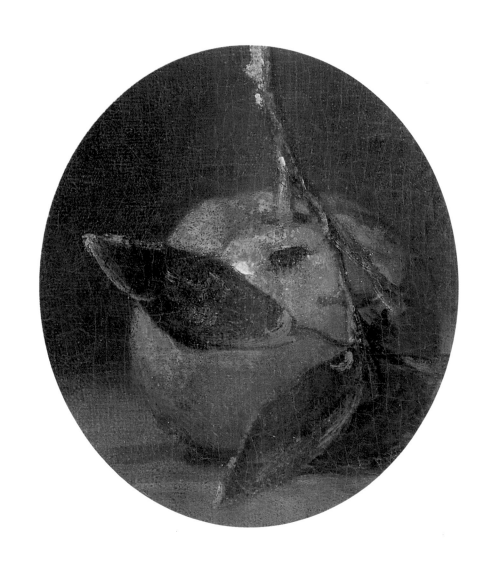

CHAPTER TWO

COLOUR, BRUSHWORK AND FEELING

*His manner of painting is unique. He applies
his colours in layers, one on top of the other,
hardly mixing them, so that his work somewhat
resembles a mosaic of juxtaposed pieces ,
similar to 'point carré' in embroidery.*

Abbé Raynal

In 1763, in a digression about paintings exhibited by Deshayes, Diderot wrote: 'what the painter grinds on his palette is not flesh, wool, blood, sunlight, or the air of the atmosphere, but earth, the sap of plants, ashes, ground stones and metallic chalks…. From this stems the individual artist's palette, his execution and his personal technique.' A few pages later, he exclaimed: 'O Chardin! It is not white, red or black that you grind on your palette: it is the very substance of your subjects; it is air and light that you dip your brush into and transfer to the canvas.' How did Chardin, 'the Salon's top colourist', render the substance of his subjects?

A note which Cochin sent to the painter Augustin Louis Belle in the 1780s gives a precise description of the 'colouring for a harmonious picture which M. Chardin used extremely well. "Lacquer; Cologne brown; ultramarine powder; *stil de grain d'Angleterre*. When the picture is done, the same colours are used for blending in. The *stil de grain* should not be visible." I have heard it said that with these tones, used variously and skilfully, M. Chardin reworked the shadows of every individual colour. He was undoubtedly the best painter of his time in terms of understanding the magical harmony of a painting.'[1]

So, Chardin used four basic colours about which eighteenth-century treatises give us some details. The basis of the 'laque' (lacquer) was an earthy substance, generally alum, to which a dye was added, usually cochineal, to obtain a red lacquer. The strength of the colour varied, depending on the amount of cochineal used, and in Chardin's time the quality of it found in Paris was very good. The 'terre de Cologne' (Cologne brown) is 'a sort of burnt umber, but a little browner and more transparent to use'.[2] 'It weakens when used with oil', but when purified by fire, 'it gives a dark brown and olive-green colour.'[3] The 'cendres d'outre-mer' (ultramarine powder), used by Chardin for its unique blue colour, is more complicated to define. Ultramarine is none other than lapis lazuli powder, an extremely expensive substance which would have been used sparingly by painters of the time. Baron Paul Henri Dietrich d'Holbach gave the recipe for it in the *Encyclopédie*, along with the proportions of linseed or turpentine oil, wax, rosin or pitch resin required to mix into the lapis lazuli powder. Blue ash extracted from copper mines could also be used, but it darkens in oil painting and becomes greenish, although it works superbly in tempera painting. 'Sometimes one finds *blue ashes* which are as beautiful as ultramarine: but when mixed with a little oil, it quickly becomes apparent that they are only ashes, because they do not turn brown, whereas ultramarine mixed with oil goes very brown.'[4] Because Chardin's blue has not turned brown and because ultramarine is in the form of powder, not ash, it is difficult for us to know from eighteenth-century documents exactly what he was using. Finally, 'stil de grain' is an 'extract of Avignon seed, mixed with chalk, the colour being fixed by using a little potash alum'. There are various shades of this, from lemon to orange to royal yellow. 'Stil de grain d'Angleterre' is a fawn or bronze colour; 'it is a chemical composition, which is used for shading and for glazing. … It is superb with oil.'[5] Watin, the author of this definition, also wrote about how to glaze colours (in *Manière de glacer les couleurs*), explaining that 'normally one only applies transparent glazes, such as lacquers, *stils de grain*, etc. Burnt umber and Cologne brown are used to glaze over browns, to give them more depth.' These colours were not simply applied to the canvas but, as Cochin said, 'reworked [by Chardin] who used them for his glazes'. We understand this to be 'the effect produced by a transparent colour applied thinly and rubbed into another which has already been painted and is dry. The colour with which one *glazes* must allow the colour underneath to come through and must give it a more brilliant tone which is more coloured and finer than it had before, and which thus contributes to the strength of the painting's harmony. One only glazes with colours which have little body, which cannot be thickened and which are transparent, such as lacquers and *stils de grain…*. The merit of a picture painted *in full colour and with impasto* exceeds the transitory brilliance of paintings where *glazing* has been skilfully applied. Colour used in the way that I have described has the advantage of not changing, and if there is some change due to the effects of time, then it is to the benefit of this way of painting boldly, because the paintings where it is used acquire a more vigorous and harmonious tone as they age, while the paintings where *glazes* have been used lose some of their harmony and the rather unstable brilliance and lightness of their *glaze*.'[6] In the context of Cochin's letter, this text shows that Chardin, a good practitioner, conformed with the methods of painting in use at the time, while achieving with these an effect which was uniquely his, in which the harmonies of colour are never accidental.[7]

On the various occasions when Chardin painted a palette, we have every reason to believe that it was his own and that the colours portrayed are those which he himself used.[8] Two of the four palettes which Chardin depicted are rectangular and appear in paintings around 1725–1730, while two are oval and are found in canvases of the 1760s. There is also an oval palette in *Monkey as Painter* (T.O.P. 93), which is dated around 1735.

The first palette is found in the centre of Chardin's *Attributes of the Painter and the Draughtsman* (T.O.P. 7; see p. 132). On the outer edge of the palette are seven colours, from black on the left, via ochre, red and four shades from brown to black, to white on the right. Underneath these, closer to the painter's body, there is a thinned down red, a yellow and a dark blue. On the left of the palette there are two bladders, one with filled with red paint and one with white. A large brush bears traces of red. Then in 1731, there is the palette in *The Attributes of the Arts* (T.O.P. 57; see p. 181 and detail p. 135), where the primary colours are on the inside, near the thumb: vermilion, Naples yellow and Prussian blue.[9] On the outer edge are the more muted colours, white, ochre, light red, ivory black and umber. According to the classical treatises, vermilion, which was expensive, was placed beside the thumb and used in very small quantities for flesh.

It is difficult to say if the palette in *Monkey as Painter* (see p. 17) has any theoretical significance; all we can see is a strong white, a little yellow and, behind the brushes, some red and some blue. These colours are echoed on the

131

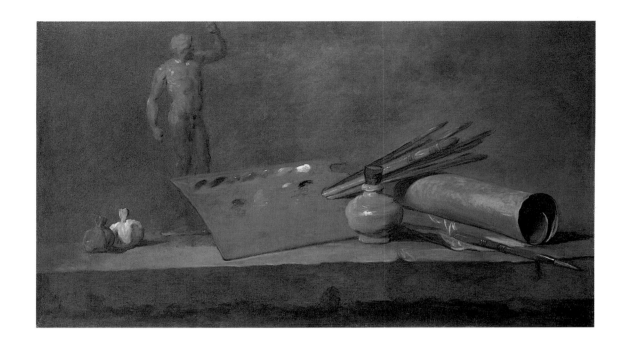

handkerchief hanging out of the monkey's pocket, various red highlights, the blue of the roller and the white of plaster.

In the *Attributes of the Arts* painted for the Château de Choisy (T.O.P. 177; see p. 182), on the edge of the palette there is a large white patch and some light touches between the yellow and the brown; on the inside, there is a bright yellow, vermilion and a long stretch of blue which may have been done with the palette knife, the handle of which is beside the palette. Finally, in *Attributes of the Arts and Their Rewards* (T.O.P. 180; see p. 179 and details pp. 115 and 133), the palette is raised up and almost as prominent as Pigalle's *Mercury*. It forms a group with the palette knife and some brushes with handles of assorted sizes and whose tips are stained with red, white and various browns. The colours are not aligned in two rows as neatly as in the other paintings. Again, there is a gradation of colour along the edge of the palette, beginning with white, beside the pot, followed by two yellows, one brighter, the other more ochre, a red and four shades of brown. On the inside are white, yellow, red and blue.

The four colours which Chardin deemed necessary for 'the harmony of a picture', namely red, blue, dark yellow and greenish brown, are found in these palettes with a subtlety of gradation which the condition of the paintings or their hanging does not always enable us to appreciate. These colours were used as much to create as to recreate tints, since, as Cochin wrote, 'He held as a principle that shadows were all the same, and that in some way the same tone should serve to break them all up. This truth is known only to painters who are colourists.' This was not a chance remark at a time when the method of rendering shadows was at the core of numerous debates: Cochin devoted a *Dissertation sur l'effet de lumière dans les ombres relativement à la Peinture* to this subject, which he read to the Académie in 1753,[10] as well as a significant part of his article on 'illusion in painting' for the *Encyclopédie*.[11]

Rabbit, Two Dead Thrushes and Straw on a Stone Table, c. 1755. Oil on canvas, 38.5 × 45 cm (15¼ × 17¾ in.). Musée de la Chasse et de la Nature, Paris.

Opposite:
The Attributes of the Arts (detail).
Musée Jacquemart-André, Paris.

Analyses in various laboratories[12] show that Chardin primed his canvases with a red-orange preparation of iron oxide mixed with oil, as was common practice. The canvas was covered with a light grey-brown ground of lead oxide mixed with kaolin[13] or chalk, and carbon black, as well as brownish earth pigments (bole).[14] This mixture produces a grey optical effect, the aim of which was to give the painting depth and resonance. On this thin ground, Chardin applied his colours, which he never used in their raw form, but mixed: lead white, Naples yellow, vermilion, ochre, burnt umber, lapis lazuli, Prussian blue, etc., in thin layers which he applied one on top of the other. To his whites, he added chalk in order to achieve a greater degree of transparency and those 'effects of directly reflected light' so admired by his contemporaries. In the version of *Soap Bubbles* in Los Angeles (see p. 124), hatching in pastel crayon is noticeable in the skin, hair and clothing of the young man. In order to emphasize certain details or increase the light, he used scumbling, a sort of impasto where brushstrokes made with a shorter brush are visible. It is also possible that he sometimes used the handle of his brush in certain grainy areas where the colour, unevenly distributed, looks as if it was mixed with sand, giving a resonant effect. He also used a short brush to paint the coat of a hare with clear highlights, rich in lead white. On top of this underpainting, he then added glazes made up of very diluted pigments. The Abbé Raynal wrote that 'his colouring is sometimes rather grey',[15] perhaps an allusion to his ground, and that 'his manner of painting is unique. He applies the colour in layers, one on top of the other, hardly mixing them so that his work somewhat resembles a mosaic of juxtaposed pieces, similar to *point carré* in embroidery.' Renou alluded to this contrast of tones when he wrote in his *Éloge* for Chardin that 'it seems that his eyes acted as a prism in breaking down the different tones of all the objects, his indescribable passages from light to shade. No one understood the magic of chiaroscuro better than he.' Cochin in turn noted that 'he sought the greatest truth possible in his tones and effects. This is why he repainted them until such time as he achieved this separation of tones which resulted from distance from the object and the reflection of everything surrounding it.' Discussing tone, Cochin referred to 'the intensity of effect in a work of art; in relation to colour, [tone] expresses the intensity of that colour, or that of all colours in general'.[16] Thus, we can understand better why Diderot wrote that he had 'seen one of his paintings of game which he never completed because the little rabbits which he was using as models had rotted and he despaired of achieving the harmony which he had in mind with any others. All the other rabbits brought to him were too dark or too light.'[17] This unfinished painting is probably *Two Rabbits, Pheasant and Seville Orange* (T.O.P. 138; see p. 136) where there is a striking difference between the treatment of the Seville orange on the left, the beautiful plumage of the pheasant lying across the composition, and the two rabbits with barely discernible fur, where we cannot even make out the hindquarters or back paws resting on the stone table. It seems likely that this part never went beyond the stage of a sketch, precisely because Chardin no longer had the model in front of him.

Chardin's proverbial slowness relates more to this perfectionism than to his handling of the brush, as he is known to have painted quickly with rapid brushstrokes.[18] In 1745, Charles Reinhold Berch wrote to Tessin that

Two Rabbits, Pheasant and Seville Orange on a Stone Table, c. 1755. Oil on canvas, 49.6 × 59.4 cm (19½ × 23⅜ in.). National Gallery of Art, Washington.

'a painting which he is working on will probably keep him busy for another couple of months. He never works on more than one painting at a time.' Mariette wrote that 'for lack of being able to do his studies and preparatory work on paper, M. Chardin is obliged to keep his model in front of him from the time of the initial sketch until he has completed the very last brushstrokes.'

MANNER AND FEELING

The mosaic or prism effect remarked on by Chardin's contemporaries relates not only to his colours, but also to his touch. 'It is not a blended touch… it seems that his brushwork is emphatic, yet nevertheless his figures have a striking truth', wrote the Chevalier de Neufville de Brunhaubois Montador,[19] and Cochin wrote that 'although in general his brushwork was not very attractive and was rather rough, there are very few paintings which could stand up alongside his'. This deliberate avoidance of a soft and blended touch led Diderot in 1763 to write his famous sentence: 'Come close and everything becomes blurred, flattens and disappears; stand back and everything is created and takes shape again.' He expanded on this in his *Essais sur la peinture* written around 1765, as follows: 'looking at the painting as closely as possible while still being able to see clearly, render the objects in all of the detail which the eye sees at this distance and paint in these details as scrupulously as the main shapes, so that as the viewer distances himself from the painting, these details fade until finally he arrives at the point where everything disappears; if we approach the painting from this distance where everything is confused, the forms slowly become discernible and gradually the details unfold, until the eye is at its initial and least distance, where it sees the tiniest and slightest variations in the objects in the painting.'

To Diderot this was the definition of 'great painting', of which he felt Chardin was the perfect example. However, this technique or method of painting, where the viewer's perception of the work changes with distance, is not an invention of Chardin's. Giorgio Vasari wrote that Titian's last works were 'executed with crudely daubed strokes and dabs in such a way that one sees nothing at close quarters, though they look perfect from a distance.'[20] In Chardin's lifetime, Sir Joshua Reynolds, writing about the irregular lines and strokes in the work of Thomas Gainsborough, remarked that 'this chaos, this uncouth and shapeless appearance, by a kind of magic, at a certain distance assumes form, and…all the parts seem to drop into their proper places.'[21] Commenting on the paintings exhibited by Loutherbourg at the Salon of 1763, Diderot compared his 'long and difficult' execution with that of other artists, both of the past and contemporary, and Chardin in particular. 'At each stroke of the fine brush, or rather of the broad brush or the thumb, the artist needs to stand back from the canvas in order to judge its effect. Close up, the work seems like a set of colours roughly applied. Nothing is more difficult than to combine this attention, these details, with what is called the broad manner. If the strokes disentangle and are seen separately the effect of the whole is lost. What art it is to avoid this pitfall! What work to bring to an infinite number of vigorous and bold strokes an overall harmony which links them and which saves the work from the pettiness of mere shapes! What a multitude of visual dissonances to create and atone!'[22]

These thoughts are inseparable from the theories of vision which were common in Chardin's time. Isaac Newton and John Locke, whose publications were quickly translated into French, examined the role of colour in our assessment of distance and the size of an object. In 1685, Philippe de La Hire (son of the painter and a mathematician) said that the apparent size of objects and the brilliance of their colours were the only means available to painters to suggest distance and that, under such circumstances, no illusion could ever be complete.[23] The debate about the distance of objects and the breakdown of colours continued throughout the eighteenth century, with Sébastien Le Clerc and Le Cat in France, Petrus Camper in Leiden and Robert Smith in London. There are echoes of it in a letter which La Tour sent to Marigny in 1763 in which the famous pastellist remarked on 'variations in the same organs such as those of sight' and drew practical conclusions from this. In the theoretical debates, some of the points relate directly to Chardin's painting. Thus, an object which reflects a red colour gives the impression that it is closer than if it were reflecting blue and it is also perceived as being smaller. Michael Baxandall illustrated these theories with *Lady Taking Tea* (see p. 200) where Chardin juxtaposes the problems of representation, perspective and colour. But the simple *Vase of Flowers* in Edinburgh (see p. 166 and detail on p. 140) is enough, I feel, to demonstrate this: the red carnation in the foreground advances and seems very large in relation to the gleaming white vase with a blue pattern; the vase, although indistinct, is still recognizable; the bouquet itself is blurred and indistinct at first glance, but its composition and variety become evident with a little distance. This demonstration could easily be extended to include other canvases, thus confirming that Chardin had mastered it perfectly, both with scientific theories and with the exceptional genius of a painter 'content to express his thought in four brushstrokes'.[24]

At the end of his essay on Chardin's life, Cochin recounts, by way of a conclusion, that Chardin became impatient with the chatter of an artist who made a great show of the methods which he used to purify and perfect his colours, whereas Chardin recognized no talent in him other than that of cold and attentive execution. He said to him '"Who told you that one paints with colours?" "With what then?" replied the astonished man. "One uses colours," M. Chardin said, "but one paints with feeling."' This exchange, which was also recounted by Diderot, is now famous and is particularly striking coming from a celebrated painter who was the greatest colourist of his time. It was used and adapted by a number of his contemporaries, including the author of the *Nécrologe*. The latter wrote that Chardin 'often told his students that the hand, the brushes and the colours were merely the instruments of painting and that principles were only the means which a painter used; that what really made an artist was genius and truth, and that you could compensate for the lack of one through intelligence and skill, but not the other.' Louis Petit de Bachaumont, on the day after Chardin's death, wrote that 'he had no style', and that he said 'one uses the hand and colours for painting; but it is not with colours and the hand that one paints'.[25]

In this concept of feeling applied to art, on the one hand the manifestation of sensitivity can be the distinguishing feature ('all painters and sculptors who succeed in portraying expression, show feeling, as expression in art may only

Opposite:
Dead Rabbit with Copper Cauldron, Quince and Two Chestnuts (detail). Nationalmuseum, Stockholm.

be produced by exquisite sensitivity'),[26] and, on the other hand, a characteristic of the execution of a painting ('because an artist is extremely aware of what serves to express the forms of nature well, and because he gives to his line that which is called feeling').[27] One understands better why C. J. Mathon de la Cour, bemoaning Chardin's giving up his 'pretty figures' in favour of still life, did so in the name of feeling, comparing the painting to 'music which [when it] imitates the sound of a bell or the noise of thunder, never pleases as much as it does when it is expressing feeling'.[28] This concept was also applied to sculpture by his contemporaries.[29]

The ideas of Chardin's close friend Cochin formed a large part of the aesthetic doctrine of the third quarter of the century.[30] Cochin gave a speech at the time of his reception into the Académie, which has unfortunately been lost, that was about works of art which he had seen in Italy. He used the opportunity to explain his thoughts on the education which should be given to future artists, 'that which makes one feel, independently of all instruction, what reserve one should have in pronouncing on works of art, which are *things of feeling and not objects of discussion*'.[31] In the years which followed, he explained his ideas further, defining painting as 'the art of rendering nature with truth and feeling based on some assumption or other'. And in the notes which he wrote to accompany the celebrated book by the Abbé Laugier,[32] he returned with vigour to the concept of sentiment, as art consisted 'of rendering the beauty of nature with feeling, that is communicating what one has felt in the manner in which this is treated', or again: 'One of the greatest beauties of art, which has even less to do with illusion, as it has no basis in nature, and because it is solely the effect of the feeling which moves the artist, is this art of working, this sureness, this easy mastery which often makes all the difference between true beauty and the mediocre which always leaves us cold.'

This theoretical context explains how Chardin could advocate the importance of feeling in relation to the work of the artisan; it is not just about people filled with emotion, but also still lifes, where feeling characterizes their truthfulness and relationship to nature.

Chardin's remark on colour and feeling illustrates his didactic attitude towards other artists, to whom he seems never to have refused to give help or advice. 'He had spirit and above all a great store of good sense and excellent judgment. He had a singular ability to express his ideas and make them understood, even in those areas of art which are most difficult to explain, such as the magic of colour and the various reasons for light effects.'[33] Diderot, who also described him as a witty man, remarked on several occasions that he 'understood the theory of his art', which he spoke of wonderfully' with 'judgment and sang-froid', and even wrote that 'possibly no one spoke as well as he on painting'. Coming from Diderot, this was no mean compliment. Throughout the *Salons*, he never missed the opportunity to cite Chardin as an example, for his comments, his ideas and his understanding of artistic problems, and it was he who reported Chardin's very critical assessment of how young artists were trained, which itself was prompted by a kind of indulgence for less fortunate or mediocre artists. 'Recall what Chardin said to us at the Salon: "Gentlemen, be kind. Of all the paintings which are here, seek out the worst and remember that two thousand unfortunates have bitten their brushes in two, despairing

Opposite:
Vase of Flowers (detail).
National Gallery of Scotland, Edinburgh.

of even doing so badly.... If you listen to me, you will perhaps learn to be indulgent".[34] In 1767, however, it seems that Chardin did not practice such indulgence in relation to Descamps, his friend. 'The good Chardin, who, as you know, took me by the hand, led me to these paintings and told me, with the nose and the curl of the lip which you know: "Behold the work of a *littérateur*."' And two years later, commenting with severity on Greuze's *Septimius Severus Reproving Caracalla*, Diderot wrote in astonishment: 'it seems that the artist was deprived, as if by magic, of that part of his talent which he should not have lost: Chardin has told me twenty times that it was an inexplicable phenomenon for him'.

It is clear that Diderot took Chardin's view before judging a work for himself. 'M. Chardin would be able to tell you more about it than me', he wrote on the subject of Nicolas Desportes. In effect, who could applaud or condemn better than Chardin, who throughout his career never ceased to bring perfection to the genres to which he devoted himself?

1. This note, which belonged to Jules Boilly, was published in *Archives de l'Art français*, vol. III, 1852.

2. Watin, *L'Art du peintre*, 1772.

3. *Encyclopédie méthodique*, vol. 4, 1791, entry on 'Terre' (earth).

4. *Encyclopédie méthodique*, vol. 4, 1791, entry on 'Cendre' (ash).

5. Watin, *op. cit.*, 1772.

6. *Encyclopédie méthodique*, vol. 4, 1791, entry on 'Glacis' (glaze) by Watelet.

7. The colours mentioned by Cochin were also used to make pastel crayons, as demonstrated in Chaperon's famous *Traité de la peinture au pastel* (published in 1788, but based on much earlier usages) and, in particular, all four colours are found in Chardin's pastels.

8. In Roger de Piles's *Éléments de peinture pratique* (Jombert edition, 1766), there is a description of the palette, 'usually oval but sometimes square'. The shape depends on the person using it…. The colours are placed on the palette before painting. The colours are arranged along the side which is furthest away from the body when the palette is held in the hand and they are placed beside each other, but do not touch each other. The middle and lower parts of the palette provide space where tints and colours may be mixed with a knife.

9. These details are taken from an article, questionable on some points, by F. Schmid, 'The painter's implements in eighteenth-century art', *Burlington Magazine*, October 1966.

10. *Encyclopédie méthodique*, vol. 2, 1788, entry on 'Repoussoir'.

11. *Encyclopédie méthodique*, 'De l'illusion dans la peinture', vol. 3, 1791.

12. Particular reference is made to the following: L. Faillant-Dumas, 'Des données de laboratoire sur Chardin', *L'Estampille*, no. 107, March 1979; and, by the same author, 'Étude de la technique picturale de Chardin' in the *Diderot et l'Art de Boucher à David* exhibition catalogue, Paris, 1985, pp. 152–53. See also J. Fronek, 'The Materials and Technique of the Los Angeles *Soap Bubbles*', in P. Conisbee, 1990.

13. Probably a similar white clay, as kaolin does not seem to have been discovered in France until about 1765, as Tamara Préaud and Antoine d'Albis have confirmed, for which I am very grateful. Chardin may of course have been supplied by a merchant who imported his colours from Germany where kaolin was used.

14. In *Woman Peeling Vegetables*, this layer is grey at the edges and beige in the centre. I would like to thank Philip Conisbee for having sent me the technical data for all of the Chardin paintings which are in the National Gallery in Washington.

15. *Correspondance littéraire*, 1750.

16. *Encyclopédie méthodique*, vol. 4, 1791, entry on 'Ton' (tone) by Lévêque.

17. *Salon* of 1769, ed. Seznec and Adhémar, vol. IV, 1967.

18. This information was given to me by E. Williams. The subject was dealt with at a symposium held in Boston in 1980 after the 1979 Chardin exhibition, the proceedings of which were not published.

19. *Description raisonnée des tableaux exposés au Louvre*, 1738.

20. Quoted by E. Gombrich, *Art and Illusion*, 1971, p. 195.

21. E. Gombrich, *op. cit.*, p. 200.

22. *Salon* of 1763, ed. Seznec and Adhémar, vol. I, 1957, p. 226.

23. *Dissertation sur les differens accidens de la vue*, quoted by M. Baxandall, *op. cit.*, 1985.

24. *Salon* of 1761, ed. Seznec and Adhémar, vol. I, 1957.

25. *Mémoires secrets*, 12 December 1780.

26. *Encyclopédie méthodique*, vol. 4, 1791, entry on 'Sentiment' (feeling) by Lévêque.

27. *Ibid*.

28. *Lettres à Madame °°° sur les peintures…, 1763*.

29. Étienne Falconet expanded this concept to the sculptor whose talent 'so essential and so rare, however much within the grasp of all artists, is for *"feeling"*… If the other studies are the basis, feeling alone is the soul'. (*Réflexions sur la Sculpture*, 1760). Once again, Chardin demonstrated his knowledge of the classical theories and ideas of his time, as feeling in painting can be related to the doctrine of imitation and of the beauty of nature. A parallel may be drawn with Nicolas Poussin, when he compared the delivery of the orator to the action rendered in the discourse or the painting: 'Quintilian', he said, 'attributed so much energy and strength to action that he considered concepts, proofs and effects useless without it, and line and colour useless too' (Bellori, quoted by Gombrich, *op. cit.*, 1971). If we replace action with feeling, we rediscover the concept that technique alone is not sufficient to produce a work of art, whatever it is.

30. See Michel, *op. cit.*, 1993.

31. *Procès-verbaux de l'Académie*, 4 March 1752. My italics.

32. M. A. Laugier, *Manière de bien juger des ouvrages de peinture*, posthumous edition of 1771 with critical notes by Cochin.

33. C. N. Cochin, *Essai sur la vie de M. Chardin*, 1780.

34. *Salon* of 1765, ed. Seznec and Adhémar, vol. II, 1960, p. 57.

CHAPTER THREE

STILL LIFE

Imagine a water fowl hanging by its leg. On a
sideboard underneath, imagine whole and broken
biscuits, a jar of olives with a cork stopper, a
decorated china bowl with a lid, a lemon, a napkin
unfolded and tossed carelessly aside, a pie on
a wooden board and a glass half full of wine.
It is here that we see that there are no
unattractive objects in nature and that
the aim is to depict them.

Diderot

Page 144:
*Still life with Carafe, Silver Tumbler,
Peeled Lemon, Apples and Pears* (detail).
Staatliche Kunsthalle, Karlsruhe.

Received into the Académie as a 'painter of animals, kitchen utensils and various vegetables', Chardin painted still life throughout his career, only ceasing when his tired eyes restricted him to painting in pastel or monochrome. He established himself in this minor genre and 'never aspired to succeed, although he would have liked to, as a history painter'.[1] Indeed, he was to become one of the greatest painters of his time in this field.[2]

Was Chardin's initial choice made purely by chance, as Mariette would have us believe? When a painter becomes famous, stories spring up about him quickly, even during his lifetime. Cochin also mentions a rabbit among his first paintings and all the obituary writers refer to *The Skate* as being an absolute masterpiece, which is what Diderot felt when he wrote in 1763 that, were he to train his son as an artist, this was the picture which he would have him copy. 'The subject is disgusting, but it is the very flesh of the fish, its skin and its blood; seeing the thing itself would affect you in the same way.'

It is generally agreed that Chardin's first still lifes date back to the years 1724–28, between his reception into the Académie de Saint-Luc and his acceptance into the Académie Royale de Peinture et Sculpture. Given their shape, some of the canvases were probably designed as overdoors; these were paintings illustrating the attributes of the arts (T.O.P. 6–9; see pp. 132 and 147). Their composition, which is a little sparse, shows the young artist's attempts to fill out a space, to experiment with diagonals and to render books, rolls and sculptures as well as possible – subjects which he was to repeat until the years 1765–70. He also painted a hound standing beside dead game, a horn and a gun in a landscape (T.O.P. 5; see p. 147) and the first of his kitchen tables (T.O.P. 10, 11, 13–15) with cauldrons, casseroles, vegetables and preparations for meals balanced rather unsteadily on a stone table with a certain lack of perspective. He painted hanging fish and a cat distracted by oysters or a salmon (see p. 26), which may have helped him prepare for *The Skate* (see p. 18), which Mariette tells us was painted as his reception piece for the Académie 'several years' before 1728 'at a time when he certainly did not think that this painting could bring him such honour'. In this horrible and magnificent painting, what is striking, apart from its huge size (114 x 146 cm [44⅞ x 57½ in.]), is the incredible way in which Chardin organizes his space: on the left is a cat, the only living thing, and, on the right, the glazed terracotta jug which recurs again and again in Chardin's painting. All of the food is placed on the left side of the picture, while on the right we see the utensils which will be used to prepare it. In the centre, the white belly of the fish, with its bloody cut, is continued in the large cloth on the table: brown, red and white, a little green on the handle of the knife, an almost imperceptible touch of blue on the oyster next to the fish. The entrails of the skate are reflected in the bottle with a stopper and on the reddened wall, particularly on the left. One would hesitate before agreeing with those who see in this painting the horror of a ghastly wound, or a

The Skate (detail).
Louvre, Paris.

The Attributes of the Arts with a Bust of Mercury. Oil on canvas, 52 × 112 cm (20½ × 44⅛ in.). Pushkin Museum, Moscow.

sexual content – or even a symbol of the Crucifixion[3] – and it is very unlikely that Chardin wanted to represent everything which is read into it today, even if he did want this painting to be representative of his talents. However, there is certainly an element of choice, a refusal to produce a purely decorative painting, although it was common to see fish of this size hung in kitchens, and seafood, painted with the same realism, was a recurring theme in northern painting in the previous century.

It was at about this time that Chardin was experimenting with his first compositions of fruit and a carafe, glasses and silver, which he studied for their reflections. His *Plate of Oysters* (T.O.P. 13; see p. 150) is remarkable for its treatment of the beaten silver tumbler and also for its reflections which are as lovely in the silver tumbler, where they have a touch of blue, as they are in the pepper mill, the oysters, the bottle and the handle of the knife. In *Basket of Grapes* and *Preparations for Lunch* (T.O.P. 14 and 15; see p. 150), the silver tumbler captures the reflection of the fish and the bread. In *Basket of Plums, Bottle, Glass of Water and Two Cucumbers* (T.O.P. 27; see p. 71), the light illuminates wonderfully the velvety smooth texture of the plums and the dark carafe with its beautiful impasto. The cucumbers are reflected in both the carafe and the glass of water, the transparency of which is rendered by an optical effect on the rounded top and bottom. The painter's signature is engraved proudly into the stone table, something which he was to do in other works of the same period. But look again and the difficulties which Chardin had in rendering perspective are visible: the stone table is not horizontal and, in particular, the top of the bottleneck, which should not be visible at all, tilts forward rather oddly. The play of light in the metal and the crystal, and the contrasts between soft, downy materials and glossy materials, are taken a step further in his *Pewter Jug with Peaches and Plums* (see p. 148) and in *Still Life with Carafe, Silver Tumbler, Peeled Lemon, Apples and Pears* (T.O.P. 32 and 33; see p. 149), which is very Dutch with its half-peeled lemon. The northern style of this canvas may explain its presence in the eighteenth century in the collection of the painter Aved, known as *Le Batave*, who owned a large number of paintings from the Netherlands,

The Hound, c. 1724–25.
Oil on canvas, 192.5 × 139 cm (75⅞ × 54¾ in.).
The Norton Simon Foundation, Pasadena, California.

147

Pewter Jug with Peaches and Plums, c. 1728.
Oil on canvas,
55 × 46 cm
(21⅝ × 18⅛ in.).
Staatliche Kunsthalle,
Karlsruhe.

Still Life with Carafe, Silver Tumbler, Peeled Lemon, Apples and Pears, c. 1728. Oil on canvas, 55 × 46 cm (21⅝ × 18⅛ in.). Staatliche Kunsthalle, Karlsruhe.

149

and also its purchase by the Margravine of Baden, who liked this genre of painting very much.

It is hardly surprising to see Chardin resume this sort of composition, this game of contrasting objects and reflections, about thirty years later,[4] although naturally with many modifications. In *Basket of Plums* (T.O.P. 154; see p. 152) and *Basket of Plums with Nuts, Currants and Cherries* (T.O.P. 173; see p. 86) he deals with opaqueness and translucence beautifully. The plums in their basket are smooth, the cherries translucent and the glass has been painted with incredibly skilful brushwork: some of the white strokes are horizontal, others vertical, with the highlights on the rim of the glass separating the transparency of the water from the transparency of the glass itself. As was the case thirty years earlier, the light falls clearly onto the cherries and the plums.

It is now 1728 and the painting is *The Buffet* (see p. 19): its composition is remarkably balanced, with the two glasses on the left corresponding to the two bottles on the right (one of the glasses has been tipped backwards, perhaps to demonstrate that he knew how to render the transparency of its round foot). The pyramid of fruit, in the centre of the buffet, is off-centre in relation to the entire picture. The porcelain bowl on the right, which together with the half-peeled lemon accentuates its Dutch influence, is there to re-establish balance and to emphasize the curved shape of the buffet on which there seems to be the trace of a bas-relief.

The astonishing *Silver Soup Tureen* also known as *Cat, Partridge, Dead Hare and Silver Tureen* (T.O.P. 39; see p. 64) marks Chardin's assured transition from compositions of fruit and silver to the still lifes of game which he was beginning to paint. The animals are placed on a curved surface, like that of *The Buffet*, in a remarkable use of space, next to a silver tureen. On the left, a cat is staring at the partridge; on the right, are an apple and two large pears similar to the fruit in the still life in Karlsruhe. The perspective leaves much to be desired – the tureen is leaning to the left and the pears are larger than the hare's head. This does not matter, given the wonderful reflections in the silver and the hare's front paws which really seem to be hanging in thin air. Around the rear paws of the hare, there is a blue band which demonstrates the subtle colouring which we find in Chardin's painting throughout his career. The treatment is rough, grainy and 'uneven'; fur and feathers are rendered by visible brushstrokes, applied alongside each other as was Chardin's technique and that of Largillierre before him.

The series of hunting trophies which followed show the influence of Desportes and Oudry, as well as of the Flemish and Dutch painters: hares, with game-bags, powder flasks and guns on a table, hanging by their paws, straight or across a diagonal, paws tied together or apart. *Dead Hare* with a gun at an angle (T.O.P. 43; see p. 151) has as its background a fragment of a landscape, which is quite mediocre, and which is probably after Oudry by whom there is a very similar painting dated 1728 (in the Musée de la Chasse, Paris). In *Dead Hare with Game-bag and Powder Flask* (T.O.P. 48; see p. 155), the entire painting appears as a brown-red monochrome, broken only by blue patches on the hare's ears, on the strap, and just visible on the game-bag and around the powder flask. The hare's fur itself is almost smooth, treated in grey, brown, red and white, each layer well spread, sometimes with circular brushstrokes.

Dead Hare with Gun, Game-bag and Powder Flask, c. 1728. Oil on canvas, 75 × 95 cm (29 ½ × 37⅜ in.). Musée de la Chasse et de la Nature, Paris.

Opposite, from left to right and from top to bottom:
Preparations for Lunch, also known as *The Silver Tumbler*, c. 1726. Oil on canvas, 81 × 64.5 cm (31⅞ × 25⅜ in.). Musée des Beaux-Arts, Lille.

Plate of Oysters, c. 1726–27. Oil on canvas, 43 × 53.5 cm (16⅞ × 21⅛ in.). The British Rail Fund, London.

Basket of Black and White Grapes with Silver Tumbler, Bottle, Peaches, Plums and a Pear, c. 1726. Oil on canvas, 69 × 58 cm (27⅛ × 22⅞ in.). Louvre, Paris.

Bowl of Plums, Peach and a Jug of Water, c. 1728. Oil on canvas, 45 × 57 cm (17¾ × 22½ in.). The Phillips Collection, Washington.

Jean Baptiste Oudry, *Water Spaniel Guarding Game*, 1728. Oil on canvas, 91.5 × 107 cm (36⅛ × 42⅛ in.). Musée de la Chasse et de la Nature, Paris.

151

Basket of Plums with a Glass of Water, Two Cherries, a Nut and Three Green Almonds, c. 1759.
Oil on canvas, 38 × 47 cm (15 × 18½ in.). Musée des Beaux-Arts, Rennes.

Basket of Peaches, Black and White Grapes, with Cooler and Stemmed Glass, c. 1759.
Oil on canvas, 38 × 47 cm (15 × 18½ in.). Musée des Beaux-Arts, Rennes.

153

Dead Rabbit, Red Partridge and Seville Orange, c. 1728.
Oil on canvas, 68 × 60 cm (26¾ × 23⅝ in.).
Musée de la Chasse et de la Nature, Paris.

Nicolas de Largillierre,
Hares with Fruit. Oil on canvas, 74 × 59.5 cm
(29⅛ × 23½ in.). Musée de Brou, Bourg-en-Bresse.

To render the fur on this light surface, there are countless thin brushstrokes, loaded with barely diluted colours, and also straight strokes and sometimes small round dabs of paint which are a little lighter than the base. One thinks here of Largillierre, mediator of the Flemish model, whose painting of *Hares with Fruit* in the Musée de Brou is reminiscent of Chardin's still lifes in the way that the fur is painted and in the contrast of fruit in shimmering colours. Largilliere's *Red Partridge in an Alcove* (see p. 121), where a partridge is hanging by a leg in front of a stone recess above some fruit and two dead birds (in the Musée du Petit Palais, Paris), comes to mind when one sees Chardin's admirable *Dead Partridge with Bowl of Plums and Basket of Pears* (T.O.P. 37; see p. 120) purchased by the Margravine of Baden in 1759, but which was certainly painted in about 1728. The plums in their silver dish opposite some pears in a more rustic basket and, between them, some fruit and foliage matching the partridge with its grey and white plumage together create a superb harmony of colour.

As well as these compositions, there is his *Two Rabbits, Grey Partridge, Game-bag and Powder Flask* of 1731 (T.O.P. 59; see p. 22), the colouring of which is similar to *Dead Partridge with Bowl of Plums and Basket of Pears* in Karlsruhe, as well as his *Lapwing, Partridge, Woodcock and Seville Orange* (T.O.P. 60; see p. 260) painted in 1732, where the orange in the foreground is contrasted with the feathers of the game, as is the case in *Duck with Seville Orange* (T.O.P. 47; see p. 21). This painting demonstrates Chardin's method of painting: its rapid execution suggests that it may have served as a study for *The Water Spaniel* of 1730 (T.O.P. 49; see p. 21), his last known 'outdoor' work. Against the wall are a gun and a hunting horn, with a water spaniel looking up at a hare and a duck. There is remarkable impasto on the spaniel's legs and its tail, some of which is beige, some almost white. The curls of its coat are painted with dark lines or in beige splotches. The body of the hare and the duck's bill are suggested with lumpy strokes. Red highlights on the stomach suggest blood without actually showing it. However, the weakness of the landscape and even the flowers could explain why from then on Chardin placed the subjects of his paintings in indoor settings.

During the 1730s, Chardin devoted a significant amount of his work to kitchen paintings. Nothing, it would seem, is simpler than these small pictures of 'ordinary and domestic' nature: a leg or a quarter of beef, a skate or mackerel hanging on a hook, above a stone table on which are placed vegetables, eggs, cheese, a plucked chicken, chestnuts or a glazed earthenware jug, a copper cauldron, a bottle, sometimes a cloth or some ordinary utensil, such as a skimmer, a pepper mill, or a pestle and mortar. These paintings, repeated identically or with varying ingredients on horizontal or vertical canvases about 30 x 40 cm [11¾ x 15¾ in.], are treated in brownish tones brightened by the white of a napkin or an egg, the redness of a piece of meat and clever reflections of the simplest objects. *The Meat-day Meal* and *The Fast-day Meal* (T.O.P. 54 and 55; see p. 157) are dated 1731. In the eighteenth century, meat days and fish days, feast days and fast days still governed the eating habits of the French and such a contrast would have been quite normal for art enthusiasts, who may even have commissioned such paintings from an artist. The difference between the two paintings is certainly clear in the objects represented: a piece

*Dead Hare with Game-bag
and Powder Flask*, 1728–29.
Oil on canvas, 98 × 76 cm
(38⅝ × 29⅞ in.).
Louvre, Paris.

155

Still Life with Haunch of Meat, 1732.
Oil on canvas, 42 × 34 cm (16½ × 13⅜ in.).
Musée Jacquemart-André, Paris.

Opposite, from left to right and from top to bottom:

The Fast-day Meal, 1731.
Oil on canvas, 33 × 41 cm
(13 × 16⅛ in.). Louvre, Paris.

Still Life with Cauldron, Cabbage, Two Eggs and Three Herrings, c. 1732. Oil on canvas, 42 × 33 cm
(16½ × 13 in.). Musée de Picardie, Amiens.

The Meat-day Meal, 1731.
Oil on canvas, 33 × 41 cm (13 × 16⅛ in.). Louvre, Paris.

Still Life with a Glazed Jug, Glass of Water, Cucumbers, Brass Cauldron and Herrings, c. 1734. Oil on canvas,
41 × 33.5 cm (16⅛ × 13¼ in.).
The Cleveland Musum of Art, Leonard C. Hanna, Jr.

of beef or some mackerel, chestnuts or eggs, wine bottles or a water jug, a slotted spoon or a grill pan. But there was also a difference in terms of the overall tonality, which is warmer in the case of *The Meat-day Meal*, colder and greyer in its pendant, *The Fast-day Meal*. Both paintings are treated in a quasi-monochrome, with more red highlights in one and more white in the other. In these small canvases, Chardin achieves a tranquil perfection, an achievement which he would continue to exploit. In 1732, *Still Life with Haunch of Meat* (T.O.P. 61; see left) perfectly summed up this simplicity and the perfect use of the objects chosen – the piece of lamb is resting on a cloth with two onions and three other items which range from brown to dark beige: a glazed jug, a copper basin with a silver lining and a pestle and mortar. The handle of a slotted spoon, the handle of the basin and the pestle form three parallel diagonal lines in the upper part, as does the line of the centre bone of the meat lower down. Chardin continues this type of spatial exploration by moving an object, or using a piece of meat or vegetables in a different way, or changing the direction of the diagonals in the composition. He would replace the marbling of a glazed pot with the whiteness of crockery (T.O.P. 83; see p. 157). This type of chromatic contrast between a brownish background, a dark table and a creamy substance occurs several times in his still lifes of the 1760s and in a similar vein he would again hang herrings over vegetables in one of his last still lifes in 1769 (see p. 176).

These few examples demonstrate how the dating of Chardin's still lifes is uncertain and even impossible if one relies solely on the subjects represented. A good example of these difficulties is given in the superb *Stone Table* in the National Gallery of Scotland (T.O.P. 141; see p. 159) which shows a white napkin, three eggs and a salmon steak, against an earthenware jug, a copper cauldron and a terrine. The painting is remarkably balanced in chromatic terms; the brown and marbled diagonal of the jug, the cauldron, the basket in the background and the earthenware pot. The greyish reflections in the napkin correspond to the skin of the salmon, the flesh of which is the same colour as the red screws attaching the handle to the cauldron, over blue highlights which echo the reflections of the eggs in the copper. This work is traditionally dated 1730–34,[5] but more recently, Pierre Rosenberg has dated it as belonging to the 1750s,[6] like *The Kitchen Table* and *The Pantry Table* (T.O.P. 146 and 147; see pp. 171 and 172). I feel that this date is far too late, because of the colour treatment and the spatial treatment of objects, because of the painting's composition which is as crowded as his works from the years 1730–40, and finally, because of its overall brown colouring without the light backgrounds and grainy impasto that he used systematically from 1734–35 onwards.

The White Tablecloth (T.O.P. 78; see p. 29) is worth mentioning for two reasons. First, it is a 'historic' work in Chardin's career, as it can almost certainly be identified as the painting which in 1732–33 prompted Aved to say to him that a portrait was not as easy to paint as a saveloy. In reporting this, Mariette added: 'M. Chardin was busy painting a picture for a chimneyboard, in which he was including a saveloy on a plate'. In addition to the slices of saveloy in the painting, the fact that it was originally shaped at the top and that its perspective was calculated to take account of the fact that it would be seen from a height, proves that it was a screen to be set into a fireplace opening.

157

Stone Table with Pitcher, Cauldron, Napkin, Eggs, Herrings, Copper Cauldron, Salmon and a Jug, c. 1733–34.
Oil on canvas, 32.5 × 40 cm (12⅞ × 15¾ in.). The Ashmolean Museum, Oxford.

Stone Table with a Jug,
Cauldron, Napkin, Eggs,
Wicker Basket and Salmon,
c. 1735–40? Oil on
canvas, 40.5 × 32.5 cm
(16 × 12⅞ in.). National
Gallery of Scotland,
Edinburgh.

The Cellar Boy, 1735 (detail). Oil on canvas,
46 × 37.2 cm (18⅛ × 14⅝ in.).
Hunterian Art Gallery, University of Glasgow.

Girl Returning from the Market, 1738 (detail).
Oil on canvas, 46 × 37 cm (18⅛ × 14⅝ in.).
National Gallery of Canada, Ottawa.

Opposite:
The Scullery Maid (detail). Hunterian Art Gallery,
University of Glasgow.

Mariette was also keen to show that Chardin, despite being a member of the Académie, did not look down on painting purely decorative work such as overdoors (although the ones which he painted for Rothenbourg were more than decoration) and chimneyboards. Oudry, too, at the height of his fame, also painted these, but he incorporated more sumptuous objects, such as those in his *Lacquer Stool* of 1742. Here we have simply a round table covered with a white tablecloth, on which are a plate, a loaf of bread, a knife and two glasses, one of which is shown on its side, as was common in seventeenth-century Dutch still lifes. On the ground, a wooden tub serves as a cooler for some bottles. There is nothing especially luxurious, and one can imagine that the screen was painted for some middle-class house whose owner only wanted to block off his fireplace during the summer months, without incurring too much expense.[7]

The White Tablecloth thus marks an important turning point in Chardin's career and we have seen that between 1737 and 1753 he did not exhibit any still lifes at the Salons. However, in the genre scenes which he began to paint from 1733 there are objects represented which only a great still life painter could have rendered in the way that he did. Consider his *Woman Drawing Water from a Copper Cistern* (see p. 31), with its hanging meat, its copper basin, the various utensils on the ground, the cistern at the centre of the canvas, naturally, and also the wooden bucket and the glazed earthenware jug, or again the large earthenware basin in which the linen of *The Washerwoman* is soaking (see p. 30). Or consider the various pitchers, barrels, cauldrons, bottles and saucepans in his *Cellar Boy*, his *Scullery Maid* and his *Woman Peeling Vegetables*, or the cistern, the pewter plate, the bottles and the stoneware jar in *Girl Returning from the Market* (see p. 212), the teapot in *Lady Taking Tea*, the plate-warmer in *Saying Grace*, the various utensils in *The Convalescent's Meal*, the bottles and the basket in *The Household Accounts*, not to mention the workbasket in *The Embroiderer* and in *The Governess*. Very often, these objects assume the same importance as the main subject of the painting, whom they help identify as a young cellar boy, a maid or a vegetable peeler. By placing figures among the objects of his repertoire, Chardin almost certainly wanted to demonstrate his twofold skill which was acknowledged early on, when the chronicler of *Mercure de France* wrote in 1737 that 'the curious were even more surprised as they did not realize that his talents stretched so far; he demonstrated the contrary'.

Chardin did not stop painting domestic objects, even though he may not have exhibited these at the Salon. In his work of this time, we can see a lightening of the background, from which the objects become quite separate, and the objects themselves are painted with a more luminous palette and with more impasto, with clearly visible blocks of paint. Along with the usual objects, he would incorporate a glazed white pot with a coloured design, which was part of this general lightening of his palette. Then came a series of very small wooden panels (17 x 21 or 23 cm [6¾ x 8¼ or 9 in.]), miniature masterpieces where Chardin would group together a cauldron, a saucepan, a pepper mill and some eggs (T.O.P. 86; see p. 162), or turn the same cauldron on its side, with a pestle and mortar, an earthenware bowl and some onions (T.O.P. 87; see p. 163) on a light grey background with gold highlights.[8]

Tinplated Copper Cauldron, Pepper Mill, Leek, Three Eggs and a Casserole, c. 1735–37.
Oil on wood, 17 × 21 cm (6¾ × 8¼ in.; reproduced actual size).
The Detroit Institute of Arts, Detroit.

Pestle and Mortar, Bowl, Two Onions, Copper Cauldron and a Knife, 1735–37.
Oil on wood, 17 × 23 cm (6¾ × 9 in.; reproduced actual size). Musée Cognacq-Jay, Paris.

Vegetables for a Stew, c. 1735.
Oil on canvas, 31 × 39 cm (12¼ × 15⅜ in.).
Indianapolis Museum of Art.

Chardin's rendering of these most ordinary objects has a rare perfection, with an almost imperceptible gradation of colour and a remarkable use of such limited space with the play of shadows used to build up the composition. For example, in the *Pestle and Mortar, Bowl, Two Onions, Copper Cauldron and Knife* (see p. 163), the shadow of the pestle and mortar which is at a diagonal to the earthenware bowl is in exact contrast to the knife seen on the right. One thinks of Diderot's much later comment on Chardin's paintings: 'The breadth of execution is independent of the size of the canvas or the size of the objects.' The size of these paintings and the choice of support may be a wink at Dutch subjects, as well as an effort to show collectors that he was just as good in this genre.

In *The Copper Cistern*, Chardin's technique and colouring, and the fact that it also involves only a slightly larger panel, makes one think that this painting (T.O.P. 88; see p. 165) was certainly painted at the same time as the previous paintings.[9] A similar cistern 'on a Chinese wooden stand' was listed in the inventory after the death of Marguerite Saintard. It is difficult to say what is most admirable in this painting, which is monumental despite its small size. However, nothing could be simpler than this cistern on a stand, where Chardin included a *cassotte* (a long-handled saucepan), a bucket of water and a glazed jug with its lid on the ground – all objects whose tonality combines various shades of brown, making the copper of the cistern stand out, while forming a sort of monochrome. The light comes from behind the viewer, projecting white highlights onto the edge of the saucepan, the rim of the bucket, the bottom of the cistern underneath the tap and the top of the near side of the lid, making the glaze of the jug sparkle. The centring is also remarkable: the cistern is completely centred in relation to the entire panel, but Chardin gives the illusion of it being more on the left, by facing the tap left, the leg of the tripod towards the right and by throwing a large shadow onto the wall, to the right of the cistern.[10]

At the same time as his efforts in other areas, Chardin perfected his treatment of still life, as *Dead Rabbit with Copper Cauldron* (T.O.P. 92; see p. 168) demonstrates. The colouring and treatment are very similar to that in *The Copper Cistern*, but its size (69 x 56 cm [27⅛ x 22 in]) is more ambitious.[11] This painting has quite an unusual background for a Chardin still life, as the stone wall is executed with rapid brushstrokes which achieve an effect of resonant colouring, like those which are assembled more regularly in his paintings with figures, such as *Girl Returning from the Market* and *The House of Cards* in London (see pp. 212 and 202). On this background is a rare monogram, *cd*, and, by way of a flourish, a knot of string holding the rabbit's legs. The rabbit's coat is painted with small brushstrokes of brown, black and white which intertwine, overlap, contrast with each other and combine to achieve a marvellous effect. Was Chardin following Largillierre's advice on painting an animal in its fur, i.e., to begin by 'impasting well with colour in main blocks … loading tints on tints, but only a little at a time'; then to work in the details with finer brushes, using a little turpentine to make the colour more liquid?[12] The indefinable colour of the fur is emphasized by the white of the tail and inside the ears (see detail p. 139), by the contrast it makes with the brightness of the cauldron, itself the fruit of a learned 'cuisine', and by the drops of blood on the ground near the rabbit's head. Only the yellow of the enormous quince, which is as big as the rabbit's head, stands out clearly.[13]

The Copper Cistern,
c. 1734. Oil on wood,
28.5 × 23 cm
(11¼ × 9 in.).
Louvre, Paris.

Vase of Flowers,
c. 1755–60? Oil on
canvas, 44 × 36 cm
(17⅜ × 14⅛ in.).
National Gallery of
Scotland, Edinburgh.

166

The Smoker's Box, also known as *Pipes and Tumbler*, c. 1737–40? Oil on canvas, 32.5 × 42 cm (12⅞ × 16½ in.). Louvre, Paris.

168

Dead Partridge, Pear and Noose on a Stone Table, 1748. Oil on canvas, 39.2 × 45.5 cm (15⅜ × 18 in.). Städelsches Kunstinstitut, Frankfurt.

Opposite:
Dead Rabbit with Copper Cauldron, Quince and Two Chestnuts, c. 1739–40. Oil on canvas, 69 × 56 cm (27⅛ × 22 in.). Nationalmuseum, Stockholm.

It was at some time during the same period, 1735 to 1740, that Chardin painted his fine *Smoker's Box* (T.O.P. 107; see p. 167) which is rather an unusual work in his repertoire. Perhaps he took pleasure in representing a personal belonging, one which is precisely described in the inventory of 1737: 'a rosewood smoking box, lockable, with steel handles, lined with blue satin, equipped with two small tumblers, a little funnel, a small candle holder and an extinguisher, four small pipe stems, all in silver and two coloured porcelain pots'.[14] Chardin was very fond of his pipe, as witnessed by the silver 'lighter box, four pipe ends and two pipe cleaners' listed in the inventory after his death. In painting these familiar and refined objects, he managed to compose one of the most erudite and pleasant of still lifes. First, he contrasts straight lines and diagonal lines: the box itself is placed diagonally across the picture, so that the base forms two triangles. The triangle on the left contains the bottle and the silver cup – one of the 'small tumblers' in the inventory – and that on the right contains the blue and white china jug, the pot enamelled with flowers and its lid bordered with silver – one of the 'two coloured porcelain pots' listed. A clay pipe, whose long handle is resting on the box, draws a different diagonal to that made by the box itself and the shadows of the objects on the left, between which it passes; a small pipe, on the right, forms another diagonal which is exactly the opposite of the first one. To complicate this game of lines even further, Chardin adds a check pattern created on the blue silk lining of the lid by the webbing which supports it. Against the grey-beige tonality of the whole painting, the white of the pipes, the foam and the china stands out clearly, and especially noticeable here is the indescribable 'Chardin blue' which is a constant feature of his painting, particularly from the years 1730–35, which shimmers here in the silk lining and in the pattern on the pot and the jug.[15]

THE 1750s: RETURN TO STILL LIFE

It is not easy to pinpoint the still lifes of the second period, those of the 1750s. First, because their presence in the Salons after 1753 does not necessarily mean that they were executed at that time. Chardin never stopped painting still lifes, even while establishing his reputation for genre scenes. There is nothing to indicate that certain paintings exhibited between 1753 and 1763 cannot be dated earlier than 1751.[16] Here one might recall the remark made by Garrigues de Froment in 1753: 'It remains for me to speak of the paintings of fruit and animals which the same artist exhibited, probably for the second time, since they were painted much earlier than *The Philosopher* (of 1734).'[17] During the 1750s, Chardin reverted to compositions of game (T.O.P. 135–138 and 140) and the wonderful *Dead Partridge, Pear and Noose on a Stone Table* (T.O.P. 128; see p. 169), dated 1748, shows how Chardin painted game at this time. The difference between these and the partridges of his great still lifes of 1728 (T.O.P. 37, 39; see pp. 64 and 120) is in the plumage which is softer, less dishevelled and has a much greater variety of colour. Here, the brown and white plumage is suggested by quick brushstrokes which require a certain distance and which, seen close up, defy analysis. The stone table and the background are also treated in brown tones which makes the red of the pear stand out, according to a formula proven time and again. And Chardin, unable to use

The Kitchen Table, 1755.
Oil on canvas, 39 × 47 cm
(15⅜ × 18½ in.).
Museum of Fine Arts,
Boston, Massachusetts.

his unique blue on the partridge or the pear, dabs it across the stone surface with the end of his brush, particularly near the bird's feet.[18]

The still lifes executed in this 'second style' may be quite clearly distinguished from the first period, by the growing vocabulary, the number of objects included and by the differences in colouring and treatment.

Exceptional, however, is the absolute masterpiece *Vase of Flowers* in Edinburgh (T.O.P. 139; see p. 166). Nothing could be simpler in appearance: white and red carnations, tuberoses, sweet peas, crocuses and small lilies make up a spring bouquet of blue, white and pink, giving a purplish effect in a long-necked blue and white porcelain vase. This is set against a background of vibrant brushstrokes, with a browner tone to the left of the vase and a lighter, greyer tone to the right. This colour is that of the wall and the deepest part of the ledge, barely indicated, which is only there to support the vase, the base of which, with broken brushstrokes, illuminates the stone with a white reflection. On the left, a few petals have fallen, on the right, there is a red carnation. Just beside this carnation, another red petal marks the edge of the ledge; on the left, between two blue and white dabs, there is a reddish stroke which has a similar effect to the drops of blood in the still-life paintings of game. Beyond a little impasto in the white flowers, which receive the full effect of the light, all of the rest is painted very lightly, with fluidity, managing to give the impression of an unfinished painting.[19]

The Pantry Table, 1756. Oil on canvas, 38 × 46 cm (15 × 18⅛ in.). Musée des Beaux-Arts, Carcassonne.

The Kitchen Table and *The Pantry Table* (T.O.P. 146 and 147; see pp. 171 and 172), exhibited at the Salon of 1757 when they belonged to La Live de Jully ('preparations for some dishes on a kitchen table; desserts on a sideboard') are dated 1755 and 1756 respectively. The first painting deals with preparations for a meal with a copper pan, a jug, a pestle and mortar, a pepper mill along with a piece of meat, a plucked chicken and a few onions – i.e., ingredients for a stew. In the second, the wooden sideboard holds everything which does not need to be brought in hot from the kitchen and which may be laid out before the meal. The salad to accompany a roast may be in the Marseilles china tureen beside the cruet. The pie will be served cold between courses. The fresh fruit, jams and crystallized fruits in glass jars and the cheese in its round wooden box will be offered as a dessert. The coffee then follows, with the sugar wrapped in blue paper, the alcohol stove, the cup and the sugar bowl resting on the small red varnished table, which he used twenty years earlier in the portrait of *Lady Taking Tea*, a copy of which Chardin owned, and the 'cruet with its stoppers' of silver, which were listed in the inventory after his death.

The success of *The Pantry Table* must have encouraged Chardin to paint, as well as a second version (T.O.P. 147A), what I will call variations, such as his *Jar of Apricots* (see p. 80) of 1756 and its pendant of four years later, *The Cut Melon* (T.O.P. 156 and 157). These belonged to the goldsmith Charles Roettiers, and were exhibited in beautiful oval frames with pediments at the Salon of 1761, and Gabriel de Saint-Aubin made sketches of them. Perfectly complementary, they contrast the glass in *Jar of Apricots* to the bottles in *Cut Melon*, the transparent glass jar to the porcelain ewer in its basin. Again, it is thanks to Saint-Aubin that we know that *Basket of Wild Strawberries* (T.O.P. 165; see p. 78) was also exhibited at the Salon of 1761, as it is not described in the catalogue or mentioned by the critics.

Jar of Olives (T.O.P. 161; see p. 83) is dated 1760, and despite the immense reputation which this picture owes in part to Diderot, we must not forget that again the subject of the painting is a sideboard, on which are placed a pie, two glasses of wine, a Seville orange, pears and biscuits in front of the jar of olives which gives the painting its name. Exhibited at the Salon in 1763 under the laconic title of 'other paintings of fruit', *Jar of Olives* is identifiable by Diderot's praise for it. Might one admit that it is difficult today to understand such a level of enthusiasm – even taking into account the fact that the work may have suffered and its colours become duller – which ranks the painting as one of Chardin's best? True, one does admire the almost linear composition, in a frieze, which is broken by the vertical jar and it is undoubtedly the contrast of materials to which the philosopher is most sensitive: the glass and the china, the wine and the water in which the olives are placed, their green colour, identical to certain patterns on the bowl, contrasted with the brown and red of the pears and the apples, with the colour of the Seville orange, the brilliance of the fruit contrasting with the smoothness of the pie and the biscuits; the whole painting is treated with a soberness which makes *The Pantry Table* seem almost showy.

If, for Diderot, *Jar of Olives* represents the essence of still life according to Chardin, critical opinion points to the Salon of 1763 as the peak of the painter's

Grapes and Pomegranates, 1763.
Oil on canvas, 47 × 57 cm (18½ × 22½ in.).
Louvre, Paris.

The Brioche, 1763.
Oil on canvas, 47 × 56 cm (18½ × 22 in.).
Louvre, Paris.

achievement in this field. While Mathon de la Cour complained that Chardin was no longer 'painting interesting pictures with lovely people, such as those which he used to paint', concluding that 'the landscapes, the fruit and even the animals are admirable, but will never attract as much interest as a good head',[20] the critic at *Mercure de France* was of the opposite opinion, praising 'the paintings of fruit and other genre subjects by M. Chardin (where) this illustrious artist seems to have renewed the entire strength of his talent. It has been recognized and must be admitted that this great painter is still *the master and the model of the genre which he may be said to have created*'.[21]

Grapes and Pomegranates and The Brioche (T.O.P. 166 and 167) are dated 1763.[22] In his *Dead Duck* of 1764 (T.O.P. 174; see p. 88), we find again the pie of his *Pantry Table*, the Meissen bowl, the glass of wine, the Seville orange, the biscuits and the jar of olives. But here Chardin breaks with domestic tradition, as above these prepared foods, he suspends a duck hanging by its leg, not yet plucked, which would normally be found in the kitchen. It is true that this was a large decorative painting (152 x 96 cm [59⅞ x 37¾ in]), belonging to a group, and Diderot explains at the time of its exhibition in 1765 that this 'painting of refreshments [is] to be placed between the first two'. Unfortunately, we do not know who these were painted for and what the subject matter of two other paintings in the scheme was. According to Diderot's description, the food for a cold meal and a dessert with their refreshments were grouped together in stone alcoves surrounded by grapes. That year Diderot began his commentary on Chardin, writing that 'although one only sees inanimate nature on the canvas, vases, cups, bottles, bread, wine, water, grapes, fruit and pies, he stands out and possibly distracts one from two of the most beautiful Vernets; it was not wise to hang these together'. Later, he comes back to this painting stating that 'if a connoisseur could only have one Chardin, he should seize this one. The artist is getting older. He has sometimes painted as well, but never better. Imagine a water fowl hanging by its leg. On a sideboard underneath, imagine whole and broken biscuits, a jar of olives with a cork stopper, a decorated china bowl with a lid, a lemon, a napkin unfolded and carelessly tossed aside, a pie on a wooden board and a glass half full of wine. It is here that we see that there are no unattractive objects in nature and that the aim is to depict them …'.

With the exception of the large canvases which, undeniably, had a decorative function, during the 1760s Chardin returned to medium-sized still lifes (32 x 40 cm [12⅝ x 15¾ in]), grouping together, as he did thirty years earlier, fruit and a glass, a cooler, a teapot, a water jug or a tumbler (see pp. 175 and 177). But the harmony is no longer the same and if the sense of space and composition are still wonderful, one must ask if the problems with his eyesight had not already begun. The colours have become harder: the almost garish red of the apples, the excessive pink in the peaches, the overly bright reflections of the greens against which he contrasts the creamy mass of a piece of china (a jug in the painting in Washington (T.O.P. 169), or a teapot in the Boston example, (T.O.P. 168)). In the two pendants in the Louvre, *The Silver Tumbler* and *Pears, Nuts and Glass of Wine* (T.O.P. 183 and 184; see pp. 175 and 178), the contrast is deliberate, but a little hard, between the red tonality of the first and the green of the second.

Above left:
Basket of Peaches with Nuts, Knife and Glass of Wine, 1768. Oil on canvas, 32.5 × 39.5 cm (12⅞ × 15⅝ in.). Louvre, Paris.

Above right:
Silver Tumbler, c. 1767–68. Oil on canvas, 33 × 41 cm (13 × 16⅛ in.). Louvre, Paris.

Below right:
White Teapot with Two Chestnuts, White Grapes and Pear, 1764. Oil on canvas, 32 × 40 cm (12⅝ × 15¾ in.). Museum of Fine Arts, Boston, Massachusetts.

Glass Tankard with Peaches, c. 1769. Oil on canvas, 37 × 45 cm (14⅝ × 17¾ in.). Newhouse Galleries, New York.

Opposite:
Kitchen Table with Hanging Mackerel, 1769. Oil on canvas, 68.5 × 58.5 cm (27 × 23⅛ in.). Collection of Mrs Phoebe Cowles, San Francisco.

However, despite its rather green colouring, one of the last known still lifes by Chardin, *Basket of Peaches with Nuts, Knife and Glass of Wine* (T.O.P. 186; see p. 175), executed in 1768, still moves us. The design is repetitive, the colour of the leaves separating the peaches rings false, the volume of the peach on the right is not properly defined. Yet the handle of the knife still juts out boldly from the table on which it casts a shadow and the white reflections on the reddish glass of water have kept their pictorial audacity.

CHARDIN'S PAINTINGS OF ATTRIBUTES

One must ask by what miracle Chardin succeeded so brilliantly with the large decorative schemes which he painted during this decade, which in 1764 rightly caused Cochin to say that he is 'the greatest painter ever known in this genre'.

Attributes of the Arts and *Attributes of Music* are dated 1765. The following year, Chardin completed *Attributes of the Arts and Their Rewards* and in 1767, his *Attributes of Civil Music* and *Attributes of Battle Music*, large decorative schemes (91 x 145 cm [35⅞ x 57⅛ in] and 112 x 145 cm [44⅛ x 57⅛ in]), all of which were royal and imperial commissions.

In this area, Chardin had had some practice, thirty-five to forty years earlier, in some paintings whose size and composition indicate that they were overdoors. The *Attributes of the Painter and the Draughtsman* and *Attributes of Architecture* (T.O.P. 7 and 8; see p. 132) depict a palette, sheaves of paper in rolls, a terracotta statuette after Duquesnoy, etc. In the *Attributes of the Arts* in Moscow, (T.O.P. 9; see p. 147), which are more those of a decent connoisseur, a plaster bust of Mercury is placed on these drawings in the centre of the table. Lightly sketched in on the wall in the background are Duquesnoy's *Children Playing with a Goat*. These canvases, which have a pure and rather naive charm, enabled Chardin to demonstrate his vocabulary, and to learn how best he could use the space given to him.

He had done this with the first paintings ordered from him in 1730 by Comte Alexandre de Rothenbourg, in which the painter addresses the arts of painting and drawing, as well as music. In one of the two paintings, Chardin placed on a stone ledge a polished jug, a violin, a musette covered in red velvet, all placed on scores, and on the right a music stand carrying a bound book on which a parrot is perched, as in *The Buffet*. The pendant shows less refined instruments: a hurdy-gurdy, a tambourine and a guitar with a blue strap; on the left, underneath the honeysuckle, a wicker basket is filled with pears. The two canvases bear visible traces of a former cutting, clearly marking that they were inserted into a panel, along with a third, which has been lost, according to the invoice sent to Rothenbourg by Chardin in 1730.[23]

It was also for Rothenbourg that the following year Chardin painted *Attributes of the Sciences* and *Attributes of the Arts* (T.O.P. 56 and 57; see pp. 180 and 181) which represent his first attempt at a more ambitious scale and he proved very successful. Although he does include a globe, a microscope and a set square in *Attributes of the Sciences*, the painting is mainly of rather luxurious items, chosen for their shape and colour, more than for their purpose, such as the blue telescope with gold rings which crosses the left side of the painting, or the tawny binding of the books which, like the set square, create the angles on which the composition is based (see detail, p. 186). The bronze incense

Peaches with White Grapes, Pear and Nuts, 1758.
Oil on canvas, 38 × 46 cm (15 × 18⅛ in.). Reinhart Collection, Winterthur.

Top:
Pears, Nuts and Glass of Wine, 1767–68.
Oil on canvas, 33 × 41 cm (13 × 16⅛ in.).
Louvre, Paris.

The Attributes of the Arts and Their Rewards, 1766. Oil on canvas, 112 × 140.5 cm (44⅛ × 55⅜ in.). Hermitage, St Petersburg.

burner on the left complements the tall Japanese porcelain vase on the right. The blue-green contrasts with the red, and luminous bursts of white on the brown of the wall, the globe and the bindings together form a muted and magical harmony.

The colours in *Attributes of the Arts* are the same, but more striking: a red velvet curtain with a gold trim, Largillierre style, the sparkling white of the antique bust, the blue of the roll and the marble surround of the bas-relief of children playing with a goat. The orange tree on the left is in a bronze pot and a sculpture on the pot depicts the Ballin design in the northern flower beds of the gardens at Versailles. Thus, in these *Attributes*, sculpture is represented throughout, symbolized by the mallet, in different forms – from whole pieces to bas-relief – and in different materials. But painting seems to be treated more ironically, as the palette is placed beside a bust with no eyes, and the crayon is held by a monkey. One thinks of the praise of travel and the tales brought back. In 1781 Sébastien Mercier wrote: 'If one has the taste for travel, while lunching in a good house, one can go far with one's imagination. China and Japan have provided the porcelain in which tea bearing the fragrances of Asia is drawing; with a spoon extracted from the mines of Peru, one takes sugar which has been grown in America by unfortunate Negroes, transplanted from Africa… down to the monkey and the parrot in the house, everything reminds us of the miracles of navigation and the hard work of man'.[24]

The Attributes of the Sciences, 1731. Oil on canvas, 141 × 219.5 cm (55½ × 86½ in.). Musée Jacquemart-André, Paris.

The Attributes of the Arts, 1731. Oil on canvas, 141 × 215 cm (55½ × 84⅝ in.). Musée Jacquemart-André, Paris.

The Attributes of the Arts, 1765. Oil on canvas, 91 × 145 cm (35⅞ × 57⅛ in.). Louvre, Paris.

The Attributes of Music, 1765. Oil on canvas, 91 × 145 cm (35⅞ × 57⅛ in.). Louvre, Paris.

The two paintings of *Attributes of the Arts* were placed over bookcases in the library at Rothenbourg's home in the Rue du Regard.[25] They demonstrate such mastery and such perfection, that one must ask why Chardin continued to paint his small kitchen subjects and why it took some thirty-five years before he received official orders for such subjects.

In 1764, as we have seen, it was Cochin who proposed Chardin for the overdoors to illustrate the sciences and the arts for the Château de Choisy.[26] Chardin marked out these vast compositions in the ovals, which had already been cut. One of them groups around a plaster representing the City of Paris – the central theme of Bouchardon's fountain in the Rue de Grenelle – the various *Attributes of the Arts* of sculpture, painting, drawing, architecture, numismatics, engraving and goldsmithing. The other painting, *The Attributes of Music*, is completely different, being centred horizontally around the musette in its red bag and the mandolin, while on the right, the hunting horn, the trumpet and the music stand form a vertical mass. The instruments chosen constitute a repertoire of instruments commonly used at the time, both indoors and outdoors. They give the painter the opportunity to create an extremely elaborate work exploring the relationships between horizontal, vertical and diagonal lines. The chromatic contrast of these two sumptuous paintings is striking: variations of blue in *Attributes of the Arts*, this typical blue, contrasting magnificently with the wood of the table, the palette, the handles of the brushes, the box, and with the bronze highlights of the jug; variations of red in *Attributes of Music* contrasting with the side of the book, the musette, its bows, its bellows and its strap, and the table cover on which the entire composition sits.

The following year, Chardin repeated his *Attributes of the Arts and Their Rewards* (see p. 179), when he completed two identical copies at the same time. Here again, the composition is centred around a sculpture, a plaster of Pigalle's *Mercury*, the same one which the young man in *The Drawing Lesson* was copying about ten years earlier, and a copy of which Chardin owned. Next to *Mercury*, on the left, are two bound books, the red sides of which we see; one has a blue bookmark and this in turn is echoed by a book bound in blue. A palette is resting on a small box, in front of which we see the black ribbon and cross of the Order of St Michael (see details pp. 115 and 133). In 1769 when a third version of the painting was exhibited, a critic wrote that 'the black ribbon seems to be falling off the table'. *Mercury* is placed on some architectural drawings; a set square is leaning against his right thigh and, in front of the sculpture, in the centre, are a protractor, medals and morocco case containing drawing instruments. The palette, which is very clear, has striking dabs of white, red and blue, which act as a reminder. The composition of these canvases and the use of objects in the space are far from the overdoors of the 1730s, despite some identical traits. The concept derived from Largillierre – the velvet curtain, the well spaced juxtaposition, the succession of motifs – has been forgotten; the composition is less 'decorative' and more narrative and it is certainly no accident that the antique has given way to contemporary sculptures by Bouchardon or Pigalle.

It was clearly the success of the paintings for the Château de Choisy which brought in the commission for the Château de Bellevue and, fully aware of this, Cochin was able to say that Chardin 'achieved a degree of perfection

Jean-Baptiste Pigalle, *Mercury*.
Marble. Louvre, Paris.

which was unique in his genre'. The skill with which he renews, on both occasions, the composition of musical instruments is admirable. Of course, in *The Attributes of Civil Music* we again find the hurdy-gurdy and the pink tambourine from the Rothenbourg *Musical Instruments with Basket of Fruit*, the violin in its pendant, and the hunting horn of the Choisy painting. But he uses these very differently, adding a tambourine, a flute and a clarinet, all on a red cover trimmed with gold. He adds round forms, the openings of the clarinet and the horn, and the ring of the latter, the top of the tambourine, the end of the hurdy-gurdy, the only straight lines being those of the bow, the side of the book and the flute. The pendant is deliberately more sumptuous with its gold tassels and shimmering fabric – blue velvet embroidered with the insignia of the Holy Spirit, the cover of the red drum fringed with gold, the gold and blue of the sign, the red cover over three quarters of the table. The reflection of the light in the drums, the cymbals, the trumpet and the trimmings give the whole a striking liveliness, perhaps reflecting the military character of these instruments.

Chardin never again had the opportunity to paint other *Attributes*. Henceforth, he concentrated on more modest subjects and sizes, giving up either voluntarily or by necessity the superb invention he displayed for the Choisy and Bellevue.

Overleaf:
The Attributes of the Sciences (detail).
Musée Jacquemart-André, Paris.

185

1. P. J. Mariette, *Abecedario pittorico*.

2. An example of how Chardin's specialization was recognized is given by Anatole France describing the mother of M. Bergeret thus: 'I have never known anyone appreciate so much the beauty of a peach or of a bunch of grapes. When I showed her the Chardins at the Louvre, she recognized that these were good. But one felt that she would prefer her own.' (*Scène de l'Histoire Contemporaine – M. Bergeret à Paris*).

3. In particular, R. Démoris, *Chardin, la chair et l'objet*, Paris, 1991 and Bois, Bonne, Bonnefoi, Damisch and Lebensztejn in 'La Raie', *Critique*, no. 315–16, August–September, 1973.

4. In particular, *Plate of Peaches, Grapes and Glass of Wine* (T.O.P. 152) and the two versions of *Basket of Plums with Glass of Water* and *Peaches, Basket of Black and White Grapes with Cooler and Stemmed Glass* (T.O.P. 154 and 155; see pp. 152 and 153) or *Glass of Water with Coffee Pot* (T.O.P. 164) and, even later, the *Silver Tumbler* in the Louvre (see p. 175) and its pendant, *Pears, Nuts and Glass of Wine* (T.O.P. 183 and 184). In *Silver Tumbler* (c. 1768), the fruit is reflected in the concave curve of the tumbler; the entire composition is enveloped in a sort of light mist, which is very different to the clarity and luminosity of the paintings in Karlsruhe (T.O.P. 32 and 33).

5. G. Wildenstein, 1933 and P. Rosenberg, 1979.

6. P. Rosenberg, 1983 (T.O.P. 141).

7. Unfortunately, we do not know the name of this person, as is the case for the many small paintings of kitchen scenes which he painted in the 1730s, and which cannot be identified in the known collections of the eighteenth century. This is undoubtedly because any references made are not sufficient to identify the work precisely, and also because these are paintings which were painted and repeated for middle-class customers to whom they were suited. Apparently they were not expensive, being much cheaper than Kalf's still lifes, for example, which were very expensive.

8. These may be the paintings which were mentioned in the inventory following the death of Marguerite Saintard, or possibly the two paintings on wood of 'kitchen attributes' in the La Roque sale. One of the two belonged to the engraver, Jean Georges Wille.

9. *The Copper Cistern* probably belonged to Jean François de Troy and featured at his sale in 1764. Unlike the early kitchen tables from 1728–32, these new paintings can be more easily identified from their descriptions in the catalogue inventories.

10. This is identical to *The Cistern*, as the painting in Stockholm is known, underneath which we see the same bucket of water and the same jug. We find the cistern again, with the bucket, in the background of *Girl Returning from the Market*. Is this sufficient reason to consider the painting in the Louvre as being preparatory for these paintings? I do not think so, no more than one can say that the various cauldrons in his kitchen scenes are studies for *The Scullery Maid*. And it is difficult to say if *The Cistern* was executed around the same time as *The Copper Cistern*, or a little later.

11. This is one of the paintings which Tessin purchased from Chardin during his time in Paris, between 1739 and 1741. From what we know of the Swedish ambassador's selection, this must have been a recent work, or even a commission, although there is no mention of this. It must therefore be dated between 1735 and 1740.

12. Oudry, Discourse of 1752, *op. cit.* Chardin had also considered these problems of technique in painting his first rabbit: 'I need to place it far enough away so that I no longer see the details. 'Above all, I have to ensure that I copy the general shapes, the tone of the colours, the roundness, the light effects and the shadows as well and as accurately as possible' (quoted by Cochin, 1780).

13. This was one of the rare still lifes from the period 1735–50, in which Chardin painted a dead animal, which he seems to have abandoned after *The Water Spaniel*. In 1753, he would again show 'a partridge with fruit' or 'with game', which may well have been painted several years earlier.

14. Quoted by D. Wildenstein, *op. cit.* 1959, and by P. Rosenberg, *op. cit.* 1979.

15. Pierre Rosenberg dates this work at about 1737, by comparing its execution and colouring with *Girl with a Shuttlecock* (T.O.P. 108). This hypothesis is perfectly plausible, although it is difficult to believe that almost twenty years separate *The Smoker's Box* from *The Pantry Table* of 1756 (T.O.P. 147), the subject matter of which is not so different. Again, this shows how uncertain the chronology of still life is, and I will give another example of this: at the 1979 exhibition, Pierre Rosenberg suggested that *The Copper Pot* (T.O.P. 143) could be the pendant of *Cauldron with Salmon Steak* (T.O.P. 142) and dated them both 1730–35. However, in his 1983 catalogue, he changes this date and the date for the still life in Edinburgh (T.O.P. 141) to 1750–60, which I feel is too late for either painting.

16. By way of example, Pierre Rosenberg showed that of a number of Chardin paintings in the Aved sale of 1766, *Partridge with Fruit*, which may be dated at around 1728 (T.O.P. 20), could be identified with one of the canvases exhibited at the Salon of 1753, in the same way as *Dead Hare with a Gun* (T.O.P. 43) which is dated c. 1730. *The Hound* (T.O.P. 5), painted c. 1725 was certainly exhibited at the Salon of 1759. Also, it has already been said that the *Head of a Wild Boar* of the 1769 Salon was highly likely to have been painted long before this date, if one relates it to the drawing of this subject which certainly goes back to the early years of Chardin's career (T.O.P. 46).

17. *Sentiments d'un amateur…*, 1753.

18. The method of painting this partridge provides chronological information about *Rabbit and Dead Thrushes* (T.O.P. 137): the birds receive the same sort of treatment and, in particular, the game is isolated on a beige background which is much bigger than that of the paintings of the 1730s, a feature which also applies to *Rabbits* in the Musée d'Amiens (T.O.P. 140) and to the *Rabbits and Pheasant* in Washington (T.O.P. 138).

19. This painting belonged to Aved. We might remark in passing that, although Aved had advised Chardin to paint subjects with figures, the nine paintings by his friend which he owned were all of still lifes. This could mean that they were less expensive, or that he thought more of these than his genre paintings. The bouquet differs from that which Chardin exhibited to the Salon in 1761, as Saint-Aubin's drawing of this shows an oval canvas with an object to the right of the vase, which is unidentifiable in the sketch. In addition, the inventory after Chardin's death mentions a 'glazed vase', but is this the same one? In any case, although the *Bouquet of Flowers*, was not, in Chardin's time, quite as unique as the painting in Edinburgh is today, and although a version of it was shown in 1761, without any critic mentioning it, this does not make dating it any easier – it could be anywhere between 1745 and 1760.

20. *Lettre a Mme °°° sur les peintures…exposées dans le Salon du Louvre en 1763*.

21. My italics.

22. It is not known if these paintings were included in the Salon that year. Various writers identify them as the two paintings lent by Comte de Saint-Florentin, 'a painting of fruit' and 'another of a bouquet' which is far from certain. They show two tables of desserts, some elements of which are similar to those in *Jar of Olives*: a Meissen porcelain sugar bowl, two glasses of wine and biscuits. The two paintings are composed in a pyramid, the summit being the porcelain water jug in one and the branch of orange blossom stuck into the *brioche* in the other. To the right and left, the objects are arranged in diagonals going towards the centre and the wine, which has already been poured in *Grapes and Pomegranates*, and which is in a Bohemian glass bottle in *The Brioche*, makes a translucent red reflection on the right which reinforces the bright red of the apples and the cherries.

23. In February 1730, Chardin received 'the sum of 6 *livres* for *fruit* purchased from M. *Chardin*, Painter who had painted overdoors for the dining room' (quoted by P. Rosenberg, 1979, chronology). This reference which supplies a date is particularly interesting for what it reveals of the work of still life painters when they received an order. It suggests that it was necessary to change the fruit several times while the painting was being executed, particularly where a slow painter like Chardin was concerned. The models for the musical and scientific instruments incorporated in these compositions would certainly have belonged to Rothenbourg.

24. S. Mercier, *Tableau de Paris*, 1781.

25. See P. Rosenberg, 1979, p. 148.

26. If Cochin quite naturally thought of Chardin for the overdoors for the games room at Choisy, he did specify that the artist would be able to paint scientific instruments, musical instruments and the tools of painting and architecture. One can imagine that Cochin knew the various Rothenbourg overdoors – we do not know where they hung at the time – and that Chardin himself had access to these, because in his *Attributes of the Arts* at Choisy, like those which he painted for Catherine II, he used the same bronze jug with gold around the rim in the form of a dog as he used in his *Musical Instruments and Parrot* in 1730.

CHAPTER FOUR

PORTRAITS AND GENRE SCENES

Yes, without doubt, it is permissible for
Chardin to show a kitchen with a servant
bent over a basin washing dishes.

Diderot

'In the collections of art connoisseurs, there are nevertheless portraits, studies of heads and other paintings which prove by their colour, their strong and graceful touch, and the knowledge of drawing which one notes in them, that no artist knew the secrets of his craft better than Chardin.' This is how Robert Hecquet[1] described the talents of the painter, 'emulator of Zeuxis, [who] had never had any serious rivals to his supremacy in the art of painting still life, a genre which he had chosen by preference.' This 'preference' is interesting, as it refers to prints of *The Morning Toilet*, *The Household Accounts*, *The Good Education* and *The Drawing Lesson*, four scenes which could in no way be described as still lifes. We have already mentioned the constant movement which saw Chardin change from still life to portraiture and genre scenes. This was the subject of comment by the critics, who regretted his still lifes when he painted scenes from everyday life, and vice-versa. In both cases, these were paintings which were on the bottom rung of the Académie's hierarchy of genres, but Chardin himself preferred 'to be the top painter in a lower genre rather than to be lost in a crowd of mediocre painters in a higher genre'.[2]

GENRE PAINTING

Claude Henri Watelet wrote that 'genre painters are artists who concentrate on representing certain objects. Individual tastes and the difficulty of embracing the full range of art are the reasons for this decision in the practice of painting.'[3] The negative connotation of this 'difficulty' is clear, and it caused La Font de Saint-Yenne to write that 'of all the genres of painting, the highest is history. The history painter is the only one who paints the spirit, the others paint only for the eyes.'[4] This view was shared by almost everyone at the time. Diderot himself, writing about Chardin, said that 'this painting, which is known as genre painting, should be the preserve of old men or of those who are born old. It requires only study and patience. No eloquence, little spirit, hardly any poetry; and that is it.'[5] However, if Chardin was often compared to La Fontaine, in contrast to history painters who were compared with Racine and Corneille, he was no lower down the slopes of Mount Parnassus. Watelet also drew a parallel between writers of comedy and 'Watteau, Lancret and other modern artists who have taken the events of ordinary life as their subject'. He concluded his article on 'Genre' for the *Encyclopédie* by exhorting young artists who were not capable of history painting to perfect their skills in the genre which suited them best. This was what Chardin had done, reluctantly, without anticipating how he would transcend this apparent limitation, and how his contemporaries would acknowledge his work: 'Painters with talents in a particular genre are not, for this reason, as open to criticism [as history painters]. The one painter whose genre is closest to that of history is *Monsieur Chardin*.'[6]

Already in 1737, a certain commissioner Dubuisson wrote to the Marquis de Caumont about Chardin's *Girl with a Shuttlecock*: 'I can see how one must

*Girl with a
Shuttlecock*, 1737.
Oil on canvas,
81 × 65 cm
(31⅞ × 25⅝ in.).
Private collection,
Paris.

Nicolas Lancret, *Fastening the Patten* (detail).
Oil on canvas, 138 × 106 cm (54⅜ × 41¾ in.).
Nationalmuseum, Stockholm.

The Morning Toilet, also known as *Le Négligé* (detail).
Nationalmuseum, Stockholm.

differentiate between such limited subjects and those others which require much more imagination, but I know which gives me most pleasure.'[7] Cochin later reported that 'Lancret, who although inferior to M. Chardin's talents, did have a certain charm in his genre, said amusingly that history painters who draw a naked foot well could not draw the same foot if it had a shoe on it.'[8]

However, around the 1750s this academic classification of genres began to break down. Some of the most famous members of the Académie took part in this movement. At the time when Chardin exhibited his domestic scenes, Oudry referred to Largillierre who 'held the skilled Flemish painters in high esteem, [because] they did not limit themselves to drawing the human body, which they left to others. It may well have been that the human body should have been supreme, but he was saddened to see many of our greatest masters draw the additional parts of their compositions so badly, and he was not ashamed to say that they had no talent for painting anything other than the nude.'[9] In relation to Chardin and Vernet, whom he considered the two best thinkers in the Académie, Cochin, in turn, wrote that 'such a distinction between genres was never made in the great Italian schools, great painters excelling as much at portraiture as at everything they undertook.'[10]

Chardin's contemporaries, when discussing his success, make frequent references to history painting. *Attributes of the Arts and Their Rewards* caused Des Boulmiers to remark that 'a history painter, if he had brought together all of the parts required, then executed his painting with a perfect sense of colour, would be the greatest artist of his century'.[11] Daudé de Jossan asked 'who would not be delighted to make a history painting as true and as incisive as this Mercury and these attributes of the arts?'[12] Cochin, recalling that Chardin's lack of education had prevented him from painting in the highest genre of all, wrote nevertheless that his 'heads in pastel prove that he was capable of this [and that] they demonstrate how he had the feeling of a great master, which he might well have been, had he been a history painter'. He completed this comment with a comparison, surprising for those who did not know his independent mind, saying that if Chardin 'had taken the same view of history painting as Caravaggio, he would have been more successful', meaning that one could equal the history painters if one could paint ordinary figures well.

Chardin's contemporaries are imprecise about the chronology of his first genre scenes. Cochin and Haillet de Couronne wrote that the day after Aved's comment, he began a painting with figures, *Woman Drawing Water from a Copper Cistern*. His success led him to repeat this in paintings 'the subjects of which are ennobled by a more sophisticated choice of people' (*The Governess* and *The Bird-Organ*). Mariette spoke of his *Soap Bubbles*, followed later by *The Copper Cistern* and *The Washerwoman*, adding, 'what really made his reputation is his painting of a governess'. Did Chardin seek to adapt his 'culinary' theme to the human figure, or was it pride which drove him to prove that he too could paint, if not strictly speaking a portrait, then at least a figure on a large scale? Following Mariette, we will study the portraits before the genre paintings, which has the advantage of a certain chronological coherence since the former (excluding the one of Laurent d'Houry and the pastels) almost all date from between 1732–33 and 1740, while the latter extend to 1751 or later, when he resumed still life painting.

PORTRAITS

Chardin began his series of portraits – almost all half-lengths – with his paintings of a young man blowing soap bubbles. There are three known versions of this (T.O.P. 97) and a fourth, which is lost, was engraved.[13] The vertical print (see right) shows a young man leaning on a stone windowsill on which there is a glass of soapy water and a straw. The bubble, which is still attached to the straw between his lips, is in the foreground in front of the sill, underneath which we see what looks like the top of the Duquesnoy bas-relief. Just behind, by his elbow, we see the head of a small child, wearing a hat with a feather, who is watching the bubble. The version in Washington (see p. 194), also vertical, has been enlarged. Honeysuckle, painted in rapid strokes, surrounds the window at the left; some is a later addition, and it is greener at the top than below, where it has been painted with a red tint, over the trace of a bas-relief. The little hand of the child holding onto the sill is not shown here. The entire painting is treated in tones of brown, against which the red ribbon in the sleeve of the jacket and two parallel blue arcs circling the left hand side of the bubble stand out. The whole painting moves from left to right. Light from the left shines on the bubble, the contours of which are admirably suggested by blue and pink reflections. The versions in Los Angeles (see p. 124) and New York are horizontal and the frame around the window has disappeared. Only the stone windowsill remains.[14] Philip Conisbee remarked that there are no *pentimenti* in any of these paintings, which would indicate that all three are based on the first version which was shown at the Salon of 1739 and which is now lost. The engraving by Fillœul (see right) is also dated 1739, as is its pendant, *Game of Knucklebones* (T.O.P. 98; see p. 195). The two paintings were still together in 1781 when they belonged to the architect Pierre Boscry, but does this mean that they were painted at the same time? Both illustrate simple occupations: the instability of the soap bubble corresponds to the uncertain journey of the knucklebones, as indicated in the verse which accompanied the engraving. In contrast to the shaded three-quarter face of the boy blowing bubbles, the face of the young girl is a true portrait, and for stylistic reasons it is possible that it was painted slightly later than *Soap Bubbles*.[15]

Lady Sealing a Letter (T.O.P. 79; see p. 196) is a unique genre scene on a large scale, which evokes the works of Jean François de Troy in its subject matter and its ambitious composition[16]. A woman wearing a dress with broad stripes, described by the Goncourt brothers as 'zinzolin' fabric, is holding a letter which she has just written in one hand and with the other hand, she holds out a stick of sealing wax to a servant who is lighting a candle. The legend on the engraving gives the subject amorous connotations:

Hâte-toi donc, Frontain: vois ta jeune Maîtresse,
Sa tendre impatience éclate dans ses yeux ;
Il lui tarde déjà que l'objet de ses vœux
Ait reçu ce Billet, gage de sa tendresse…

(Hurry, now, Frontain: see your young Mistress, / Her tender impatience sparkles in her eyes; / She longs for the object of her vows / To receive this letter, a pledge of her affection.)

Pierre Fillœul, *Soap Bubbles* (*Les Bouteilles de savon*), 1739. Engraving after Chardin.

Soap Bubbles, c. 1732–33.
Oil on canvas, 93 × 74.5 cm
(36⅝ × 29⅜ in.). National
Gallery of Art, Washington.

Game of Knucklebones,
c. 1734. Oil on canvas,
81.5 × 64.5 cm
(32⅛ × 25½ in.).
The Baltimore Museum,
Mary Frick Jacobs
Collection.

195

196

It has already been said that the boy blowing bubbles was clearly the model for the servant. His mistress, whose profile is similar to that of the woman in *Lady Taking Tea* (see p. 200) and whose hair is identical, must be Marguerite Saintard, Chardin's first wife. Her dress is made of the same fabric with white and blue-grey stripes bordered by a thin red stripe, 'a costume evocative of the late Madame Joffrin [and] which makes this piece truly interesting and original', as we read in the catalogue of the sale after the death of Hubert Robert,[17] who painted Madame Geoffrin at her desk, with a servant and in her striped dress. But it is certainly Chardin's wife here; he shows her wearing a coat dress, the folds of which are draped over the cane chair, her head dressed for going out and not for being at home, and wearing a necklace. The red curtain with its gold cords and tassels and the beautiful table coverings all contribute to the richness of the décor.[18]

In announcing the engraving, *Mercure de France* of May 1738 referred to the 'naive and true expression', a phrase which echoes Mariette's remark on *Soap Bubbles* that Chardin had 'tried to give [the young man] a naive air'. This concept of naivety, which comes up so often in critiques of Chardin's work, should be placed in the context of the time. On Chardin's death, Cochin wrote that one was struck by 'the truth and the naivety of [his] poses and compositions. Nothing seems deliberate and yet all of these conditions were fulfilled with an art all the more admirable for being so discreet.' It was also mentioned by the editor of *Mercure de France*: 'nature is imitated with such accuracy and naivety, that some connoisseurs feel that the painter has successfully found the means of capturing nature and extracting from her that which is most naive and most touching.'[19] If this quality is so closely linked by contemporaries to the painter's work, it is also because to them it seemed to define the man. Thus, in 1755 when Cars's engraving after Cochin's portrait of Chardin was put on sale, *Mercure de France* noted 'the resemblance which has been captured beautifully. This naivety which forms his character and which reigns in his works is striking'. The print's legend takes up this image:

De quoi pourrait ici s'étonner la nature?
C'est le portrait naïf de l'un de ses rivaux.
Il respire en cette gravure
Elle parle dans ses tableaux.

(What could surprise nature here? / This is the naive portrait of one of her rivals. / It breathes in this engraving / Nature speaks in his pictures.)

The concept is clearly defined by the Chevalier de Jaucourt in the *Encyclopédie*: 'Naivety is the language of beautiful spirit and of simplicity full of light. It is the source of charm in discourse and is a supreme result of art in those to whom she is not natural… The naive is the opposite of the calculated… [it] emerges from the beautiful spirit, without the assistance of art; it may neither be compelled nor detained.'[20] Diderot wrote that 'not everything that is true is naive, but everything that is naive is true. Almost all of Poussin's figures are naive, i.e., they are perfectly and purely that which they should be. Almost all of Raphael's old people, his women, his children and his angels

Opposite:
Lady Sealing a Letter, c. 1732–33.
Oil on canvas, 146 × 147 cm (57½ × 57⅞ in.).
Schloss Charlottenburg, Berlin.

197

Joseph Aved, *Self-portrait*, 1727, engraved in 1762 by Guillaume Philippe Benoist.

are naive, that is to say they have a kind of originality in their nature, an innate grace which no institution has ever given them.'[21] These definitions help one understand why one may call naive, that is to say natural, faces and poses such as those of *Soap Bubbles* or *Lady Sealing a Letter*, which are the antithesis of exaggeration.

The 'chemist in his laboratory' exhibited at the Salon of 1737 (see p. 119), engraved in 1744 under the title of *Le Souffleur* (*The Prompter*; see p. 199), and exhibited again in 1753 as 'a philosopher reading', raises different questions.[22] The painting was commissioned by the Comte de Rothenbourg, probably after his return from Madrid in 1734. When the ambassador died in April 1735, he had not paid Chardin, who took back 'a picture of a *philosopher* commissioned from him by the late Comte de Rottembourg… to dispose of it as he saw fit.'[23] The sitter was identified by Elie Fréron, in his report on the Salon of 1753: 'the portrait of M. Aved, friend of M. Chardin, is easily recognized'.[24] Was this so 'easy' that no one else had noticed until then? The painting is dated *4 XBRE 1734*,[25] which seems to me to be directly related to Aved's election to the Académie a few days earlier. But why would Rothenbourg have ordered a likeness – even if Aved was a painter who had worked for him? Even supposing that he had seen *Lady Sealing a Letter*, the *Portrait of Laurent d'Houry* or a version of *Soap Bubbles*, why would he have approached Chardin for a portrait? However, the real question is whether *The Philosopher* may be described as a portrait.

Aved did paint some self-portraits.[26] One of them, engraved by Guillaume Philippe Benoist, is dated 1727. The portraitist, aged twenty-five, looks at us with an air of juvenile pride; his wig of long curls is tied back at the neck with a satin bow. Chubby cheeks, a well drawn nose and bright eyes characterize a pleasant face which it is hard to imagine could have become the rather bloated, ageless man of the portrait seven years later. It seems certain that the painting never belonged to Aved. It never left Rothenbourg's home from the time of its execution to the Comte's death. Chardin then took it back and exhibited it when the Salon opened again and there is every reason to believe that it belonged to him then and also in 1744 when an engraving was made. Nine years later, when the painting was shown again at the Salon, it belonged to Boscry, the architect.[27] It would seem that Chardin did not set out to paint a portrait: rather, this Rembrandtesque composition is a fantasy or 'fancy' portrait, like those Fragonard was to do some thirty-five years later. Perhaps Rothenbourg, after his attributes of the arts, the sciences and music, wanted an allegory of philosophy or alchemy. While the objects on the table are not carefully painted, the grainy treatment of the books, the inkwell and, in particular, the hourglass, where amazing shades of blue and red blend together, makes this 'still life' a piece of pure painting. In a work which is almost monochrome, these colours make the sleeves of the dressing gown over which the philosopher has thrown his greatcoat bordered with fur, the table covering, the curtain and his scarf stand out strongly.

In common with all the other 'portraits' of the years 1732–35 (with the exception of *Game of Knucklebones*), *The Philosopher* does not show the sitter full face. It is as if, at this time, Chardin did not know how or did not wish to paint anything else.

In 1735 Chardin painted his first wife, Marguerite Saintard, taking tea (see p. 200), a peaceful masterpiece to which Michael Baxandall devoted one of his studies, concentrating mainly on the problems of vision and colour.[28] His conclusion is applicable to all of the portraits and genre scenes, i.e., that 'Chardin is one of the great eighteenth-century narrative painters: he can and often does make a story out of the contents of a shopping bag. He narrates by representing not substance – not figures fighting or embracing or gesticulating – but a story of perceptual experience masquerading lightly as a moment or two of sensation…. that narrative of attention is heavily loaded: it has foci, privileged points of fixation, failures, characteristic modes of relaxation, awareness of contrasts, and curiosity about what it does not succeed in knowing.'[29] In fact, nothing is happening: a woman with a placid profile is looking at the porcelain cup into which she has just poured some tea. In her right hand, she is holding a silver spoon, while in her left hand, which is not clear, she is holding the saucer. Steam rising from the tea merges with the steam from the teapot to form a slight haze, separating the foreground from the wall, against which is placed a red table. Some faint arabesques have been painted onto the sides of the table which suggest *chinoiserie* without actually representing it. The same applies to the blue pattern on the white porcelain. Chardin is not trying to render the details of the décor precisely; he is happy, as in his *Vase of Flowers* in Edinburgh (see p. 166), to make the object recognizable, without being too specific. His approach is quite different when it comes to rendering the fabric of the woman's dress, her criss-cross shawl and her bonnet, all of which are painted very precisely. Particularly admirable is his rendering of the woman's black muslin spotted shawl, lined with the same blue fabric, which allows the painter to alternate the two colours: the blue on her neck, the blue where the shawl is turned up above her elbow and the blue of the bow, crossed with her black sash, to which Chardin has given a certain transparency. The bow on her bonnet is painted in the same blue, while her powdered hair and her earring, painted with the same small circular brushstrokes which we saw in the coat of the *Water Spaniel* of 1730 (see p. 21), are in a bluish white which makes the transition from the white bonnet to the blue of the top of the shawl. Several problems with perspective are immediately obvious: it is not clear how the woman is sitting, nor how the back of her chair sits in relation to the table, and the teapot looks as if it is about to fall. However, this is of little importance in relation to the chromatic harmony of the painting: the clear black of the shawl, the gleaming brown of the teapot, the green-grey stripes of the dress bordered by a red identical to that of the table, and the blue of the bow, the lining of the shawl, the porcelain and the drawer of the table.

This portrait had a pendant (T.O.P. 102) which seems to have been Chardin's first attempt to depict a young boy building a *House of Cards* (see right). This painting is exactly the same size as *Lady Taking Tea*. We see the boy's left profile, and his body down to his knees. His arms are in front of him and his hands, which are holding the cards, are in the same position as those of the woman holding the tea cup. The green cover corresponds to the red table, the brilliant white of the block of cards with their crisp edges contrasts with the round, brown shape of the teapot. The bright wall behind the woman, divided by vertical monochrome lines, is repeated in a darker form in *House of*

François Bernard Lépicié, *Le Souffleur* (The Prompter), also known as *Philosopher Reading*, 1744. Engraving after Chardin.

Lady Taking Tea, 1735. Oil on canvas, 80 × 101 cm (31½ × 39¾ in.). Hunterian Art Gallery, University of Glasgow.

Cards, where the light source is a window on the left which is mostly covered by a curtain held back by sashes and a tassel similar to those in *The Philosopher*.

The success of this composition is witnessed by the studio replicas and its various engravings, and also by the fact that Chardin would deal with the subject again, with different variations. One of these (T.O.P. 103 – the only one not to have been engraved) is unfortunately too worn for us to be able to draw any stylistic or chronological conclusions. Meanwhile, the *House of Cards* in Washington (T.O.P. 109) was exhibited at the Salon of 1737 as a pendant to *Girl with a Shuttlecock* (T.O.P. 108; see p. 191). The boy's dark brown hair is tied back with a bow which is painted in the same blue as the apron over his brown frock coat. The games table is covered with a bright green cover, which reminds us how rarely Chardin used this colour, and we can see how he enjoyed painting the heads of the screws in the wood and how he makes the drawer knob stand out with a dark shadow. The cards are folded in two and their alignment forms more of a wall than a house. Their white backs, like the boy's collar, contrast with the red of the hearts, the counter on the table and the lining of the right sleeve of the boy's coat; their crisp fold, along with the corner of the table and the card which is sticking out of the drawer, gives the whole composition an angular stiffness. In Chardin's final *House of Cards* (T.O.P. 105; see p. 202), the young boy with chestnut coloured hair, wearing a tricorne is seen in profile from the right.[30] In his left hand he is holding the card which he is about to add to the pile. The harmony of the picture is softer, with light brown and beige dominant, broken only by the muted green of the felt cover and the blue of the scarf.

The case for *Girl with a Shuttlecock* (T.O.P. 108), dated 1737, being the pendant of *House of Cards* is supported not only by the measurements of the paintings and the fact that they are facing each other, the girl looking to the left and the boy to the right, but also by their entry on the same date into the collection of Catherine II. Also, there are two replicas in the Uffizi, which it seems have always been kept together. How well they complement each other is emphasized by the choice of colours: as well as the milky white of the apron, the bright tones of *House of Cards* match the blue trim of her brown dress, the blue ribbon holding the scissors and pin cushion, the feathers in the shuttlecock and the flowers in her bonnet. In both paintings, the blue is juxtaposed with a rather faded pink and with white, creating a porcelain effect echoed in the girl's colouring, her blue eyes and her lightly powdered hair. Only the muted red of the girl's racket and the pin cushion vary from these light tints.

The same girl may also have been the model, a little later, for the *Schoolmistress* (T.O.P. 104; see p. 123), probably a pendant for 'the son of M. Le Noir', not only because both were engraved by Lépicié, but because their scale, their colouring and even, I would say, their sensitivity, are in perfect harmony. In this case, the *Schoolmistress* and her little brother would both be members of the Le Noir family. Here again, the colours have great subtlety: the pale wood of the furniture picks up the white of the child's corselet and the bottom of his cap, the red and blue embroidery on the cap in turn corresponding to the ribbon on his elder sister's bonnet and the blue of her blouse. The light is brighter in the right-hand side of the picture and the background behind the girl's fichu, apron and bonnet. This luminous effect includes a

House of Cards, c. 1735.
Oil on canvas, 81 × 101 cm (31⅞ × 39¾ in.).
Private collection, Britain.

201

House of Cards, also known as *Son of M. Le Noir Building a House of Cards*, *c.* 1740. Oil on canvas, 60 × 72 cm (23⅝ × 28⅜ in.). National Gallery, London.

Child with a Spinning Top, c. 1738. Oil on canvas, 67 × 76 cm (26⅜ × 29⅞ in.). Louvre, Paris.

Pierre Louis Surugue, *The Inclination of Her Age*, 1743.
Engraving after Chardin.

Jean Baptiste Massé, *The Godefroy Brothers with Jacques Fallavel*. Red chalk drawing, 56 × 42 cm
(22 × 16½ in.). Musée Nissim de Camondo, Paris.

calculated angle of vision, our eye resting on the girl in the foreground, her silhouette and on the knitting needle which she is using to point out the letters of
the alphabet. In contrast, the rendering of the child in the background is deliberately soft, giving the sense that the eye has not yet focused on him. Is this
painting really a double portrait, or is it a genre scene which has been given the
dimensions of a portrait? The doubt lingers, as it does for the other paintings of
comparable style and format executed between 1737 and 1742.

The only one of these paintings where the model has not been identified is
The Young Draughtsman (T.O.P. 112; see p. 205). In both versions (in the
Louvre and in Berlin), dated 1737,[31] there is the same harmony of the white
frock coat, with the blue of the smock underneath just visible, the same blue as
the sheet of paper on which this young man has drawn a caricature of the head
of an old man. The only bright note is the red of the ribbons binding his drawing book. The end of one of these ribbons on the table is treated like a trace of
blood beside dead game in a still life.

At the same Salon in 1738, Chardin showed two other portraits of chil-
dren. The first was a 'portrait of the son of M. Godefroy, Jeweller, watching
his top spinning', which appears to have been hung beside *The Young
Draughtsman*. The second was a 'portrait of the small daughter of M. Mahon,
Merchant, with her doll'. The latter is known to us only through its engraving,
The Inclination of Her Age, which leads us to think of it being the same format as
Girl with a Shuttlecock or the various versions of *House of Cards*. The face with its
clearly defined features, seen almost in full, is a real portrait.[32]

In *Child with a Spinning Top* (see p. 203), the space is divided into two
equal parts. The space on the left is reserved for inanimate objects: books on
the table, a quill resting in an ink pot, a roll of paper and the top itself, while a
red crayon holder is peeping out of the half-opened drawer. The space on the
right is occupied by the little Gabriel – whose beautiful curls around his face
we admire, along with the blue bow tying back his hair, the embroidered blue
and silver waistcoat and his brown frock coat. He is standing in front of a wall
covered in a beige, green and red striped fabric. In this portrait, as in the one of
his brother, Charles, holding a violin (see p. 206), the hands are quite remarkable, especially as these are usually the weak point of Chardin's figures.
Charles's fingers are resting on the strings of his violin as though he had just
finished playing, while Gabriel's thumb and forefinger are still squeezed
together, having just sent the top spinning.

Chardin's portrait of *Madame Le Noir Holding a Book* which he showed at
the Salon of 1743 has disappeared and we know it only through its engraving,
called *The Moment of Meditation* (see left). The young woman is portrayed down
to her knees, sitting in a finely furnished room. She is elegantly dressed and is
holding a half-open book on her lap. Again, this painting is halfway between a
true portrait and a genre scene. What difference is there, except in scale,
between *The Moment of Meditation* and *The Amusements of Private Life* painted
only a few years earlier, representing 'a woman sitting nonchalantly in a chair
and holding a book in her hand…'?

In the years which followed, Chardin painted only two true portraits. In
1746, he exhibited a portrait of André Levret which was 'as big as life'. Its
small medallion engraving gives the impression that it was designed for the

The Young Draughtsman, 1737. Oil on canvas, 81 × 67 cm (31⅞ × 26⅜ in.). Gemäldegalerie, Staatliche Museen Preussischer Kulturbesitz, Berlin.

Young Man with a Violin,
c. 1736–37. Oil on canvas,
67.5 × 74.5 cm
(26⅝ × 29⅜ in.).
Louvre, Paris.

Pierre Louis Surugue, *The Moment of Meditation*, 1747.
Engraving after Chardin.

frontispiece of one of the books published by this famous physician, 'obstet-rician to the Dauphine'. This portrait, which was missing for a long time, has just reappeared. Originally rectangular, it was made into an oval, possibly so that it would match its engraving. Unfortunately, the canvas has been damaged, but it is obvious that Chardin clearly intended this to be a proper portrait, giving the eyes an attentive look, drawing the mouth firmly and giving his face an expression of kindly authority (see right). Eleven years later, he exhibited the medallion portrait of another famous doctor, the surgeon Antoine Louis. This portrait is known to us through its engraving by Simon Miger (see p. 281) and it is comparable to the thirty or so medallions made at about the same time by this engraver after the drawings of Cochin, representing different categories of important men, artists, academicians, men of letters, clergymen, members of parliament and members of society.[33] Included were eight surgeons and five doctors. In addition, Madeleine Pinault has noted that Diderot, in his entries in the *Encyclopédie* on medicine and surgery, referred to the work of Antoine Louis, who had himself contributed numerous articles, and that of André Levret, who was responsible for many improvements in the science of obstetrics.[34] Chardin thus found himself part of the intellectual movement of the Enlightenment; although he himself did not directly belong to a circle of writers or thinkers, he was in contact with the theoreticians of his time and the fact that Levret and Louis chose him as their portraitist was certainly not by chance.

GENRE SCENES

In Chardin's genre scenes, as in the portraits, one can again distinguish various categories: people on their own, portraying a type – a draughtsman, or a blind man, for example; or an occupation – a scullery maid or a woman doing the household accounts. These can involve scenes with two or three people, which was another way of illustrating daily life of the time. In total, there were about twenty subjects, painted over eighteen years, which formed the basis of Chardin's fame.

His transition from still life to genre scenes is marked with *Woman Drawing Water from a Copper Cistern* (T.O.P. 80; see p. 31). In this painting, Chardin includes his whole repertoire, and adds two people into the 'décor', which serves to open up a new space. These figures do not yet have individuality, or even a face: at most we see two shadowy profiles, like mirror reflections of each other. The child in the background is very poorly handled. In *The Washerwoman*, which may have been painted a little later, the woman and the child are more individual (see p. 30). The little boy in rags who is sitting blowing bubbles may have been Jean Pierre Chardin, who was born in 1731. The background is a complete success, where in the doorway we see the silhouette of a woman hanging a white sheet, which picks up the headdress and the apron of the woman in the foreground, as well as the washing in her barrel.

It was around this time, between 1734 and 1737, that Chardin painted a series of small figure paintings, each one of which depicts an occupation or a trade. Examples (see pp. 50 and 51) are his *Embroiderer* which has always been paired with his young *Draughtsman* (which should not be confused with the portrait of 1737; T.O.P. 84 and 85). The rigorous composition of these small panels, which are not even 20 cm (8 in.) high, stands out, giving the space a certain monumentality. There is none of the smooth technique of similar Dutch subjects, but an execution in large brushstrokes with grainy impasto. Chardin is not interested in the faces: *The Embroiderer* is portrayed through her dress, her apron, her headdress, in the red table covering behind her, in the piece of work on her lap and above all by her work basket in the foreground on the right, from which she is selecting a ball of wool. *The Draughtsman*, who is seen from the back, is clearly finding it difficult to earn a living, considering the old frock coat which he is wearing, complete with holes – the pretext for a lovely dab of red in the middle of all the brown – and his clumsy boots. Seated on the ground, he is concentrating on copying a drawing of a male nude in red chalk which is hanging on the wall. This is one of the young students, 'pencil in hand, back bent for a long time over a portfolio', who runs the risk at the age of nineteen or twenty of still being 'without a profession, without resources and without standards',[35] an impression reinforced by his association with the embroiderer, depicted as a worker in a simple medium.[36]

These paintings, or copies of them, were exhibited again in 1759, and were praised by the *Journal encyclopédique*: 'Of the two paintings which

Portrait of André Levret, Surgeon, c. 1746.
Oil on canvas, 65 × 54 cm (25⅝ × 21¼ in.).
Private collection.

207

Jacques Fabien Gautier Dagoty,
The Embroiderer, 1742–43. Engraving after Chardin.

M. Chardin exhibited this year, those which merit the most attention are two small ones, one of which represents a young man copying a drawing and the other a girl doing some needlepoint. We only see the young draughtsman's back. Despite this, the artist has so well captured the truth and the nature of the young man's situation that, when looking at the picture for the first time, it is impossible not to feel that he is concentrating very hard on his task. The girl working on her tapestry is bending down to choose some wool. In the girl's head and her rather dreamy attitude, the artist has captured the satisfaction of semi-idleness and the repose of one who is not upset at having to pause in her work for a moment, although she does not want to stop completely. In both of these paintings there is a harmony of light which indicates great beauty to the viewer who only sees half of the scene.'

Although it is dangerous to try to compare paintings with others which are known only through their engravings, copies, or photographs, it seems that *Blind Man Begging* (T.O.P. 89) can be included with these small panels. A version of this on wood has been destroyed and it is known to us through an enlarged painting in the Fogg Art Museum and through an engraving (see p. 60). At the Salon of 1753, this small painting was commented on by the Abbé Laugier and Abbé Garrigues de Froment. Laugier wrote that 'we see a blind man standing, with a stick in his hand and holding a small dog on a leash. His pose, the tilt of his head and the way he moves his stick are truly the movements of a blind man. His dress, both in its shape and in its grime, clearly identifies the figure as an inmate of the Hôpital des Quinze-Vingts.'[37] Garrigues de Froment wrote: 'however trivial the choice of subject, however esoteric it might seem…, through his art and magic, the artist has succeeded in completing a very piquant little picture. This is the good part. However, I must point out that there is not enough play in the folds of his garment, although its colour is very true, and the blind man's dog looks very like the one belonging to the diligent mother. This is the bad part.'[38] Despite the late date of its exhibition and its engraving (1761), it is likely that this 'very piquant little picture' had been painted long before, around the same time as *The Draughtsman* and *The Embroiderer*, possibly marking the beginning of paintings depicting minor trades.[39]

Then Chardin changed direction again. He gave up all of the small panels which seemed to have brought him success and it was on canvases of about 46 x 37 cm (18⅛ x 14⅝ in.) that he began to paint his figures, either alone or in groups, captured performing ordinary, everyday actions. The first of these, painted between 1735 and 1738, were three humble scenes in which a single figure is using the utensils which Chardin had already portrayed elsewhere. In this group of paintings, his *Cellar Boy* (T.O.P. 113; see p. 210) is the sole portrayal of a man in a world of women and young girls. Like its pendant, *The Scullery Maid* (T.O.P. 114), the *Cellar Boy* is painted in a monochrome of brown, beige and off-white, against which the bright red of the painted metal bottle-carrier stands out (see detail, p. 160). Each object has its own harmony of colour, where brown, grey, black and even blue dominate alternately. In this long, pale figure the face is individualized, and Chardin has taken care to define the mouth and eyelids clearly. *The Scullery Maid* (see p. 211) opposite is leaning towards him, washing a pan. Around her, varying shades of brown provide a backdrop for the pale colour of her dress and her yellowish apron. The only gleam is on the inside of the cauldron (see detail p. 161) and the only new colour is the blue of the ribbon round her neck and the blue of her petticoat, which is identical to the blue ribbon holding the young cellar boy's keys. The sobriety of the overall colouring gives this young woman a certain distinction which is out of keeping with her occupation, and one wonders if Chardin may have 'dressed up' a member of his entourage, most likely the woman who served as the model for *The Governess*.[40]

The Scullery Maid is dated 1738, like *Woman Peeling Vegetables* (T.O.P. 116; see p. 42), who attracts our sympathy. She has paused in her task, distractedly holding in her hand a knife and a turnip, the peelings of which are falling down her apron onto her skirt. Sitting, slightly stooped, she is lost in thought, with a rather abandoned, lonely air. Beside her, the block on which she must have killed a fowl still bears a trace of blood. The perspective is faulty, with everything seeming to slide downwards to the left.

I suggested earlier that the three small panels of *The Blind Man*, *The Embroiderer* and *The Draughtsman* were part of the same series. Here (particularly with *Girl Returning from the Market*), there is even more of a sense of a coherent series of domestic works, which should certainly be considered in relation to the *Cries of Paris* engraved after Boucher (by Simon François Ravenet and Le Bas) and after Bouchardon (by Caylus) from 1736 (see p. 213), not to mention Cochin who made similar drawings at this time. Among Bouchardon's *Studies of Common People* were a *Scullery Maid*, *People Shelling Peas* and a *Walnut Seller* whose spirit was very similar to that of Chardin's paintings.

With *Girl Returning from the Market* (T.O.P. 115; see p. 212), Chardin took a step forward in his representation of domestic tasks.[41] This woman is not trapped in her humble world like *The Scullery Maid* or *Woman Peeling Vegetables* – she is coming in from the world outside, bringing provisions with her. The door opening onto the street is still ajar and in the doorway we can just see the head of a man, talking to a girl in profile. Thus, the composition has been enlarged to include other people and also a new space. Certainly, the place where the woman has stopped is quite different from the kitchen or the laundry of the previous pictures. Perhaps it is a pantry, given the bottles on the ground, the jar of fat, the pewter plate and the sideboard on which the woman is leaning. The frame of the door is as simply refined as her clothes – the sleeves held up by a pink bow, her pink stockings, her pink and grey striped fichu, the medallion hanging on a velvet ribbon, all of which indicate the affluence of this servant or cook, which is emphasized by the verse with which Lépicié accompanied his engraving:

A votre air j'estime et je pense,
Ma chère enfant sans calculer,
Que vous prenez sur la dépense
Ce qu'il faut pour vous habiller.

(By the look of you, I guess and think, / My dear child, without doing any sums, / That you help yourself from the expenses / To what you need for clothes.)

Jacques Fabien Gautier Dagoty,
The Draughtsman, 1742–43.
Engraving after Chardin.

209

The Cellar Boy, 1735.
Oil on canvas,
46 × 37.2 cm
(18⅛ × 14⅝ in.).
Hunterian Art Gallery,
University of Glasgow.

The Scullery Maid,
1738. Oil on canvas,
45.4 × 37 cm
(18 × 14⅝ in.).
Hunterian Art Gallery,
University of Glasgow.

Girl Returning from the Market, 1738.
Oil on canvas, 46 × 37 cm
(18⅛ × 14⅝ in.).
National Gallery
of Canada, Ottawa.

But here again, Chardin changes course and, despite the success of *Girl Returning from the Market*, he interrupts his series of representations of people glimpsed performing humble tasks. He resumed it eight years later, however, with four 'scenes from middle-class life', showing the occupations or pastimes of women at home. In between, he painted the pictures of woman and children which added most to his reputation.

There are no men in these paintings, neither fathers nor tutors. Norman Bryson sees a clear division of labour here, between the woman who maintains the home and the man – Chardin – who paints. But Chardin took pains to portray domestic scenes in such a way that the presence of the painter does not disturb the order of the scene. He operates in female space, without effort or disruption – as if there were a sort of osmosis between the work of the painter and the house which surrounds him.[42] In this world, the lives of children up to the age of nine or ten years old were still run by women. Furthermore, the ideas of Jean Jacques Rousseau were becoming known and, increasingly, school was given up in favour of 'reserving for one's innermost private hearth the formation of sensitivity, and the teaching of values and behaviour'.[43] This teaching was the task of the mother, who managed the education of her daughter and her young son, took care of their clothing, taught them social graces, good manners, domestic tasks and religion.[44] In these charming scenes, small episodes from life which we witness in *The Governess*, *The Diligent Mother*, *The Morning Toilet* and *Saying Grace*, Chardin tenderly and mischievously illustrates the flaws of early childhood: idleness, carelessness, coquetry, etc.

Mariette and Cochin both see *The Governess* (see p. 43) as Chardin's most popular picture and the critics are not short of praise for the painting and its engraving, stressing the accuracy of the expressions. The woman is sometimes called the mother, not the governess, just as the woman in *Saying Grace* was called a governess in Pesselier's verses, published in 1741. In the end, there is no difference between all of these women who run their homes and look after their children and one wonders if Chardin's model for *The Governess*, *The Scullery Maid* and *Woman Peeling Vegetables* was not in fact the woman who ran his own home. In *The Governess*, the pleasant little boy in the brown frock coat with streaks of blue paint, with his brown stockings and his blue bow, has a contrite expression which ties in with the kindly reprimand of his mother, the whiteness of whose bonnet, fichu and apron accentuates her blue striped dress. The red velvet chair, the elegant parquet floor, the sober wooden panelling on the walls, the wallpaper or tapestry glimpsed through the door and the games table all denote refined comfort. In his portrayal of the relationship between mother and child, in his analysis of expressions and movements, as in his use of space, Chardin has reached the summit. In *The Morning Toilet* (see p. 47), the very young mother and her little daughter form a triangle in the centre of the picture; on the left we see a dressing table and, on the right, the sideboard and clock listed in the inventory after Marguerite Saintard's death. The little girl is wearing a light blue jacket with a white lining over a pink dress. Her muff is blue and white and her mother is tying a blue bow around her white bonnet. The mother's dress echoes these colours, which highlights the black mantilla under which we see her profile, absorbed, while her daughter is looking in the mirror. We see the child's round and rather ungainly face again

Caylus, *Woman Scouring a Pot*, c. 1737. Engraving after Edmé Bouchardon.

213

in *The Diligent Mother* (see p. 218); here Chardin has demonstrated, using two comparable subjects and certainly the same models, how he could make two very different pictures. In *The Diligent Mother*, around the white mass of the two figures is the refined décor of a room closed off by a partition, but which still opens up to the outside by a door at the back. The colours of the décor are also found in the tapestry on the mother's lap, in the lilac-grey stripes of her dress, her blue stockings and her white shoes with pink bows, in the little girl's blue and ivory blouse and in the ribbons around their bonnets.

The same sketch (T.O.P. 119) seems to lie behind both *The Diligent Mother* and *Saying Grace* (see pp. 32, 54 and 215). On the left we see the two children, but in *The Diligent Mother* the girl standing is holding in her hands one end of a piece of fabric and her mother is holding the other. Finally, Chardin produced the composition known today, which he repeated at least twice in a vertical format and then horizontally (T.O.P. 120).[45] At the same time Chardin painted *Card Games* and *Game of Goose* (see pp. 48 and 54), two compositions of groups of children, this time without an adult, and engraved in pairs (T.O.P. 95, 96). In each of these, we see a little girl, a small boy and a slightly older boy; in *Card Games*, the latter may even be a young tutor.[46] In 1748–49, Chardin painted two similar pictures for Queen Louisa Ulrica and he also made versions for La Live de Jully. These pictures are the last which he devoted to subjects of childhood and they represent a sort of pinnacle. *The Drawing Lesson* (T.O.P. 126; see p. 217) shows a young adolescent, seated, his sketch book on his knees, copying a plaster of *Mercury* by Pigalle. A companion is standing looking over his shoulder. *The Good Education* (T.O.P. 127; see p. 216) is a variation of *The Diligent Mother* and the girl seems to be hesitating while her mother is making her say her catechism. As in the first *House of Cards*, the light enters from a window on the left, partly concealed by a velvet curtain, illuminating the mother's striped dress, the blue dress of her daughter, their bonnets and the tablecloth which is too white, giving the scene a rather artificial, milky white light reminiscent of a Daniel Chodowiecki composition.

The Drawing Lesson was exhibited in 1748, before it went to Sweden. It was praised by the Abbé Gougenot who wrote that 'the emulation between the two young men could not have been portrayed better. The figure which they are copying is M. Pigal's *Mercury* [see p. 184].[47] The artist has let it be known by his choice that our School is able to supply the purest models for teaching drawing.'[48] However, the Abbé added that Chardin was still criticized 'for not giving enough relief to his flesh. In his new painting, this fault applies to all of the figures.' On the other hand, when Chardin exhibited a second version in 1753, Estève criticized 'the location of the scene, a poor garret rendered with great accuracy. In it are two figures with very long legs, common faces and a disgusting air…. The marble group which decorates the painting has a very unnerving effect. It is well drawn, without having any distinctive feature. The contour is lost in the true rendition of the colours'.[49] The Abbé Garrigues de Froment did not share this view. However, although he liked the painting, he was critical about its pendant: 'seen closer, the repetition of the girl reciting her catechism, which she does not know, is not as piquant as its composition suggests it should be. The artist has contrasted lights which are too bright, with too little colour, with shadows which have precisely the correct tone.

Saying Grace,
c. 1741–42.
Oil on canvas,
49.5 × 41 cm
(19½ × 16⅛ in.).
Louvre, Paris.

The Good Education, 1749. Oil on canvas, 41 × 47 cm (16⅛ × 18½ in.). Museum of Fine Arts, Houston, Texas.

The Drawing Lesson, 1748. Oil on canvas, 41 × 47 cm (16⅛ × 18½ in.). Fuji Art Museum, Tokyo.

The Diligent Mother, 1740.
Oil on canvas, 49 × 39 cm
(19¼ × 15⅜ in.).
Louvre, Paris.

218

There is a sort of fog which does not lift, either from close up or from a distance and which I believe I am right to see as the effect of brushwork which is too soft and too indecisive.'[50] The Abbé Le Blanc remarked that 'there is such expression in the young girl's head that one feels one can almost hear her speak; her internal distress at not knowing her lessons is clear from her face.'[51] The Abbé Laugier wrote of the face of the mother 'seated and listening with the rather teacherish expression which one has when listening to a lesson being recited', and describes the expressions of the two as having 'charming naivety'.[52] Cochin, meanwhile, responded vigorously to Estève's criticism as follows: 'From this fine description [that of Estève], would you not imagine a garret crossed with beams and rafters, with tumble-down walls, indeed all of the filth which one would find in a *poor garret*? Do you imagine characters with lowered heads in the style of *Ostade* with pallid colouring? To what else could the term disgusting be applied? Pupils dressed in dirty or torn clothing! Well, sir, there is nothing of the sort; the scene is not even located in a *garret*, but in a room or anteroom, and it is simply furnished in the manner of a place devoted to study. There is nothing common or disagreeable about the heads, indeed they are quite refined. The colouring of the faces is lively and fresh, as is normally the case at sixteen or eighteen years of age. If these students have long, slender legs, it is because this is a distinctive characteristic of adolescence. Finally, they are neatly dressed as is usual for children of the middle classes, whose resources are just enough to ensure comfort for all the time it takes to study the arts, but which are not plentiful enough for the student to be able to slacken. These are the best circumstances for educating excellent artists. Otherwise, all of the accessories in this painting are also suited to the subject, there being no low objects which indicate poverty or which degrade the art which they are studying. Those who would consider this poorly formed would seem unaware that each age has its particular graces.'[53]

The genre scenes painted by Chardin from 1745 to 1750 are praised for their truth and their naivety, as was the case, as we have seen, for his portraits. It was certainly La Font de Saint-Yenne who defined this quality best. In 1747, he admired in *The Amusements of Private Life* 'the talent for rendering with a truth which is his alone, and which is uniquely naive, certain moments in life which are not in the least interesting and which do not attract attention in themselves, and some of which are not worthy of the artist's choice or of the beauties which one admires in them'. He came back to this point in 1754, writing that 'he adds to his particular talent for seeing in nature the naivety and delicacy which she hides from others, a talent for rendering with a truth of illusion which always seems new and which is attractive regardless of the mediocrity of the subject.'[54] The definition of naivety is enriched here with a new significance, linked more to the action or the person represented than to the intrinsic qualities of the painter. We find this particularly in Watelet's reflections on naivety: 'the naive only belongs to the qualities which are associated with ingenuousness, simplicity, candour, perhaps even with a sort of physical weakness… naivety, pleasant in childhood and youth, vanishes with advancing age. In women, it continues to please for a long time, because their retiring life, simple and free from business, leaves them inexperienced for a long time.'[55] We see well how the concept of naivety applies perfectly to

219

Chardin's subjects, as he only paints women and children. And one understands why Mariette wrote in 1749 that 'the talent of M. Chardin is only a renewal of that of the Le Nain brothers. Like them, he chooses the simplest and most naive subjects and, to be honest, his choice is even better.'[56] Elsewhere he wrote that the paintings of the Le Nain brothers 'please as much in their execution as by the naivety of the characters which they present'.[57] And it is true that one finds in the subjects of the Le Nain brothers some things in common with Chardin; the interest in children and their occupations (the *Little Card Players*), similar themes (*Saying Grace*), or again the representation of domestic occupations in an interior (*The Three Ages*). In fact, beyond the concept of naivety, the interesting thing about the eighteenth-century parallel drawn between Chardin and the Le Nains is to find a source for Chardin's subjects outside the perennial reference to the Low Countries, linking Chardin to a French tradition and to known models. Jacques Thuillier remarks that in *The Peasant Family* 'the most singular trait is the absence of any subject'.[58] This judgment could certainly not be applied to Chardin; however, in good academic tradition, one is tempted to say of his paintings that 'his compositions have no purpose. They do not express any passion and consequently are lacking in one of the most moving aspects of painting, namely action.' What Caylus wrote about Watteau could be applied to the genre scenes painted by Chardin.[59]

What can one say about paintings such as *The Amusements of Private Life* or *The Household Accounts*, *The Convalescent's Meal* and *The Bird Organ*? Four women (or the same woman four times – probably Françoise Marguerite Pouget, Chardin's second wife) are seen reading a novel, doing the household accounts, cracking a boiled egg or teaching a canary to sing – in short, captured in their lives which are 'retiring, simple and free from business'. This image was so normal for Chardin's contemporaries that no one was surprised by it; on the contrary, it helped him achieve fame. The fact that these paintings were commissioned by the Courts of Sweden and Vienna and, even better, by the French king, underlines this. The first two show the limits of Chardin's inspiration around 1745, as the subjects planned were to illustrate *L'Education douce* and *L'Education sévère*: instead, he shows an idle woman in one, and in the other a woman preoccupied with her household accounts. In *The Amusements of Private Life* (T.O.P. 123; see p. 52) the woman, who for once is looking at the viewer, is lying back in a red velvet armchair with a book in her lap. La Font de Saint-Yenne calls her 'amiably lazy', and goes on to describe her as 'a woman in rather casual and fashionable clothing, with quite a sweet face wrapped in a white scarf tied under the chin hiding the sides of her face'.[60] Two years later, after its exhibition at the Salon, another critic wrote that the painting – or, most likely, its engraving, as the original was by then in Stockholm – 'has a sort of languid air which comes from the woman's eyes, which she has fixed on a corner of the picture; we can tell that she is reading a novel and the tender feelings which this has aroused are making her daydream about some person whom she would like to see arrive soon. Is there anything more touching than this small painting, which is as good as the best of the Flemish School and which would enhance the most discriminating collections.'[61]

In its pendant, *Household Accounts* (T.O.P. 124; see right), the woman is wearing an apron and the muslin scarf in *Amusements* has been replaced with a bonnet. She is sitting at her desk on a simple wooden chair, facing the window on the left where the light is coming from. She is checking a list of expenses on her lap against sheets of accounts on the table. Unfortunately, the painting has been very badly damaged and its reputation relies wholly on the engraving which Le Bas made of it (see p. 280), after it had left France, based on a drawing by the Swede Jean Eric Rehn. Chardin would certainly not have wanted to send a 'portrait' of his wife to Louisa Ulrica, but it was undoubtedly convenient to use her as a model and, besides, it is easy to imagine that she who called herself the 'Lady Treasurer of the Académie' treated his household expenses with care and that would have kept the list of outgoings up to date.[62]

The Convalescent's Meal, also known as *The Attentive Nurse* (T.O.P. 125; see p. 223), was executed at about the same time as *The Household Accounts*, and like it has a simple domestic theme. The setting comprises a table partly covered with a large cloth, a wooden chair and a fireplace. The standing woman is removing the shell from a boiled egg. She is wearing a light green, pink, reddish-pink and white striped skirt, a white blouse with a pink floral print and a pink apron. A wonderful sketch exists of this painting (T.O.P. 125A; see p. 222) which helps us understand how Chardin worked on his compositions and his colours, as well as the objects which he included in his paintings. This sketch, which is about the same size as the final work, is almost monochrome with its beige and brown tones, against which the black bonnet, the touch of blue on the shoe and some pink highlights on the woman's blouse stand out. The apron is white, like the fichu, the napkin over her arm and the tablecloth. Two red highlights on her nose and her lips give her a curiously animated face, smiling more than in the final version. Seemingly small changes in the placing and the type of objects make a considerable difference to the sense of space and give the woman a certain monumentality.

There is only one copy of each of these three paintings, which is exceptional for Chardin. All left France as soon as they were completed, or very soon after, which prevented replicas being made. This was not the case for *The Bird Organ* (see p. 59), which was commissioned by the King's Direction des Bâtiments. There are two known versions of this (T.O.P. 133 and 133A), which show Madame Chardin with her usual head covering, wearing a dress made of the same material as the blouse in *The Attentive Nurse*. Turning the crank of a music box, or bird organ, she is looking at a canary in its cage.[63] Chardin took the opportunity of this *Woman Varying Her Pastimes* to pay homage to Charles Antoine Coypel by hanging two framed engravings of his work on the wall. The one seen in full is Lépicié's engraving of *Thalia Driven Out by Painting*, a clear allusion to Coypel, who had long been torn between painting and the theatre, for which he had written many plays. The engraver took care to inscribe on the frame, in small letters, the word *Thalia*, enabling the work to be identified.[64]

It seems that in 1753, Chardin received an order from the King's Direction des Bâtiments for 'a painting of the same size as that which is known as a woman varying her pastimes, valued at 1,500 *livres*, the choice of subject to be made by the author', and Lépicié noted that 'he was working on it'. Although this commission was very flattering, it was never completed and *The Bird Organ* remains the final work of this type painted by Chardin, whose fame

The Household Accounts, c. 1747.
Oil on canvas, 43 × 36 cm (16⅞ × 14⅛ in.).
Nationalmuseum, Stockholm.

221

The Convalescent's Meal, also
known as *The Attentive Nurse*.
Sketch, *c.* 1747.
Oil on canvas, 45 × 35.5 cm
(17¾ × 14 in.).
Private collection.

The Convalescent's Meal,
also known as *The
Attentive Nurse*, c. 1747.
Oil on canvas, 46.2 × 37
cm (18⅛ × 14⅝ in.).
National Gallery of Art,
Washington, Samuel H.
Kress Collection.

223

increased from this time on, as he resumed his still life painting until the year 1770, which marked a new turning point in his work.

PASTELS

In exhibitions or articles, drawings have been attributed to Chardin for their subject matter rather than their style: for example, a *Man Wearing a Tricorne* which belonged to the Goncourts, or a *Lady Taking Tea* which is really by Jeaurat.[65] In fact, the definitive list of drawings by Chardin is short and it confirms Mariette's remark that 'he did not concentrate on drawing'.[66] Therefore one is all the more surprised to see him, from 1770–71 on, devote himself to pastel and succeed in this medium, which involves drawing more than painting, as few other artists would in the eighteenth century. This turn-around has been explained by the fact that Chardin was no longer able to tolerate the pigments used in his paints. This may well be true, but one must also remember that pastel remained accessible to artists having problems with their eyesight. La Tour recounted that he came to this technique because he was too short-sighted for painting and Rosalba Carriera used pastel until the end of her life, although she wore spectacles and had been operated on for a cataract. Chardin also wore spectacles and it is possible that he came to pastel because it was a practical technique for those with failing eyesight.[67] Finally, pastel may be applied rapidly; it enables portraitists to shorten the time of sittings, and this would have been a considerable advantage for an artist who worked as slowly as Chardin.

Chardin's *Self-portrait with Spectacles* is dated 1771 (T.O.P. 191; see p. 228) and it was exhibited at the Salon that year as a 'study of a head', without the name of the model being specified. In it, we find the colours used so often in his painting: the light brown of the jacket, the pink and blue checked scarf, the blue ribbon tied around his white headscarf. Above his spectacles, clear eyes look at the mirror without indulgence. What is most surprising in this portrait, as in the other portraits which we know, is the boldness of the grey, blue and white strokes of the crayon hatching the flesh, marking the shadows cast by the spectacles under the nose and on the cheek by his ear lobe.[68] His study of the head of an *Old Man* (T.O.P. 192; see p. 96) is also dated 1771, and is most likely to have been exhibited at the Salon with the self-portrait. Looking at this head which could be that of a hermit, the muted colouring, the audacity of the green and blue hatching marking the flesh, one understands why Cochin, speaking of these different types of heads, of 'young people, old people and others', life-size, said that in them Chardin 'was very succesful due to his skill and his manner which was broad and easy – in appearance at least, for in fact it was the fruit of a great deal of reflection and he was a hard man to satisfy. These works show that he had a feeling for greatness and that he could have been a history painter had he so desired.'[69]

One may also think that, in drawing these heads, Chardin was contradicting the letter he had been sent by Baillet de Saint-Julien who, complaining that artists neglected the study of the passions, wrote: 'You, Sir, if you have not made such a study, it is because the rare and unique genre which you have created, and possibly perfected, has no call for it. You have been concerned with the knowledge of characters that it requires; and that study is as valid as the

François Bernard Lépicié, *Thalia Driven Out by Painting*, 1733. Engraving after Coypel.

Opposite:
Self-portrait, also known as *Chardin at the Easel*, 1778–79. Pastel, 40.5 × 32.5 cm (16 × 12⅞ in.). Louvre, Paris.

Study of a Head, also known as *Portrait of the Painter Bachelier*, 1773. Pastel, 55 × 45 cm (21⅝ × 17¾ in.). The Fogg Art Museum, Cambridge, Massachusetts, Bequest of Grenville L. Winthrop.

other, if I may say so to you.'[70] Further on, he asks Chardin, 'why do your colleagues have so little success with characters and with the study of passion? It is because they do not practise it.'

Did Chardin want to prove that he was also able to represent passion and thus equal the history painters? In 1773, he also made a study of a Rembrandtesque head: a man with a decisive face, wrongly said to be Bachelier, the painter (T.O.P. 193; see left), wearing brown clothes with a pleated ruff, a baldric and a medal on a chain and a red velvet hat with a blue bow.[71] Here again, the crayon casts shadows on the face, suggesting a beard, mixes grey, red and brown tints in the fabric and recreates the same harmonies of colour as in oil painting. All of these pastels are executed on blue paper, roughly prepared with brown so as to obtain an unevenly shaded base.

Self-portrait with Eye-shade and the first version of *Portrait of Madame Chardin* (T.O.P. 194 and 195; see pp. 8 and 229), which date from 1775, were surely designed to be a pair, as the pinkish tones in his beige-pink jacket, scarf and ribbon are answered by the blue ribbon in his wife's bonnet. Chardin's gaze, behind his spectacles, reveals a certain arrogance. The portrait of Madame Chardin is dazzling: Chardin paints her in a dress with reddish stripes. The black shawl edged with a frill, the transparency of her fichu, underneath which we see a blue ribbon, and the bluish tints on the edges of her bonnet all demonstrate an incredible mastery of pastel, which is best in his treatment of the face. Chardin paints this old woman without any concessions, her closed lips certainly hiding missing teeth. He includes dark circles, shadows, blemishes and reddened eyelids. In 1776, he made a second version (T.O.P. 195A) as well as another *Head of an Old Woman* (T.O.P. 196; see p. 227) which is a copy of a portrait of Rembrandt's mother – at the time the original was in the Baudouin collection before it was acquired by Catherine II. At the Salon the following year, Chardin again exhibited three studies of heads in pastel, including his portraits of a young girl and a young boy (T.O.P. 198 and 199; see pp. 100 and 101), and the critics praised his 'broad and skilled touch'. It is striking to see the artist, who was almost eighty years old, return to the subject of children, which he seems to have abandoned for more than thirty years. He did so again with *Little Jacquet* bought at the Salon of 1779 by Madame Adelaide. The two pastels of 1777 included Chardin's favourite colours: there is the blue of the girl's apron-corset and the ribbon holding back her chestnut hair; the red, beige and blue stripes of the sleeves of her dress; the white of her muslin scarf, shaded with blue; and the liquid transparency of her pearl necklace. Her young brother's costume echoes these colours: a pink jacket with large silver buttons, a blue belt, the pleated collar, and the strange black straw hat topped with a large black bow. The treatment of the fabrics, the hair and the faces, which Chardin executes with grey hatching, all demonstrate his absolute mastery of the medium.

In 1778 or 1779 Chardin painted his last self-portrait (T.O.P. 201; see p. 225). This final effigy is also his last known work. Old and sick, the artist had lost none of his mastery, nor his evocative power. This ruthless portrait of an old man with an absent look is both a testament to the artist and a celebration of drawing. The crayon marks out the skin in parallel hatching and shadows are made by rubbing his thumb into the pastel. Although the hand is a little misshapen, it is firmly holding the stick of red crayon with which Chardin was preparing to draw on a sheet of blue paper attached to a thin frame.

While so many portraits depict both the artist the work in progress, Chardin – whom no one ever saw paint – has kept his secret to the end, by showing us only the support for his picture.

PENDANTS IN CHARDIN'S WORK

There are a great number of pendants in Chardin's work, including a dozen 'pairs' of genre scenes, about twenty still lifes and at least two sets of pastels. These may have been executed in a thematic way, or they may have been commissions.[72] Announcements of engravings helps us to know which paintings were considered pendants, although they may not have been painted at the same time.[73] The Salon catalogues also specify if pendants were involved. Thus, of the paintings exhibited between 1753 and 1763, *Game of Goose* and *Card Games* 'were pendants', as were *The Diligent Student* and *The Good Education* and also a number of still lifes, which were not always described very precisely ('two paintings of fruit', etc.). Sometimes the information is drawn from a commentary on the exhibition – for example, in October 1738, *Mercure de France* described a 'Young woman, sitting on a rush-seated chair, doing needlepoint, has paused in her work, her gaze fixed on the draughtsman'; it gave clear details of how the two canvases were to be hung as a pair. Sometimes it is the sale catalogues which enable us to see which works were presented as pendants. For example, at the second Geminiani sale in London in 1743, the two paintings of *The Embroiderer*, one small one and a larger copy made between 1737 and 1738, are mentioned; each painting is accompanied by 'its companion', namely the two paintings of a *Draughtsman*. In 1779, the Trouard sale catalogue mentioned 'two pendants: each shows a young boy in half-length – one is amusing himself blowing soap bubbles and the other is building a house of cards'. These paintings are not true pendants, but their juxtaposition in the collection clarifies for us what collectors regarded as pairs. *Jar of Apricots* and *The Cut Melon* were painted four years apart; however, their oval shape, identical frames and particularly the fact that in one the light comes from the left, while in the other it comes from the right, show that these were true pendants and it seems likely that Roettiers, having purchased the first, had commissioned the second from Chardin. *Dead Pheasant with Game-bag* (T.O.P. 159) dated 1760 appears to be the pendant to *Dead Hare with Wallflowers* (T.O.P. 160), but a comparison of their composition and scale (see pp. 230 and 231) makes it unlikely that they were executed with this in mind.

More interesting still are the mentions of pendants where one painting is by Chardin and the other by a different artist. This was not an unusual phenomenon in the eighteenth century.[74] This is how Chardin came to paint a 'replica of *Saying Grace* with an addition, to pair with a Teniers in the collection of Madame ***', which was mentioned in the catalogue of the Salon of 1746. An example of the contrary process comes from the Vassal de Saint-Hubert sale catalogue of January 1774. We see the following entry under number 105: '*Simon Chardin*, A blind man from the Quinze-Vingts begging with his dog, ... a canvas ten inches three lines [27.5 cm] high by six inches nine lines [18.5 cm] wide' (see p. 235). Number 106, by '*M. Fragonard*', is described as follows:

Head of an Old Woman, 1776. Pastel, 46 × 38 cm (18⅛ × 15 in.). Musée des Beaux-Arts, Besançon.

Self-portrait, also known as *Portrait of Chardin with Spectacles*, 1771. Pastel, 46 × 37.5 cm (18⅛ × 14⅞ in.). Louvre, Paris.

Portrait of Madame Chardin, 1775. Pastel, 46 × 38.5 cm (18⅛ × 15¼ in.). Louvre, Paris.

Dead Pheasant with Game-bag, 1760.
Oil on canvas, 72 × 58 cm (28⅜ × 22⅞ in.).
Gemäldegalerie, Staatliche Museen
Preussischer Kulturbesitz, Berlin.

'A painting on copper the same size as the one above, and which was executed as its pendant. It depicts a woman leaning on a post with a hurdy-gurdy, with two small dogs playing near a column in the background…' (see p. 235). This is Fragonard's *Fanchon, the Hurdy-Gurdy Player*.[75] Thus Vassal de Saint-Hubert, who collected the work of both Chardin and Fragonard, commissioned from Fragonard a pendant to pair with his copy of *Blind Man Begging*.

REPLICAS AND COPIES

The catalogue of Chardin's *œuvre* shows twenty-one still lifes and eighteen genre scenes of which two or three versions existed, excluding the self-portraits and the portraits of Madame Chardin in pastel.[76] This practice was so widespread that it was suggested to Louisa Ulrica of Sweden that she acquire replicas of existing paintings and the Margravine of Baden also considered this solution. By keeping a painting in his studio to serve as a model, and by repeating it almost identically, it was certainly easier for Chardin to increase his output without having to arrange new sittings and without having to replenish his game, vegetables, meat or fish too often. Thus Fleischmann informed the Margravine of Baden that 'the paintings which Chardin has made for the Abbé Trublet are not currently in the latter's possession, having been shown at the exhibition of paintings at the Louvre [in 1759] and since then, Chardin has taken them back and kept them at his studio'. This was obviously so that he could make the copies which we know (T.O.P. 154 and 155; see pp. 152 and 153), but it also meant that this was considered quite usual and that connoisseurs accepted that the painter would copy works which they owned.

More surprising is the existence of copies from the very beginning of his career. In the inventory after the death of Marguerite Saintard in 1737, there were 'two paintings on canvas representing animals and fruit *which are two copies after originals by the said M. Chardin*'.[77] At the La Roque sale in 1745, there were 'two paintings, one of which shows a cook returning from buying provisions; it is the original by M. Chardin and it has been engraved… the second painting depicts a mother giving her child his lessons and correcting its faults. The latter is a copy which has been retouched in several places by M. Chardin.' Four years later, in 1749, the inventory after the death of Claude Nicolas Rollin mentions 'two pictures painted on canvas, copies of Chardins, one of a Pupil and the other of a Governess'. If these were the paintings from the La Roque sale, it seems that the supposed original became a copy in a very short time! Even more surprising, taking into account the personality and the taste of the collector, is the fact that in 1741 – i.e., shortly after the originals were presented to Louis XV – Tessin sent to Stockholm two copies of *The Diligent Mother* and *Saying Grace*, bearing an inscription on the back, possibly in Chardin's own hand:[78] 'After the original painting by Chardin in the King's collection / 1741'. At the time, these copies were valued at 180 *livres* by Tessin. Finally, two paintings exhibited 'for sale' at the Salon of the Académie de Toulouse in 1769, were described as 'a painting of musical instruments by Chardin' and 'a painting of mathematical instruments by the same'.[79] In the absence of any other information, one might suppose that these were copies of two of the Choisy paintings.

A passage in Pierre Henri Lévêque's article on 'Copies' in the *Encyclopédie* refers directly to Chardin: 'A picture made after another picture. Where the master himself makes the copy, the second painting is known as a *double* [replica]. Some copies exist which are so skilfully executed that it is difficult to distinguish them from the originals. There are some which have been made, under the eyes of the master, by skilled pupils and which have been touched up by him…. Many artists humbly admit that they could be deceived by these *copies*. Dealers are a long way from admitting the same and there are amateurs who express themselves similarly to the dealers…. M. Chardin ensured that he would never be fooled by *copies* which may have been made of his pictures. It must be admitted that not all painters are as difficult to copy as M. Chardin.' This sentence concludes the entry. It explains perhaps the huge number of paintings mentioned during the artist's lifetime as being 'in the taste', 'in the genre' or 'in the style' of M. Chardin, demonstrating amply that, like Watteau, Chardin had truly created a genre which was admired and sought after. A good example of this is given by the *House of Cards* in the Musée Cognacq-Jay: it is a copy, probably painted towards the end of the eighteenth century, of an engraving by Fillœul, embellished with elements from the *Young Draughtsman*.[80] This mix of two themes clearly shows what was sought after in Chardin and the reason for a market of copies and pastiches after his most popular subjects.

Dead Hare with Wallflowers and Onions, c. 1760.
Oil on canvas, 73 × 60 cm (28¾ × 23⅝ in.).
The Detroit Institute of Arts.

tiftes , on ne peut trop en confidérer le *faire* & le bon coloris, tout annonce la célébrité de l'Auteur.

Charles Natoire.

104 L'Ange qui conduit Tobie tenant un poiffon. Ce tableau eft dans le goût de *le Moine*, fon coloris & la légereté de la touche font honneur à l'Auteur, il eft fur toile qui porte quinze pouces trois lignes de haut fur onze pouces fix lignes de large. 360 *pavel [...] pour tous*

Simon Chardin.

105 Un aveugle des Quinze-vingt faifant la quête avec fon chien, une chaife eft à gauche ; de l'archi-tecture fait le fond de ce favant tableau qui eft fur toile de dix pouces trois lignes de haut fur fix pouces neuf lignes de large. 1700

M. Fragonard.

106 Un tableau fur cuivre de même grandeur que le précédent , & qui

a été fait pour pendant : il repré-fente une joueufe de vielle appuyée fur une borne , deux petits chiens jouent proche d'une colonne qui fait partie du fond. L'Artifte fait voir par ce morceau fes talents dif-tingués tant dans le deffein que dans le coloris & la belle intelli-gence de la lumiere.

107 Deux morceaux du même Artifte; ce font des payfages chauds & d'un bon ftyle , enrichis de figures agréa-bles & d'animaux fur des plans dif-férents , ils font fur toile , & cha-cun porte treize pouces fix lignes de haut fur dix-fept pouces de large. 2000 *quewt*

Joseph Vernet.

108 Un autre dans des rochers, plu-fieurs fabriques , des Matelots qui font du feu , un homme qui pêche à la ligne & autres figures. L'effet de ce tableau eft au clair de lune ; fon mérite eft fupérieur , il eft fur toile de dix-huit pouces de haut fur vingt-quatre pouces de large. M. *Marce-nay de Guy* l'a très bien gravé dans le goût de *Rembrandt.*

Gabriel de Saint-Aubin, drawings in the Vassal de Saint-Hubert sale catalogue, 1774.

1. It was Robert Hecquet who brought the Le Bas *œuvre* to the Bibliothèque Royale and who annotated it (Bibliothèque Nationale, Cabinet des Estampes, *Ee 11*, fol.).

2. *Le Nécrologe des hommes célèbres de France*, 'Éloge Historique de M. Chardin', 1780.

3. *Encyclopédie méthodique*, vol. 2, 1788. Entry on 'Genre'.

4. *Réflexions sur quelques causes de l'état présent de la peinture…*, 1747.

5. *Salon* of 1765, ed. Seznec and Adhémar, vol. II, 1960, p. 111.

6. Gougenot, *Lettre sur la peinture, la sculpture et l'architecture à M°°°* (by a Society of Amateurs), 1748.

7. Quoted by P. Rosenberg, 1979, catalogue no. 72.

8. *Essay* on the life of Chardin, 1780. For this comparison which is often made between Lancret and Chardin, one might consider a note written in 1740 by Algarotti, the connoisseur, when he was drawing up an acquisitions plan for the Museum of Dresden and planning commissions to be placed with leading contemporary artists: 'Non si sono anno verati in questa nota se non se i Figuristi, lasciando stare i Pittori d'Architettura, come Orlandi in Bologna, Panini in Roma, Canaletto e i suoi imitatori in Venezia, cosi pure si sono lasciati i Pittori di Paesi come Zuccarelli in Venezia, *que'di bambocciate come Chardin in Parigi, e Lancret imitatore di Watteau*' (quoted by G. Brunel in *Tiepolo*, 1992, p. 133).

9. First discourse by Oudry on colour, *op. cit.*, 1749.

10. Third discourse delivered in 1778 to the Académie de Rouen on 'the methods of studying nature'.

11. *Mercure de France*, October 1769.

12. *Sentiments sur les tableaux…*, 1769

13. See *Soap Bubbles by Jean Simeon Chardin*, Los Angeles County Museum of Art, 1991.

14. In the version in the Metropolitan Museum, New York, there is a little honeysuckle on the left which has been poorly executed. The paint on the boy's forehead is like a sort of milky skin. The painting in Los Angeles is a little bigger, creating the impression of a large amount of space on either side. It seems to have been executed more quickly and less work has been done on the hair.

15. One of the horizontal versions of *Soap Bubbles* passed through several public sales in the eighteenth century as the pendant of *The Schoolmistress*. This was certainly because of its size, but also because of the presence of a child in the background (see P. Rosenberg, 1983, T.O.P. 104).

16. The painting appears to be dated 1733, but the last figure is not quite legible and the engraving gives a date of 1732.

17. 5 April 1809, no. 31. Hubert Robert owned a version of this painting.

18. The exceptional nature of this painting may explain the smaller copies made by Chardin (T.O.P. 79A), one of which was offered to the Margravine de Baden in 1759 by Fleischmann, who said that it was 'one of the prettiest pieces in his collection'.

19. *Mercure de France*, October 1740.

20. *Encyclopédie méthodique*, entry on 'Naïveté' (naivety), 1765.

21. Diderot, *Pensées détachées sur la peinture*, in *Oeuvres esthétiques*, ed. P. Vernières, 1968.

22. The verse which accompanied the engraving makes a specific link between the sitter and chemistry or alchemy to be precise.

23. Quoted by P. Rosenberg, 1979, catalogue no. 62.

24. 'Exposition des tableaux…', *Lettres sur quelques écrits de ce temps*, 1753.

25. This date is also on the engraving.

26. See G. Wildenstein, *Le Peintre Aved*, Paris, 1922.

27. It seems to be accepted that this was not a second version, although Pierre Rosenberg's argument that Garrigues de Froment specified that it was painted in 1734, because he wrote his report in front of the painting, is debatable. The engraving bears this date and the critic may have been referring to this.

28. M. Baxandall, *Patterns of Intention*, Yale, 1985, 'Pictures and Ideas: Chardin's *A Lady Taking Tea*'.

29. M. Baxandall, *Patterns of Intention*, Yale, 1985.

30. This painting is of 'the son of M. Le Noir amusing himself building a house of cards', the title under which it was shown at the Salon of 1741. It was engraved in 1743, the same year that Chardin exhibited the portrait of Madame Le Noir and it was a pendant for *The Schoolmistress* (T.O.P. 104) which had been exhibited at the Salon in 1740 and was also engraved by Lépicié. For stylistic reasons, Rosenberg dates this canvas 1735–36. before *Girl with a Shuttlecock* and, therefore, before the *House of Cards* in Washington. But it is hardly likely that Chardin would have exhibited at the Salon, without giving his identity, this portrait of the Le Noir boy whom he would have painted five or six years earlier when the boy, who looks about ten here, would only have been four or five. Furthermore, insofar as this painting is part of a series of portraits of the Le Noir family, it is logical to think that it was painted shortly before its exhibition. On the other hand, this child could also be the small boy in *The Governess*, a painting of 1738, which would date Chardin's links with the Le Noirs a little earlier.

31. One of these was exhibited at the Salon of 1738 as a 'young draughtsman sharpening his pencil', with a pendant of 'a young woman doing some embroidery', a painting which has been lost and which does not seem to have been engraved. (D. Carritt, *art. cit.*, 1974). The differences between the two paintings are minimal and involve only details.

32. More information is available to us about the Godefroy family than the Mahon family. The father of *Child with a Spinning Top*, Charles Godefroy, who died in 1748, was a banker and jeweller. He was associated with the draughtsman and miniaturist Jean-Baptiste Massé, a friend of Chardin, when he was having the paintings of the Galerie des Glaces engraved. He may have been related to the master painter J. F. Godefroy, who had died in a duel in 1741, and whose widow was an appointed restorer of the king's paintings. A drawing by Massé, dated 1736 (in the Musée Nissim de Camondo, Paris) shows Charles and Gabriel, the two sons of the jeweller, with Jacques Fallavel, who was close to Massé and the executor of his will. On the left is the small boy whom Chardin painted two years later playing with a top (T.O.P. 111); on the right, we see his elder brother, whom Chardin painted holding a violin (T.O.P. 100). Charles Théodose was born in 1718. In 1759 he became *Capitoul de Toulouse*, with the title 'Seigneur de Villetaneuse', and he took over his father's work assisting Massé with his engraving. He also devoted himself to music, which is certainly the reason why Chardin painted him holding a violin and bow, in front of a volume of *Minuet*. X-rays of the painting have shown that its size was altered, probably so that it would be the same size as the portrait of his brother, Auguste Gabriel. The latter was born in 1728 and his portrait was probably painted in 1738, the year when it was exhibited, if we are to go by the apparent age of the model. But the commission which Charles Godefroy – who also owned two still lifes by Chardin – placed for two portraits of his young sons could date back a little earlier. The *Young Man with a Violin* must be about eighteen to twenty years old, which would indicate that it was painted between 1736 and 1738, and that the modifications to the canvas were made after *Child with a Top* was painted.

33. See C. Michel, 1993, p. 172.

34. M. Pinault, *L'Encyclopédie*, 'Que sais-je?', 1993.

35. Chardin's famous text on apprentice painters was reported by Diderot in his comments on the Salon of 1765.

36. However, such an association may have been quite normal for the public, as in 1738 *The Young Draughtsman* who, in the paintings in the Louvre and in Berlin, appears as a young amateur from a good family, has as its pendant another 'young woman working on a tapestry'. Unfortunately, we do not know what she looked like.

37. *Jugement d'un amateur sur l'exposition des tableaux…*, 1753.

38. *Sentiments d'un amateur sur l'exposition des tableaux…*, 1753.

39. On the other hand, consider *The Little Soldier* and *Little Girl with Cherries*, which were exhibited at the Salon of 1737 as 'a small child with the attributes of childhood' and 'a little girl playing with her lunch'. These were both small panels 20 x 18 cm (7⅞ x 7⅛ in.) which may be considered as another attempt to render figures in a small format, or types – children in this case. 'Among the first paintings of people by Chardin' (P. Rosenberg), they may also have been earlier than 1737, and there is nothing to stop one

thinking that this little boy with his drum and drumstick is the painter's son.

40. These two paintings perfectly ilustrate the celebration of gestures put forward by Patrick Drevet (in *Huit petites études sur le désir de voir*, Paris, 1991), although Chardin's *Boy* is not a waiter. 'What gesture could be humbler, simpler, more familiar and more tedious than the gesture of this servant! However, it suffices that it is that of a man or a woman who is anxious to do well and whom I have studied carefully for their poetry… Drawing back his hand, the servant does it so slowly that he gives the impression of trying to fade away, without disturbing the fragile light which he has just created or disturbing the air suddenly filled with expectation, with the care which one would take not to let the flame of a candle flicker…. The presence of objects which he has put down is very real because they are simply accepted as is his routine gesture of laying them down.'

41. Chardin made two copies of this painting in 1738, as well as one the following year. One of the versions was bought by the Prince of Liechtenstein and another by Frederick II.

42. N. Bryson, *Looking at the Overlooked*, Harvard, 1990.

43. 'Formes de la privatisation', in *Histoire de la vie privée*, under the direction of P. Ariès and G. Duby, vol. 3, 1986.

44. Reference is made, among others, to E. Snoep-Reitsma, 'Chardin and the Bourgeois Ideals of his Time', *Nederlands Kunsthistorisch Jaarboek*, 1973, which gives a good bibliography of books published in France and England between 1720 and 1735, and even earlier, about the education of children and the role of women.

45. The two versions in the Louvre hardly differ at all – the chief differences are in the colour of the mother's skirt and the ribbon of her bonnet, as well as modifications to space. The first version has a better use of space thanks to the tiled floor, which is absent from the second. In general, the treatment of objects is better: the hands and faces are more refined and, in the version presented to the King, the brushwork is much looser.

46. Insofar as one can make a judgment from the engravings, it would seem that the little girl in *Card Games* is the same as the child in *Saying Grace*, while the boy with no hat in *Game of Goose* could be the same little boy who is being scolded in *The Governess* (see p. 54). The two paintings belonged to the same collector, the enigmatic banker Despuech. Although *Card Games* and *Game of Goose* were exhibited together at the Salon of 1743, the former had already been exhibited in 1739, which enables us to group these pendants with his series of genre paintings with children.

47. Pigalle's *Mercury*, 'regarded as the most beautifully composed figure to come out of the French School', was the sculptor's reception piece for the Académie in 1744. Its monumental version, ordered by Frederick II, was on display in 1748 in Pigalle's studio, in the courtyard of the Old Louvre, before going to Prussia and the plaster was exhibited at the Salon that year. With regard to its use by Chardin, who owned a copy of it at the time of his death, W. McAllister Johnson noted rightly that the 'existence of Mercury in an ordinary studio demonstrates the use of

Salon models throughout the artistic hierarchy' (W. McAllister Johnson, 'Visit to the Salon and Sculptors' Ateliers during the Ancien Régime', *Gazette des Beaux-Arts*, VI/CVV, July–August 1992). Baillet de Saint-Julien gave this interesting commentary: 'one cannot be too grateful for the thought in his painting and it is difficult to say whether he does himself or M. Pigalle most honour' (*Réflexions sur quelques causes présentes…*, 1748). This sculpture was unanimously considered a return to models inspired by nature, as opposed to classical antiquity. This explains the significance attached to it and the praise for Chardin's choice.

48. *Lettre sur la peinture, la sculpture et l'architecture…*, 1748.

49. *Lettre à un ami sur l'exposition des tableaux…*, 1753.

50. *Sentiments d'un amateur…*, 1753.

51. *Observations sur les ouvrages…*, 1753.

52. *Jugement d'un amateur…*, 1753.

53. *Lettre à un amateur en réponse aux critiques…*, 1753.

54. *Réflexions sur quelques causes de l'état présent de la peinture…*, 1747, and *Sentiments sur quelques ouvrages de peinture…*, 1754.

55. *Encyclopédie méthodique*, vol. 2, 1788, entry on 'Naïf' by Lévêque.

56. This priority was not recognized by Jacques Thuillier when he wrote of *The Peasant Family* that 'all anecdote is suppressed… a painting is organized. But so sober in means compared with a Chardin, that it would make the latter seem light and verbose' (preface to the Le Nain exhibition catalogue, Paris, 1972).

57. *Abecedario…*, entry on 'Le Nain'.

58. Thuillier, *op. cit.*, 1972.

59. Caylus, *Vie de Watteau*, read to the Académie in 1749.

60. *Réflexions sur quelques causes…*, 1747.

61. La Font de Saint Yenne (*Observations sur les arts et sur quelques morceaux de peinture…*, 1748) recognized in this painting the classical theme of reading a novel. The terms which he used set the scene in an affluent interior: a comfortable seat, warm and light clothing. The languor of her look, emphasized by the commentary, although it is not very clear in the painting, reflects how 'men of the eighteenth century conceived of the act of a woman reading, which had become something quintessentially private; only the painter could break into her quiet solitude.' (R. Chartier, 'Les pratiques de l'écrit' in *Histoire de la vie privée*, *op. cit.*, 1986.)

62. In Stockholm, there is an anonymous gouache of Ulla Tessin, the ambassador's wife, at her desk; the space around her is filled with sculptures and paintings. On the left is a bookcase and behind her, on a piece of Chinese furniture, is the pagoda which Gersaint, the dealer, used as a sort of emblem. This work is especially interesting because it depicts Madame Tessin seated at her desk, holding a pen with which she is writing in a ledger, and there is a harmony between the reading and the holding of

the account books such as that found in the paintings Tessin commissioned from Chardin for the Queen of Sweden. Although we do not know the date of this gouache, it is tempting and realistic to recognize in it an echo of Chardin's work.

63. This instrument is a very simple organ, the cylinder of which, operated by a crank, plays different tunes. In 1745, Hervieux de Chanteloup 'trainer of the Princess de Condé's canaries', published a *Nouveau Traité des Serins de Canarie*, in which he recommends the use of such a bird organ over the flageolet, to which, however, he devotes two pages of music 'to teach canaries by means of the flageolet'. Certainly, these tunes would have been part of the organ's repertoire.

64. See E. H. Turner, '"La Serinette" by Jean-Baptiste Chardin: a Study in Patronage and Technique', *Gazette des Beaux-Arts*, VI/XLIX, April 1957 and S. J. Taylor, 'Engravings within Engravings: Symbolic Contrast and Extension in some Eighteenth-century French Prints', *Gazette des Beaux Arts*, VI/CVI, September, 1985.

65. See E. Dayot and L. Vaillat, *Chardin et Fragonard*, 1907. See also J. Mathey, 'Les Dessins de Chardin', *Albertina-Studien*, 1964, no. 1.

66. See P. Rosenberg, *Chardin: New Thoughts*, II: 'The Issue of Chardin as a Draftsman'.

67. In a letter to Marigny in 1763, La Tour described 'the difficulty of short and weak vision, forcing one to be only two or three feet away from the model, obliged to stretch and bend down, and turn to the right and left, in order to see close up what one can only see properly from a distance!' (quoted by G. Wildenstein, *La Tour*, 1928, p. 65). This letter, the aim of which was to obtain a higher payment, was trying to establish that the work of the pastellist is more difficult than that of an oil painter; however, the letter insists that the former works much closer to the model than the latter.

68. The success of this portrait is proved by the engraving made by Chevillet and the second version by Chardin in 1773 (in the Musée des Beaux-Arts in Orléans).

69. *Essai sur la vie de M. Chardin*, 1780

70. *Lettre à M. Ch… sur les caractères en peinture*, 1753.

71. The fur hat and chain are those of the costume of the treasurer of the Académie de Saint-Luc, a post held at the time by Bachelier.

72. For example, although *The Washerwoman* was probably executed after *The Copper Cistern*, we do not know if it was La Roque who wanted to have a pendant for the first painting. However, these paintings were always shown together and were engraved as pendants.

73. With two exceptions, *Girl with a Shuttlecock* and *The House of Cards*, *The Amusements of Private Life* and *The Household Accounts*, the engraving of pendants was always entrusted to the same engraver.

74. A good example is Restout's *Jacob and Laban* which was painted as a pendant to Lemoyne's *Jacob and Rachel*, belonging to the collection of the Comtesse de Verrue.

234

75. J. P. Cuzin, *Jean-Honoré Fragonard*, 1989, cat. D. 35. The Vassal de Saint-Hubert version has disappeared, but there is a second, larger version on wood in the Fogg Art Museum, with a *Blind Man* attributed to Chardin, which was enlarged in order to be a pendant. Both belonged to the Duclos-Dufresnoy collection in 1795 (cf. J. P. Cuzin, cat. 366).

76. P. Rosenberg, *Tout l'Œuvre peint*, 1983. There are several versions of *The Blind Man* and *Saying Grace*, as was the case for other compositions, and the Salon catalogues mention subjects where another version had already been exhibited, or was in a particular famous collection. In 1746 and 1761, it was repetitions of *Saying Grace*; in 1735, *The Draughtsman* and *Young Girl Saying her Lessons*, which belonged to La Live de Jully were 'repeated after originals' belonging to the king of Sweden; in 1769, a 'repetition with changes' of *Girl Returning to the Market* belonging to Silvestre, while the Abbé Pommyer lent his version of *Attributes of the Arts and Their Rewards*. In 1773, Silvestre also lent his *Woman Drawing Water from a Copper Cistern*, 'a copy of that belonging to the queen of Sweden'.

77. My italics.

78. According to P. Rosenberg, in his 1979 exhibition catalogue.

79. R. Mesuret, *Les Expositions de l'Académie royale de Toulouse de 1751 à 1791*, 1972.

80. T. Burollet, *Musée Cognacq-Jay – Peintures et Dessins*, 1980, no. 20.

Gabriel de Saint-Aubin, drawings in the Vassal de Saint-Hubert sale catalogue, 1774 (details).

CHAPTER FIVE

THE ARTIST
AND ENGRAVINGS

*Chardin's originality carries over
from his painting to his engraving.
Once you have seen one of his paintings,
you remember it and
recognize it everywhere.*

Diderot

'The public were eager for his paintings and, since their creator painted only for his own amusement and, consequently, very little, the public anxiously tried to compensate for this with prints engraved after his work.'[1] La Font de Saint-Yenne's comment on the success of engravings after Chardin's paintings is confirmed by Mariette, although he denounced its negative side: 'The prints which have been engraved after the paintings of M. Chardin were no less successful: they have become fashionable prints which, like those of Teniers, Wouwermans and Lencret; have dealt a fatal blow to serious prints such as those of Le Brun, Poussin, Le Sueur and even Coypel. The general public enjoy seeing the events which occur daily in their own homes, and do not hesitate to give these preference over more sophisticated subjects, the knowledge of which requires a certain study. I do not wish to contemplate whether this is detrimental to taste.'[2] The study of prints after paintings by Chardin is linked to any analysis of his success, the subjects which he favoured and his output. It helps us to understand any symbolism which Chardin himself, as well as his public, may have given to his works and, more specifically, whether or not these discreet scenes of morals concealed a meaning which is not clear to us today.

The first thing to be said is that none of Chardin's still lifes was ever engraved. One can understand that a dead hare or kitchen utensils were not sufficiently characteful or interesting to give rise to an engraving. The same would not be true, however, in the case of the attributes of the arts or the sciences which Chardin painted on various occasions, the overdoors depicting sculptures, vases and various cleverly arranged objects; and their absence is all the more surprising since when Oudry painted similar compositions, such as an *Allegory of the Arts*,[3] bringing together a plaster bust, musical instruments, a palette and a plant in a vase, he did not hesitate to have these engraved by Gabriel Huquier in a *Recueil de dessus de portes* (Book of Overdoors), published in 1737. There was nothing of the kind for Chardin. On the other hand, from the time of the reopening of the Salons, the paintings which he exhibited quickly became the subject of engravings. Almost all of his genre scenes were engraved, and these prints were regularly exhibited at the Salons, including that of 1742 when Chardin did not submit any paintings.[4] Between 1737 and 1747, prints of no fewer than twenty-nine pictures were announced, starting in 1737 with *House of Cards*, which was engraved by Pierre Fillœul in the same year that it was exhibited. At the Salon in August of the following year, 1738, Chardin exhibited *Lady Sealing a Letter* (see p. 196), the engraving of which had already been announced in May. The engraver needed access to a work for several months, or even longer, so in view of the success of the paintings exhibited in 1737, and bearing in mind his plans to exhibit *Lady Sealing a Letter* in 1738, Chardin probably let Étienne Fessard have it during the previous autumn or winter, so that it would be available for sale at the Salon.[5] *The*

Page 236:
Lady Sealing a Letter (detail).

Pierre Fillœul, *House of Cards*, 1737.
Engraving after Chardin.

Schoolmistress (see p. 123) was exhibited at the Salon of 1740, at the same time as its engraving by Lépicié, which clearly indicates that it must have been painted before that date. In the same year, Chardin exhibited *The Diligent Mother* (see p. 218); Lépicié's engraving (p. 241), also dated 1740, mentions that the painting was part of the King's collection. As Chardin had presented his painting to the King on 17 November, it is certain that the engraving, or at any rate its legend, was made after this date. *The Morning Toilet* (see p. 47) was exhibited at the Salon of 1741. Its engraving by Le Bas was announced in December, after Tessin had sent the original to Sweden. It is clear that in this case the engraver, who was a great friend of Chardin, two of whose paintings he owned, had begun to work on his print in the artist's studio, while the latter was putting the final touches, or retouches, to his canvas. *The Amusements of Private Life* (see p. 52), another painting destined for Sweden and for which Louisa Ulrica was waiting impatiently, was exhibited at the Salon in August and September of 1746 and on 5 October, Chardin wrote to Tessin that he could take it, but that he would like to have time to have it engraved 'which would take until the Spring. This favour would be very much appreciated by me, as I have a certain debt to the public on account of their recognition of my work'.[6] This engraving (see p. 241), dated 1747, was announced in June and exhibited at the Salon. Chardin dedicated it to Countess Tessin, and its legend indicates that 'the original painting is in the Gallery at Drotningholm in Sweden and is a pendant to another painting made in 1747 by the same artist of a lady who is checking her household accounts'. This painting is *The Household Accounts* (see p. 221), delivered by Chardin in February 1747 with *The Amusements of Private Life* and which, for this reason, could not be shown at the Salon. In announcing the engraving, the chronicler of *Mercure de France* remarked that 'it was regrettable that the various paintings by M. Chardin, such as *The Copper Cistern*, *The Washerwoman* and *The Morning Toilet* were going to foreign countries and are lost to us'. From 1753, when the engraving of *The Bird Organ* was shown (see p. 241), although Chardin showed as many still lifes as genre scenes and portraits and the number of engravings decreased – ten in thirteen years – and they did not follow the exhibition of the originals quite so promptly. It must be said that several of these paintings were either second versions or paintings which had already been exhibited, and it is sometimes difficult to tell which version was engraved.[7]

Between 1759 and 1779, there were no further engravings after Chardin,[8] the reason being that he had abandoned genre scenes in favour of still lifes. The promotion of engravings was directly related to the success and the fame of the paintings which they copied, and it worked best when the prints were executed more or less simultaneously with the painted originals.[9]

In listing the works exhibited by Chardin at the Salon of 1738, the Chevalier de Neufville de Brunhaubois Montador spoke of the certainty that 'the service of having these engraved would shortly be made available to the public',[10] insisting on the importance of this being executed properly.[11] According to *Mercure de France*, it seems that 'prints after paintings by M. Chardin are always successful'.[12]

Diderot wrote that Chardin's 'originality carries over from his painting to his engraving. Once you have seen one of his pictures, you remember it and

Étienne Fessard, *Lady Sealing a Letter*, 1738.
Engraving after Chardin.

François Bernard Lépicié, *The Schoolmistress*, 1740.
Engraving after Chardin.

239

Pierre Fillœul, *Game of Knucklebones*, 1739.
Engraving after Chardin.

recognize it everywhere. Look at his *Governess with her Children* and you have
seen his *Saying Grace*.' This was probably due more to the pictures' subject-
matter than to the prints' quality, for the different engravers varied in skill.
What is certain is that the engravings were popular because they disseminated
Chardin's scenes of private life. They became Mariette's fashionable prints in
which the public recognized themselves, as they did in the paintings exhibited
at the Salon. The result was that the engravings were valued almost as a substi-
tute for the original.[13]

Certain scenes from everyday life, which had been painted on a larger
scale, were also engraved, such as the various versions of *House of Cards*, *Soap
Bubbles*, *Game of Goose* and *The Schoolmistress*. What is more surprising to see is
portraits of those close to Chardin, such as *A Lady Taking Tea* or *The Moment of
Meditation*, being treated as scenes of everyday life. It was the legends included
underneath the engravings which transformed these portraits into the genre
scenes so appreciated by the public. These all-purpose verses, often composed
by Lépicié or by Charles Étienne Pesselier, a poet and contributor to *Mercure
de France* and the *Encyclopédie*, trivialized the subjects by diminishing the originality of Chardin's scenes, which are quite different to their seventeenth-
century Dutch or French predecessors. The result was that paintings such as
The Morning Toilet, *Household Accounts*, *House of Cards* and *Lady Taking Tea* were
included in the Le Bas catalogue alongside Teniers and Wouwermans.[14]
Chardin's prints sold for about one *livre* a piece, an attractive price, given that
engravings after Flemish artists were selling for three or four *livres*.[15]

The feeble rhymes, like those on the bottom of engravings after Watteau,
are supposed to explain the hidden meaning of a scene. Thus, for instance, in
the case of *Lady Taking Tea*: 'Que le jeune Damis serait heureux, Climène, / Si
cette bouillante liqueur / Pouvait échauffer votre cœur, / Et si le sucre avait le
vertu souveraine / D'adoucir ce qu'en votre humeur / Cet amant trouve de
rigueur.' (How happy the young Damis would be, Climène, / If this boiling
liquor / Could warm your heart, / And if the sugar had the sovereign virtue / Of
sweetening that which in your mood / That lover finds unyielding.) Lépicié,
engraver of 'The Son of M. Le Noir Building a House of Cards', enriched his
engraving with a commentary on the 'aimable enfant que le plaisir décide'
(sweet child moved by pleasure), asking him 'Quel est le plus solide / De nos
projets ou bien de vos travaux?' (Which is more solid, / Our plans or your
efforts?) The engraving of the portrait of the 'little daughter of M. Mahon' was
given the title *The Inclination of Her Age* and it is to Pesselier, who also wrote
verses accompanying *The Antiquarian*, *The Painter* and *The Morning Toilet*, that
we owe the following: 'Sur les frivoles jeux, dont s'occupe cet âge, / Gardons-
nous de jeter des regards méprisants; / Sous des titres plus imposants, / Ils sont
aussi notre partage' (At the frivolous games which command this age's attention, / Let us not cast scornful glances: / Under more imposing titles / They are
also our concern).[16]

Lépicié signed the verse accompanying *The Philosopher*, *Child with a
Spinning Top* and *The Moment of Meditation*, a portrait of Madame Lenoir
'holding a book'. The latter reads: 'Cet amusant travail, cette lecture aimable /
De la sage Philis occupent le loisir. / Quand on sait joindre l'utile à l'agréable /
L'innocence est toujours la base du plaisir' (This enjoyable work, this

agreeable reading / Occupies good Philis' leisure. / When one can combine the useful with the pleasing / Innocence is always the basis of pleasure). In these verses, models have given way to stereotypes. Their names have disappeared, most likely because they would not have been well enough known to add any interest or value to the engraving, which was content to illustrate the games of childhood, the pleasures of reading, or indeed the uncertain results of alchemy. One understands why, in front of the portrait of Levret (see p. 207) which was exhibited in 1746, La Font de Saint-Yenne remarked that 'the public would despair to see him abandon or even neglect an original talent and creative brush to give himself over with complacency to a genre which has become very common or without even the excuse of need',[17] i.e., to devote himself to true portraits, which were certainly better paid, to the detriment of the 'genre portraits' mentioned. It is understandable, too, how Mariette reproached Chardin for his subjects being too widely distributed in engravings, which he compared with Lancret's romantic subjects and seventeenth-century northern subjects. The comparison was made frequently, like the references to Dou and Teniers in the engravings' announcements, which may have helped to sell them.[18]

The success of these engravings is proven by the accounts of contemporaries and by their presence in the best collections of the time, such as that of Madame de Pompadour, who owned twenty-three prints, perfectly classified according to the catalogue of her sale, where they are listed by name of the engraver and with reference to their pendants.[19] In a different area, some of these were used for *trompe l'œil* compositions; this is how Lépicié's engravings of *Saying Grace* and *The Amusements of Private Life* were copied, most probably by Gabriel Moulinneuf, in two *trompe l'œils* 'with broken glass', a genre which

Laurent Cars, *The Bird Organ*, 1753. Engraving after Chardin.

Louis Surugue, *The Amusements of Private Life*, 1747. Engraving after Chardin.

François Bernard Lépicié, *The Diligent Mother*, 1740. Engraving after Chardin.

241

was very popular in the last thirty years or so of the century.[20] Finally, it is no accident that *The Embroiderer* and *The Draughtsman* featured among some coloured prints made between 1741 and 1745 by Jacques Fabien Gautier Dagoty, who invented a process whereby he tried to make real facsimiles of oil paintings, to be attached to a canvas, stretched on a frame and varnished. The result (see pp. 208 and 209) is rather mediocre, but it is clear that the printmaker wanted to give the impression of real paintings by displaying the signature *M. Chardin P.*, at the top in the background, while his own signature, *Gautier S.*, appears at the bottom.

Was Chardin's public aware of the 'messages' contained in these genre scenes, or did they only see pretty, endearing subjects? E. Snoep-Reitsma has studied the relationship between these engravings and various earlier models, taken from seventeenth-century northern painting and from early eighteenth-century French painting, and he shows how Chardin adapted to the taste of contemporary Parisians for subjects with uplifting or erotic subtexts.[21] Philip Conisbee writes that Chardin, like other French contemporary painters who were unable to paint history subjects, made do with genre subjects with moral or satirical undertones, adapting the conventions of earlier northern painting to the spirit of the time.[22] This remark was prompted by *Soap Bubbles*, a conventional evocation of human fragility and vanity. The same message, according to the verse which accompanied the engravings, lay behing *Child with a Top* and the various versions of *House of Cards*. The women in *Lady Sealing a Letter* and *Lady Taking Tea* are supposed to be thinking of their lovers; and *The Morning Toilet, Game of Knucklebones* and *The Diligent Mother* are references to coquetry, frivolity and idleness, which were considered to be female attributes, in contrast with *The Household Accounts*, where the verse emphasizes the woman's exceptional character: 'Quel prodige! Une femme à des soins plus flatteurs / Dérobe un temps qu'elle donne au ménage. / Ce tableau simple du vieux âge / Est pris dans la nature et non pas dans nos mœurs.' (What a prodigy! A woman from more flattering cares / Has stolen time which / She gives to household affairs. / This simple picture of the old days / Is taken from nature and not from the ways of today.) Did Chardin himself give his engravings the meanings which their verses suggest and on which some commentators rely today? Cochin's engraving of *Little Girl with Cherries*, a painting exhibited at the Salon of 1737, was accompanied by the following verse: 'Simple dans mes plaisirs, en ma colation, / Je sçai trouver aussy, ma récréation' (Simple in my pleasures, my refreshment, / I also know how to find my recreation). Should we, like Snoep-Reitsma, query the meaning of this 'recreation' by recalling the erotic significance of cherries in seventeenth- and eighteenth-century painting and make this painting into a warning about the dangers of luxury?[23] I find it difficult to believe that such an erotic connotation was considered by Chardin when he painted this little girl sitting on a chair looking at the bunch of cherries in her hands, and where he has captured the seriousness of a child beautifully. The same applies to the theme of soap bubbles. The text accompanying the engraving takes the form of advice: 'Contemple bien, jeune garçon, / Les petits globes de savon: leur mouvement si variable / Et leur éclat si peu durable/ Te feront dire avec raison / Qu'en cela mainte Iris leur est assez semblable.' (Consider well, young boy, / The little soapy spheres: their movement

Charpentier, *The Good Mother*, c. 1744. Engraving after Champagne?

so changeable / And their sparkle so short-lived / Will make you say, with reason, / That in this they resemble many an Iris.) Chardin has adapted an old subject in his own way. But this was one of his first paintings with figures, where he wanted to demonstrate his skills by painting the soft transparency of the bubble, the creamy white of the soapy water and, particularly, the impasto on the face, the blurred focus of the small boy in the background – all suggest that the technique of painting is more important than meaning.

We do not know what sort of contracts Chardin had with his engravers and how much he earned from the sale of the prints, which must have brought in a considerable income.[24] At most, we know that it was not the painter but his engravers who applied for the *privilège*, or official permission to publish, the engravings which they made and sold.[25] Chardin would certainly have been consulted about the verses accompanying these prints, but, although he may have approved them, did this mean that he actually planned to give his paintings the same symbolism? I have shown that this was probably not the case. However, he is unlikely to have disapproved of these texts, as despite their ordinariness, their presence underneath a print would certainly have helped it sell better, by bringing it into line with the vast stock of images sought by the public.

Pierre Dupin, *Cat and Cheese*. Engraving.

That the engravings after subjects by Chardin constituted a well liked genre is confirmed by the proliferation of paintings which they inspired and also by copies or counterfeits of these subjects. Emile Bocher has discovered about ten prints by Weiss, Charpentier, Pierre Dupin and Jacques Couché that bear the name of Chardin, as inventor or as painter, the vulgarity and awkwardness of which show that they are mediocre works 'in the manner' of Chardin.[26] Dupin, for example, engraved with the signature *Chardin pinx.* a *Cat and Cheese* which is a nasty plagiarism of the engraving of *Little Girl with Cherries* (see p. 41). The difference is primarily in the pose of the two girls: the gentle seriousness of the little girl's concentration as she holds the cherries contrasts strangely with the awkward position, the harsh folds of the apron and the ugly profile of the girl holding her cat in her lap. The same applies to *The Little Horseman*, compared with Chardin's *Young Soldier* (see p. 41). There are many of these examples which amply demonstrate that Chardin, like Watteau earlier with the *fête galante*, had really created a genre which became an essential part of art in his time.[27]

CHARDIN AND THE DECORATIVE ARTS

There is one final area where Chardin's models became known through engravings: this was the decorative arts, an area which also drew on Watteau for sources.[28] In the case of Watteau the diversity and number of prints, and the fact that they include designs for ornaments, figures and elaborate compositions, enlarged their potential use in porcelain or decorative painting, the leaves of folding screens or overdoors, ornamental cartouches or fans. The number of engravings after Chardin is more limited – about forty – and all have the same type of subject. It seems, however, that the groups or even single figures in interiors, were very quickly seen as so many usable motifs. The 'broken glass' *trompe-l'œil* pictures derived from *Saying Grace* and *the Amusements of Private Life* have already been mentioned. *The Cellar Boy* can be found at the top

Pierre Dupin, *The Little Horseman*. Engraving.

The Household Accounts.
Meissen porcelain. Musée Cognacq-Jay, Paris.

The Amusements of Private Life. Meissen porcelain.
Musée du Petit Palais, Tuck Collection.

The Governess. English porcelain box.
Musée du Petit Palais, Tuck Collection.

of one of the pages of George Bickham's book of calligraphy, *The Museum of Arts – Universal Penmanship*, published in London in the years 1740–45, i.e., very shortly after its engraving by Cochin in 1740.[29]

Chardin is unlikely to have known the groups modelled by Johann Joachim Kändler at Meissen during the years 1756–58, from prints after his famous originals. It has been possible to identify three of these (but there are probably more). These are *The Household Accounts*, *The Amusements of Private Life* and *The Morning Toilet*. All three are in the style of Le Bas's engravings and their colours differ from those of the paintings. A rococo style is present which is completely foreign to the originals: the table legs are curved and sculpted in extravagant fashion, including that of the dressing table which is not visible in *The Morning Toilet*. The young mother is not wearing a cloak or the black cape which suits the story, and the translation into porcelain completely changes her pose and her behaviour. The same is true of *The Household Accounts*, where the woman, dressed in a ravishing floral jacket, seems to be busy writing to her lover, rather than checking her accounts.[30] In addition, these groups rest on rococo pedestals which increase their ornamental character. A nineteenth-century Dresden china group reproducing *Saying Grace* from the engraving (i.e., in reverse from the painting) is certainly a copy of a piece of eighteenth-century porcelain, which must be added to this short list. Finally, *The Governess* features, again in reverse like its engraving, on the cover of a painted enamel box, made in England during the second half of the eighteenth century.

These few examples illustrate how a design could, in a few years, lose its original meaning. Not only has the spirit of Chardin disappeared, but also the meaning given to it by the engraver; there remains only a design, which is certainly attractive, but which is devoid of any reference to a form of art (painting), a country, or a theme. Perhaps this is the price of true genius.

1. La Font de Saint-Yenne, *Réflexions sur quelques causes de l'état présent de la peinture en France…*, 1747.

2. *Abecedario pittorico*, 1749.

3. Oudry exhibition, Paris, Fort Worth, 1982–83.

4. Two exceptions were *The Convalescent's Meal* and *The Embroiderer* (lost), which were not engraved. The engravings, listed under the engraver's name in the catalogue, were exhibited at the Salon in the window recesses. They were scarcely visible to the public and were never commented on by critics. It is, therefore, from announcements of their appearance in *Mercure de France*, the advertising element of which should not be ignored, that we learn of them most often.

5. A catalogue of engravings made after Chardin's paintings is given at the end of the book.

6. Quoted by J. Heidner, *op. cit.*, 1982.

7. A perfect example of this is *The Drawing Lesson* and *The Good Education*. The former, shown at the Salon of 1748 'as a pendant to those which have left for the Court of Sweden', was sent in November 1749 to Stockholm, with its pendant which was not seen in Paris. Their engravings by Le Bas, marked *Chardin pinx 1749*, were not exhibited until the Salon of 1757. In the meantime, second versions of these paintings which belonged to La Live de Jully were shown at the Salon of 1753 ('the draughtsman exhibited for the second time with changes' in relation to the version in Sweden, according to the catalogue). Clearly, Le Bas, who did not go to Sweden, engraved La Live de Jully's pictures, with their owner's consent. This did not prevent Chardin from dedicating the engravings to the Queen of Sweden, indicating that the works belonged to her collection.

Today, only one pair of these paintings is known (T.O.P. 126 and 127). In 1979 they were still part of a private Swedish collection and, for two plausible reasons, Pierre Rosenberg took them to be the La Live de Jully paintings. The first was their frames, which are similar to those of other works owned by the same man. The second is differences between *The Drawing Lesson* and its engraving. However, these differences show that these pictures – now in Houston and Tokyo – must be the royal paintings and that, in giving a prestigious location in the inscriptions on the engravings of the La Live de Jully pictures, Chardin and Le Bas knew very well that the Queen of Sweden would not notice this small deception, which would increase the value of the engravings by virtue of their owner. It is amusing to read in *Mercure de France* of October 1760 that 'the patronage given by the rulers to the arts gives so much glory to artists that we must mention here the honour which the Queen of Sweden has just bestowed on M. Chardin. This princess, who is aware of the respectful attention paid to her by this artist in dedicating the engravings of two of his paintings to her, chosen from many in Her Majesty's collection, has honoured him with a magnificent medal bearing an imprint of his portrait'.

8. With the exception of 1761, when Pierre Louis Surugue exhibited his *Blind Man Begging* (see p. 60).

9. This change may also be linked to a more general trend towards engravings of 'noble' subjects, after years when only pleasing subjects were favoured. In 1762 the Académie decided to engrave all reception pieces, although it was not until the Salon of 1779 that many of these engravings could be seen (see W. McAllister Johnson, 'La Gravure d'Histoire in France au XVIIIᵉ siècle', *Revue de l'Art*, no. 99, 1993).

10. *Description raisonnée des tableaux…*.

11. He also wrote that these engravings should be 'as well executed as *M. Boucher's Cook* by M. *Aveline…*', which is interesting because it applies to a genre subject similar to those by Chardin.

12. Written in October 1747 in relation to the engraving of *The Moment of Meditation*.

13. The announcement of *The Bird Organ* is a good example: 'The engraver has carefully arranged and kept all of the refinements. He expresses the delicacy of balance and broad expanses of the painting. As for colour and how to render it accurately in engraving, he understood how to do this and how to contrast different types of work. Thus, the engraving shows the paleness of a blonde woman's skin, contrasting with a bonnet and a muslin mantilla; a boldness in the painting which has been truly and accurately rendered in the engraving, which possibly proved more difficult' (*Mercure de France*, November 1753).

14. Although the last two engravings are by Fillœul, they were sold at the Le Bas studio.

15. See T. Crow, *op. cit.*, 1985, p. 137.

16. These verses are mainly those which Pesselier addressed to Chardin when sending him a poem about *La Nature et l'Art* dedicated to him in 1748 (*Fables nouvelles*, 1748, Book II, Fable XVI, 'To M. Chardin of the Académie Royale de Peinture').

17. *Réflexions sur quelques causes…*, 1747.

18. Some engravers of Chardin's work also specialized in engravings after Flemish and Dutch artists. François Bernard Lépicié was the main engraver of his work: between 1739 and 1745 he engraved and wrote verses for about ten paintings, from *The Governess* to *Saying Grace*. This did not prevent him from engraving *Vertumnus and Pomona* then attributed to Rembrandt, as well as several works by Netscher and Teniers. As for Chardin's friend Jean Philippe Le Bas, who in 1741, for his reception piece at the Académie, had engraved Aved's portrait of Cazes, only four engravings after Chardin can be attributed to him, which is low compared with the ninety or so engravings which he made after Teniers, ten after Nicolaes Berchem, eleven after Jacob van Ruisdael, as well as those after Adriaen van Ostade, Paulus Potter, Adam Pynacker and Philips Wouwermans. The Surugues also made engravings after Rembrandt's *Young Girl at the Window*, *The Philosopher Meditating* or *Contemplating*, as well as *Rembrandt's Father*, all three being part of the collection of the Comte de Vence, who also owned Chardin's *Scullery Maid* and *The Cellar Boy*.

19. See E. Campardon, *Madame de Pompadour et la cour de Louis XV*, 1867.

20. Trampisch sale, Paris, 5 March 1986, no. 164.

21. E. Snoep-Reitsma, *op. cit.*, 1973.

22. P. Conisbee, *op. cit.*, 1990.

23. E. Snoep-Reitsma, *op. cit.*, pp. 212–17.

24. To see how the relationship between the painter and his engravers operates, a study by F. Arquié-Bruley is interesting, i.e. 'Documents notariés inédits sur Greuze', *Bulletin de la Société de l'histoire de l'art français*, 1981, 1983, although it is about an artist who had organized the business of having works engraved in a remarkable way and can therefore only give us information of a general nature about Chardin.

25. See P. Fuhring, 'The Print Privilege in Eighteenth-Century France', *Print Quarterly*, vol. II, no. 3, September 1985 and vol. III, no. 1, March 1986.

26. See E. Bocher, *Jean-Baptiste Siméon Chardin*, in *Les Gravures françaises au XVIIIᵉ siècle*, 1876. Some, engraved by Charpentier with *J. B. S. Chardin pinxit*, have been shown to be fake but another edition gives the name of a certain Champagne as the painter. This is the case with the prints entitled *The Good Mother*, *The Mousetrap* and *The Spoiled Child*.

27. On a rather different note, there is the print engraved in 1777 by Juste Chevillet who also engraved Chardin's *Self-portrait with Spectacles*. It is marked *J. B. S. Chardin pinx.* and portrays a young girl standing in a drawing room, in front of a fireplace, wearing a flounced dress. According to the title of the engraving, she is *Marguerite Siméone Pouget* (E. Bocher, *op. cit.*, no. 44), probably a niece of Madame Chardin and Chardin's goddaughter, since she bears his name. In an oval frame over the fireplace hangs the portrait of Chardin wearing spectacles, after an engraving. Despite this, and although this engraving was done during Chardin's lifetime by the son-in-law of his friend Wille, it seems impossible to attribute the design to Chardin. Could this be a form of praise to the old master and is it possible that the portrait was shown to him? This cannot be not ruled out.

28. See M. Roland Michel, *Watteau, un Artiste au XVIIIᵉ Siècle*, 1984, p. 291 ff.

29. To my knowledge, this is the only model after Chardin used by Bickham who, in his many successful publications, took his illustrations from prints and illustrations of iconology, collections of portraits or landscapes, and pieces of furniture as well as from Watteau, Lancret, Philip Mercier and Hubert-François Gravelot.

30. Thérèse Burollet has pointed out amusing differences in the text of the accounts books of known versions of this. In one, tea and coffee are listed, in another different wines; the names of towns are also listed and even the transport of food (in *Musée Cognacq-Jay – II – Porcelaines*, Paris, 1983, no. 24).

CHAPTER SIX

PAINTING IN CHARDIN'S TIME

He said to me one day, modestly,
that painting was like an island and that he had
moved around its edges. However, all of his paintings prove
that he explored every inch of it and that he left the
mark of his success everywhere.

Hecquet

'arivaux is the most original genius in France. ...To write as he writes, one would have to be him. He writes the way Chardin paints: it is a genre, a taste which one admires and that no one else can achieve; their copyists can only produce monsters.'[1] This text is dated 1745. Three years later, a similar comparison was made between Chardin and Thomas Germain Joseph Duvivier: 'Some artists, seduced by the fine touch and great purity of draughtsmanship which distinguish his works, have wanted to follow in his footsteps; but they have succeeded no better than those who, inspired by the success of M. Chardin's work, have tried to imitate him.'[2]

The special nature of Chardin's talent was thus recognized, as well as his influence on many artists who, without him, would have painted differently. This phenomenon is comparable to the adoption of the *fête galante*, after the disappearance of Watteau, by his followers, namely, Lancret, Pater, Bonaventure de Bar and Octavien.[3] But, unlike Watteau, who died before his work was engraved, Chardin's work was widely distributed during his lifetime.

GENRE SCENES AFTER CHARDIN

When Chardin exhibited genre paintings in 1737, he surprised the public and the critics. But if his pictures pleased, it was more because of their spirit and their treatment than for the originality of their subject matter, which was similar to that of other painters, such as Jean François de Troy, Delobel, Jeaurat and Lancret, who had exhibited his *Lady Taking Coffee* in the same year as Chardin's *Lady Taking Tea*. In 1739 Boucher painted *Lunch* (see p. 249), which shows two women and two children in an elegantly decorated room, in a mood that Chardin would not have disowned.

In the years which followed, a number of painters, both famous and unknown, produced works whose subject matter or composition seemed to derive from Chardin's work. Among the artists from the Académie de Saint-Luc, in 1753 Pierre Allais showed *A Woman at her Toilet Arranging her Daughter's Dress* and Bizet showed *Young Girl Feeding a Canary* and *Young Boy Drawing*. In 1762, Jean François Coquelet exhibited *A Cook* and *A Young Baker* and in 1752, Pierre Simon Dequoy showed *A Scullery Maid*. Finally, in 1756 Simon Liégeois showed *Lady Playing a Bird Organ*.

Pierre Louis Dumesnil the Younger, who was also a member of the Académie de Saint-Luc, showed paintings of women and children at its Salon. In 1762, he exhibited a *Cook Drawing up her Shopping List* and a *Wine Merchant's Boy Washing Bottles*. Some paintings by Dumesnil are known to us, which has enabled us to see what he owed to Chardin, both in his subjects and in the way that he rendered them. *The Catechising Priest* gives an indication of where the artist sought his models.

In the 1740s, Louis Aubert drew and painted studios showing young artists grinding colours and preparing canvases. But he also devoted himself to

Page 246:
Copper Pot with Casserole, Pestle and Mortar,
Three Eggs, Two Onions, Two Leeks and Cut Cheese (detail).
Mauritshuis, The Hague.

Pierre Louis Dumesnil, *The Catechising Priest*, 1752.
Oil on canvas, 33 × 41 cm (13 × 16⅛ in.).
Private collection.

the more domestic scenes, of which *The Reading Lesson* of 1740 (see p. 251) is the best example. In addition to the subject matter, we find all the elements which contributed to Chardin's success at that time.[4]

Philippe Canot, history painter, decorator with the Menus Plaisirs and a member of the Académie de Saint-Luc, became known through his charming interior scenes in the style of Chardin, such as *Child's Windmill* or *The Pinwheel*,[5] *Le Gateau des Roys* (The Epiphany cake) and *The Dancing Teacher*, which was engraved by Le Bas in 1745.[6]

Again, it was Le Bas who engraved *The Merchant* by Descamps: the influence of his friend Chardin is undeniable here, as it is in *The Nurse from Caux*, also by Descamps. In 1767 Diderot wrote that it is 'flat, foolish, stupid, dull, rigid and devoid of expression, a thousand miles away from early Greuze and ten thousand miles from Chardin who once worked in this genre'.

But the best person in 'this genre' is undoubtedly Étienne Jeaurat, an exact contemporary of Chardin, who from the 1740s painted domestic interiors of women at various tasks, paintings which were immediately distributed by engravers looking for scenes of everyday life. In 1744, Lépicié engraved *The New Mother* and *Afternoon* (see p. 251) and wrote the quatrain for *Tea* engraved by Balechou. None of these compositions would exist without prints inspired by Chardin. Although the model is recognizable, the spirit of Jeaurat is quite different. The charming *Woman Preparing Salad* (see p. 262) which he exhibited at the Salon of 1753 is not at all comparable to Chardin's *Woman Peeling Vegetables*, who is lost in thought (see p. 42).

The links between Chardin and Greuze are of a different nature, even though the two artists were compared when Greuze first appeared at the Salon of 1755. 'His style is half way between Chardin and Jeaurat. He paints the village middle classes. Little people, but a grand manner.'[7] Thus, it is not a question of subject matter. In 1757, the parallel was usually drawn between the colouring of the two painters. 'The works of both artists were put side by side in order to facilitate comparison of this painter with M. Greuze. They win and lose in turn. If one considers colour, M. Chardin is better. His paintings are vigorous, all of the objects are mirrored in one another and the result is a transparency of colour which livens up everything which his brush touches. M. Greuze is most certainly a colourist, but to give effect and relief, he uses his blacks too much. Meanwhile, M. Chardin seems to remove them everywhere…. To compare these two geniuses, M. Greuze seems to have more fire, to be drawn more to the high style. But he does not always have M. Chardin's originality. He has generally more sureness of drawing and more expression than him, which is a considerable advantage; he is fortunate when he can add the magic of his colours, because he must still regard him as his master in this area!'[8] These comments were prompted by the four 'paintings in Italian costume', portraits, *Neapolitan Sailor* and *Boy Studying His Lessons* (see p. 250), the only painting which can be compared to Chardin for its soberness and for the meditative air of the young boy frozen in time. Diderot extolled the virtues of a painter capable of being 'simple and true like Chardin, moving like Greuze'. In 1763, writing about *The Paralytic*, he praised 'its fine, strong colour, although it is not that of Chardin', In 1765, he went even further in his comments about the colour of the two artists, writing that Chardin 'is above Greuze by the

François Boucher, *Lunch*, 1739.
Oil on wood, 81.5 × 65.5 cm (32⅛ × 2⅞ in.).
Louvre, Paris.

Jacques Philippe Le Bas, *The Dancing Master*.
Engraving after Philippe Canot.

Jacques Philippe Le Bas, *Shelling Peas*. Engraving after Jean Baptiste Greuze.

Jacques Firmin Beauvarlet, *The Scullery Maid*. Engraving after Jean Baptiste Greuze.

Jean Baptiste Greuze, *Young Boy Studying his Lessons*.
Oil on canvas, 61.8 × 48 cm (24¼ × 18⅞ in.). National Gallery of Scotland, Edinburgh.

Pierre Antoine Baudoin, *Reading*.
Gouache, 29 × 22.5 cm (11⅜ × 8⅞ in.). Musée des Arts Décoratifs, Paris.

Louis Aubert, *The Reading Lesson*, 1740.
Oil on wood, 32.5 × 22.8 cm (12⅞ × 9 in.). Musée de Picardie, Amiens.

François Bernard Lépicié, *Afternoon*, 1744. Engraving after Étienne Jeaurat.

Hubert Robert, *Eat Up, Little One*, 1773. Oil on wood,
23 × 27 cm (9 × 10⅝ in.). Private collection, Paris.

Pierre Alexandre Wille, *Anticipation of Pleasure*.
Engraving.

whole distance between the earth and the sky, but only on this point'. Whether in fact the two artists can meaningfully be compared is debatable. It is true that Le Bas engraved Greuze's *Shelling Peas* and Beauvarlet his *Scullery Maid* (see p. 250) in the same year that Chardin showed his for the second time; true also that Greuze placed young women and their children in kitchens (*The Spoilt Child* and *Silence!*). But the spirit of these works is totally different to that of Chardin's compositions. The desirable women in Greuze's paintings and his turbulent children have nothing in common with Chardin's respectable, reserved women and his serious, still children, and it is not only their colour that makes them as different from each other as the distance between the earth and the sky. Nor is there anything in common between the sentimental effusiveness of Greuze, the tears which he draws, the pity or the horror which he inspires, and the way in which Chardin renders a scene or a person with attentive sensitivity.

The draughtsman and engraver Pierre Alexandre Wille, a pupil and emulator of Greuze, was no less inspired by Chardin when he painted in his *Anticipation of Pleasure* a woman taking chocolate or tea, while his wife was painted by Jean Antoine Peter, around 1775 'sitting next to a table, holding a book'. This theme was also painted by Baudoin in a charming gouache called *Reading* (see p. 251). Set in a refined interior, half way between a boudoir and a study, we see maps, books and a globe, as well as a guitar resting on a dog's kennel, and a young woman lying back in an armchair. She has let fall the book which she was holding, which was no doubt responsible for her sensuous meditation. The theme is the same as that of *The Amusements of Private Life* (see p. 52), but the difference is striking, both in terms of the how the book is being read and in the choice of accessories and clothing. Reasonable distraction has become abandon, with all of the latter's erotic implications.

Even Hubert Robert invites comparison with Chardin. When he exhibited his *Italian Kitchen* at the Salon of 1767, Diderot described the painting in detail and wrote that the servant 'could not be more natural or more true. This figure is from one of Chardin's early small paintings'. And when in 1773 Robert painted the exquisite *Eat Up, Little One*, which portrays a woman in an elegant room holding out a spoon to a little girl standing in front of her, how can one fail to think that this painter of ruins must have known the work of the painter of *Saying Grace*?

THE SPREAD OF GENRE PAINTING THROUGHOUT EUROPE

Chardin's works portray the limited world of mid-eighteenth-century bourgeois Paris – whose members happily identified with his paintings. The French character of Chardin's art is even more apparent when compared with the work of other European painters who were painting in the same genre: Chodowiecki in Germany, for example, and particularly Chardin's direct contemporaries in London and Venice, namely William Hogarth (1697–1764) and Pietro Longhi (1702–85). Both of these, Longhi in particular, established their reputation in painting contemporary genre scenes or family groups, peasant as well as middle class and aristocratic. Longhi illustrated, sometimes with indifferent success, little theatrical scenes in which the participants, like actors, face the viewer. For example, his *Visit to the Lord*, with its detailed representation of the cup, the porcelain teapot and the furniture, or its pendant, *Visit to the Lady*, dated 1746,[9] whose comparison with *The Amusements of Private Life*, a painting commissioned in 1745, is limited to the subject matter only, namely a woman sitting in an armchair, holding a half-open book.

The real difference between these painters is in their concept of time – continuous or arrested. Hogarth, like Longhi, creates powerful or charming scenes where the characters, or rather actors, look as if the curtain is just about to drop. They have stopped for a moment, just long enough for the painter to picture them before they resume their activity. In Chardin's work, this suspended time is the moment of reflection, intimacy, dialogue or monologue. His women are motionless in the time needed to recover their spirits, to rest or to think, without this interruption seeming at all conventional or theatrical.

A young boy is seen in profile from the left, sitting at a table (see p. 254). He is wearing a red frock coat with a grey velvet collar, his long curly hair tied back with a bow; in his left hand, he is holding a slice of bread and with his right hand, he is taking some butter with a knife. In the foreground, the drawer of the table is half open, and a few sheets of paper are sticking out. The boy's pose and his absorbed expression are the same as those of *Child with a Spinning Top* (see p. 203) and perhaps that is why this painting, which is the same size as Chardin's, was attributed to him for so long.[10] However, it is a portrait which Jean Étienne Liotard painted of his son around 1770, heavily influenced by Chardin's picture, which he clearly knew. In Paris around 1750 Liotard painted his portrait of a *Young Woman in Turkish Costume Reading a Book* (see p. 254) and also the painting known as *The Countess of Coventry* (in the Musée d'Art et d'Histoire, Geneva). It is difficult not to think that, despite the eastern dress, he was trying to pay homage to the painter of *The Amusements of Private Life*, by showing these young women meditating or reading in an interior. *Making Hot Chocolate* was exhibited at the Salon of the Académie de Saint-Luc in 1752. Here again, despite a rather smooth, Netherlandish treatment, it is impossible not to think of Chardin, given the quiet concentration of this young woman who is stirring a spoon in a porcelain cup on the table. Finally, how can we not think of Chardin's self-portraits, when contemplating Liotard's *Self-portrait with Hand on Chin* in which the ageing artist, wearing a simple blue

Daniel Chodowiecki, *A Painter's Collection*, 1772. Engraving.

Pietro Longhi, *Visit to the Lady*, 1746. Oil on canvas, 61 × 49.5 cm (24 × 19½ in.). The Metropolitan Museum of Art, New York, Frederick C. Hewitt Fund.

253

jacket and a red hat, looks at himself frankly in the mirror, and does not avoid showing wrinkles or his sagging flesh.

STILL LIFE AND 'VICTIMS OF CHARDIN'

Faced with still-life painters whose talents could not, in his opinion, match up to those of Chardin – the undisputed master in the genre – but whose failing was simply that they lacked his touch, his colouring and his sense of composition, Diderot in 1763 invented the concept of 'victims of Chardin'.

In 1753, on the occasion of the last Salon in which Oudry participated, Garrigues de Froment wrote that 'if it were a case of having to compare the method of execution of M. Chardin in the genre of animal painting to that of M. Oudry, I believe I would be right to say that the former is bolder and more picturesque and that the latter is more relaxed, but more studied, more caressed…'[11] Cochin takes this comparison further: 'One will easily recall two bas-reliefs copied by M. *Chardin* and by M. *Oudry*. The latter is a very skilled man and he paints with ease. The illusion in both paintings is equal and one is obliged to touch each of them to be certain that they are indeed paintings. Artists and people of taste could not see any inequality between the two works. But the painting of M. *Chardin* was as much above that of M. *Oudry* as the latter is himself above the mediocre. In what lay the difference, if not in that execution which could be described as magical, witty and full of fire, that inimitable art which characterizes so well the work of M. Chardin?'[12]

From 1755, critics, artists and collectors recognized the absolute supremacy of Chardin in still life, and it was also in this area that painters who relied on his teaching learnt most from him.[13] In this regard, a letter from Vernet, after Chardin's death, shows well how young artists built up their repertoire and their style: 'Mademoiselle Harisson has been basing her work on Mademoiselle Vallayer-Coster; I procured some Chardins for her so that she would learn better how to work from nature.'[14]

When Thomas Germain Joseph Duvivier, son of the medal engraver, exhibited paintings of fruit in the Place Dauphine in 1761, *L'Avant-Coureur* wrote that 'it is easy to see that he has carefully studied the works of M. Chardin; with the advice of a skilled man and the application to put these to use, one can hope for rapid success'. This must refer to two still lifes with fruit whose subject matter, composition and sense of space clearly show Chardin's influence.[15]

Unfortunately, we do not know what the three still lifes exhibited at the Salon of 1799 by a Madame Peigné, who presented herself as a pupil of Chardin and Gerard Van Spaendonck, looked like.

In 1779, included in the sale of Peters, the painter, who also owned paintings by Chardin, were two still life paintings by Antoine de Marcenay de Ghuy, co-founder with Peters of the short-lived Salon du Colisée where he had exhibited the two works in 1776. 'In one, we see peaches in a bowl, a pot of dripping and a glass of liqueur on a table; in the other, a basket of plums, cucumbers, apples and a bottle'. This description, accompanied by one of Saint-Aubin's sketches, indicates the model to which Marcenay had referred.

Allowance must be made for what was, after all, traditional iconography and a common fund of subject matter. It is tempting to mention Nicolas Henri

Opposite, from left to right and from top to bottom:

Jean Étienne Liotard, *Self-portrait of the Elderly Artist with Hand on Chin, c.* 1770–71. Pastel on parchment mounted on canvas, 63 × 52 cm (24¾ × 20½ in.). Musée d'Art et d'Histoire, Geneva.

Jean Étienne Liotard, *Young Woman in Turkish Costume Reading a Book,* 1753. Oil on canvas, 50 × 56 cm (19⅝ × 22 in.). Uffizi, Florence.

Jean Étienne Liotard, *Making Hot Chocolate.* Oil on canvas, 47 × 39 cm (18½ × 15⅜ in.). Earl of Bessborough's collection, Stansted Park, Hampshire.

Jean Étienne Liotard, *Portrait of Jean Étienne Liotard, Eldest Son of the Painter, Buttering Bread, c.* 1770. Oil on canvas, 63 × 70 cm (24¾ × 27⅝ in.). Naville Collection, Geneva.

Thomas Germain Joseph Duvivier, *Still Life with Basket of Strawberries.* Oil on canvas, 47 × 37 cm (18½ × 14⅝ in.). Private collection.

255

Nicolas Henri Jeaurat de Bertry, *Military Attributes*,
c. 1757. Oil on canvas, 130 × 96 cm (51⅛ × 37¾ in.).
Musée National du Château de Fontainebleau.

Roland Delaporte, *Still Life*.
Oil on canvas, 53 × 65 cm (20⅞ × 25⅝ in.).
Norton Simon Museum, Pasadena, California.

Jeaurat de Bertry, received into the Académie in 1756 on presenting two paintings of *Kitchen Utensils* (in the École des Beaux-Arts, Paris) and one of *Military Attributes* (see p. 256); Antoine Le Bel, who in 1757 exhibited *Preparations for a Lunch*; and Michel Honoré Bounieu, whose *Ingredients for a Stew* entered the Louvre as a Chardin – but is it really correct to speak of them as emulators of Chardin?

With Michel Bruno Bellengé, 'painter of vegetables, flowers and fruit, and a victim of Chardin',[16] we touch the heart of the subject. However, this artist, whose models were used for Savonnerie carpets, mostly painted flowers in vases, with drops of dew and small insects in a style which is closer to Dutch painting than to Chardin. Diderot saw merit in him and even commented favourably on his painting of *Vases and Fruit* exhibited in 1767: 'around this second vase are peaches and fruit. Chardin, yes Chardin, would not look down on this piece'. On the other hand, his opinion on Nicolas Desportes is more ambiguous. After describing him in 1763 as 'a painter of fruit and one of Chardin's victims', two years later Diderot paid the nephew of the great Desportes a backhanded compliment: 'this is not without colour and truth, Monsieur Desportes, wait until Chardin is no longer here and then we will look at you'. He then added: 'you have seen how hard and raw this was; well, of the twenty thousand people who have been drawn to the Salon by our painters, I would say that not even fifty would be able to distinguish these paintings from those by Chardin'. An elitist view, perhaps, to which Diderot returned in relation to Roland Delaporte: 'Tell those who pass by Roland de La Porte without stopping that they do not have the right to look at Chardin. However, it is not the touch, the strength, the truth or the harmony of Chardin; it is quite the opposite, i.e. a thousand leagues and a thousand years removed. It is this small imperceptible distance which one senses and which one never crosses.' However, several canvases by Delaporte were attributed to Chardin, the most famous of these being his *Orange Tree* in the Staatliche Kunsthalle, Karlsruhe (see p. 258), praised on the occasion of the Salon of 1763.[17] Diderot, who judged that 'it is easier to go from the Notre-Dame bridge to Roland de La Porte, than from Roland de La Porte to Chardin', judged this artist's paintings severely. None of the still lifes exhibited in 1765 found favour in his eyes: 'Poor victim of Chardin! Compare Chardin's Masulipatan [textile] to the latter's, and how that will seem to you to be hard, dry and starched', or again: 'Another victim of Chardin. But M. Roland de La Porte, console yourself: may the devil take me if anyone but you and Chardin suspects it.' And in 1769: 'You believe you are almost there and you are right: but you will never bridge the gap.'

Without aspiring to bridge the gap, one painter did come close: Anne Vallayer-Coster, who was becoming famous during the last years of Chardin's life. She was received into the Académie in 1770 with *Musical Instruments* (see p. 259) and *Attributes of the Arts* (both in the Louvre, Paris), which Cochin described to Marigny as being 'in Chardin's genre' and were praised by Diderot: 'Excellent, vigorous, harmonious: it is not Chardin, but while it is below the level of that artist, it is greatly above that of a woman.' The choice of subjects, five years after the overdoors which Chardin had painted for Choisy, is no accident and their composition loosely refer to Chardin, as do her *Instruments of Military Music* (1771),[18] or again her *Bust of Minerva with Military*

Copper Pot with Casserole, Pestle and Mortar, Three Eggs, Two Onions, Two Leeks and Cut Cheese, c. 1735–40?
Oil on canvas, 33 × 41 cm (13 × 16⅛ in.). Mauritshuis, The Hague.

Roland Delaporte, *The Orange Tree*.
Oil on canvas, 60 × 49.5 cm (23⅝ × 19½ in.).
Staatliche Kunsthalle, Karlsruhe.

Attributes (1777) with the crosses of the Orders of St Louis and St Michael projecting from the edge of the table in the foreground.[19] Vallayer-Coster dealt with other subjects similar to Chardin's as well: bas-reliefs (see p. 262), kitchen tables, fruit and vegetables, and dead game in particular, which she painted brilliantly and which brought her great success with connoisseurs. The Marquis de Marigny owned her 'red partridge and a rabbit hanging by its feet' and the painter Alexandre Roslin owned a painting of 'game with a gun and a powder flask'. The reference to Chardin is very clear in this type of still life. In 1769, she soberly assembled a dead hare, hanging by its feet, beside a brown stoneware jar and a wicker basket. The painting (see p. 259) is almost monochrome, in brown and beige tones; the light is reflected on the jar and lights up the white belly of the hare, whose downy fur contrasts with the darker coat of its back, which is painted in almost hair by hair.[20] But it is in a painting exhibited at the Salon of 1787 that she best expresses her debt to Chardin. In *Hunting Trophy with Dead Hares* (see p. 259), she assembles two hares on a stone table, their criss-crossed bodies reminiscent of Chardin's *Two Rabbits with a Game-bag and Powder Flask* (T.O.P. 140), a game-bag, a barrel of powder and, in the foreground, the edge of a powder flask. The composition, the overall colouring in tones of beige, light brown and dark brown, and above all the blue braid of the game-bag and the blue cord of the powder flask hanging over the edge of the table in front, are all a direct reference to Chardin and pay homage to him.

This homage continued over the years, transcending the changes in taste and manner that are designated for convenience as neo-classicism and romanticism. In the middle of the nineteenth century, at the time when François Bonvin, Philippe Rousseau and Théodule Ribot were drawing inspiration from ideas of still life and indeed from some of Chardin's genre scenes,[21] his works were sought after by collectors and connoisseurs. This is the time when La Caze,[22] Marcille and Laperlier purchased canvases, without always making the distinction between the manner and the genre, the quality and the subject – in short, between original paintings by Chardin and works which were sometimes wrongly attributed to him.[23] This was also the time when Jules and Edmond de Goncourt had no difficulty in re-establishing Chardin among the leading lights of his century.[24]

How is it that over the course of time this phenomenon has continued and that our admiration and feelings remain as strong as those of Chardin's contemporaries? Throughout this book, I have considered attempts to analyse his method of painting, specify which pigments he used and establish which models inspired his compositions. The answers to all these questions are not completely satisfactory and cannot serve as explanations. The questions asked during the eighteenth century are those we ask today. How did he paint, what methods did he use to render the velvety skin of fruit, the sparkle of a glass or silver, or the texture of an animal's fur? How did he achieve the contrast of his tones, his shadows and reflections and his graduated colours?

If, unlike the visitors to the Salon, we can no longer identify with Chardin's characters, we are interested in their occupations, and we remain touched by their simplicity, by their lack of any frivolity and by their timelessness. The attitude of *Woman Peeling Vegetables*, the activities of *The Attentive*

Anne Vallayer-Coster, *Dead Hare with Stoneware Jar*,
1769. Oil on canvas, 74.5 × 61 cm (29⅜ × 24 in.).
Private collection.

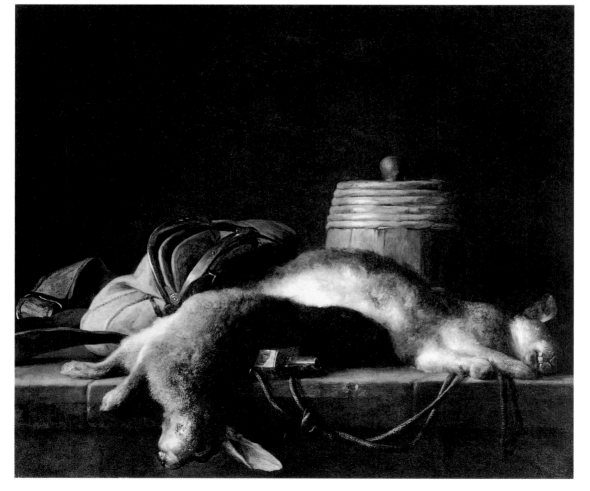

Anne Vallayer-Coster, *Musical Instruments*, 1770.
Oil on canvas,
88 × 116 cm (34⅝ × 45⅝ in.). Louvre, Paris.

Anne Vallayer-Coster, *Hunting Trophy with Dead Hares*.
Oil on canvas, 54 × 64.6 cm (21¼ × 25⅝ in.).
Private collection, London.

*Lapwing, Grey
Partridge, Woodcock and
a Seville Orange*, 1732.
Oil on canvas,
58.5 × 49.5 cm
(23⅛ × 19½ in.).
Musée de la
Chartreuse, Douai.

Nurse, like the affectionate scolding of his mothers, or the absorption of his children's occupations, are timeless.

However, the way in which Chardin represents these seems so linked to the time when he was painting that, of all the artists of the eighteenth century, he is the one to whom historians today refer most. Whether the issue is letter-writing, food or clothing, the education of children or their games, private life including attitudes and culture, the decor of middle-class homes, functional or decorative objects, Chardin's images, the objects which he assembled, and the scenes which he reproduced serve to illustrate an environment which has been transposed and recreated.[25]

'These peaches, these nuts, this wicker basket; these grapes, this drum, this bottle with its cork stopper, this copper cistern, this wooden mortar, these smoked herrings, / There is no honour, no merit in choosing such subjects. / No effort, no invention; no proof here of a superior spirit. More a proof of laziness or poverty.'[26] However, Francis Ponge added, 'undertake to treat the most ordinary of subjects in the most ordinary way: here your genius appears.' Oddly, the poet joins the historian here to recognize the mark of genius in the representation of everyday nature frozen in its objects and gestures and rendered alive and real. Through fruit or animals, furniture or crockery, as in his ordinary scenes where people are captured in an ordinary occupation, or a particular piece of clothing, each painting totally expresses this 'truth', unanimously praised by Chardin's contemporaries.

Words wear thin in the attempt to describe, while the eye marvels in front of a subject which discourages analysis and defies time. Beyond the subject, which is sometimes merely anecdotal, beyond the elaborate grouping of objects, beyond the calculated harmony of colours, Chardin offers pure painting for our enjoyment.

> Certes le temps s'écoule, mais pourtant jamais rien n'arrive.
> Tout est là.
> Tout l'avenir, aussi bien, – dans le moindre fragment d'espace.
> Tout y est lisible,
> Pour qui veut bien, pour qui sait bien l'y voir.[27]

> (Certainly, time passes, but nothing ever happens. / All is here. / All the future as well – in the smallest fragment of space. / All can be read here / By whoever wants to, by whoever is able to see it.)

1. F. L'Honoré, quoted by Deloffre, in Marivaux's *Théâtre complet*.

2. *Lettre sur la peinture…*, 1749.

3. R. Rey, *Quelques satellites de Watteau*, Paris, 1931.

4. This type of subject showing people indoors was a speciality of some of the engravers of Chardin's work, notably Lépicié and Le Bas. It is half way between genre painting and the painting of scenes of private life and ensured the spread of a sort of typology of the Parisian interior around the middle of the century. Chardin was involved in this in the same way as Jeaurat, Canot, Descamps and Lépicié.

5. This painting is known through the catalogue of a sale in Paris, 15 March 1944, no. 7.

Jacques Firmin Beauvarlet, *Woman Preparing Salad*. Engraving after Étienne Jeaurat.

6. The little poem at the bottom of the latter engraving is signed Moraine, the author of the verse accompanying *Blind Man Begging*. Once again, it gives the scene a meaning, which is not immediately apparent, but which the engraver must have felt was needed if the print was to sell better. Moraine also signed the verse accompanying the engraving of *The Reader* engraved by Gaillard after Gravelot, in which a young man is reading a novel to a young girl: 'Oui cette jeune Angloise a droit de te charmer / Et tu lui lis, Damon, sans doute l'art d'aimer…' (Indeed this young Englishwoman is right to charm you / And you Damon, are probably reading her the art of love…).

7. Estève, *Seconde lettre à un partisan du bon goût…*, no date.

8. 'Lettre à l'auteur. Sur les tableaux actuellement exposés au Louvre', *Observations périodiques sur la physique, l'histoire naturelle et les arts*, 1757, an anonymous text which is often attributed to Renou.

9. See T. Pignatti, *L'Opera completa di Pietro Longhi*, Milan, 1974.

10. A. de Herdt in the Liotard drawings exhibition catalogue, Geneva and Paris, 1992, no. 138.

11. *Sentiments d'un amateur…*, 1753.

12. *De l'Illusion dans la peinture*, text written between 1765 and 1770, *Recueil de quelques pièces concernant les arts*, vol. II, 1771, read to the Académie in 1772 and republished in the *Encyclopédie méthodique* in 1788.

13. In 1780, Cochin wrote that 'his advice was extremely useful to those sought it; and many times without touching the works of artists who had confidence in him, he taught them how to give harmonious balance to paintings which seemed to be lacking in this.'

14. Letter to Descamps in 1784 and reproduced by Lagrange, *op. cit.*, 1864, p. 457.

15. These two paintings, dated 175[9], were sold at Sotheby's in Monaco on 5 December 1992, no. 56.

16. Diderot, *Salon* of 1761, ed. Seznec and Adhémar, vol. I, 1957.

17. Mathon de la Cour, *Lettre à Madame °°° sur les peintures…*, 1763.

18. M. Roland Michel, *Anne Vallayer-Coster*, Paris, 1970, cat. no. 259.

19. M. Roland Michel, *op. cit.*, cat. no. 264.

20. A balanced composition of a hare, a partridge, ham, colza and a copper basin is also dated 1769 (in the Musée des Beaux-Arts, Rheims).

21. For more details, see G. P. Weisberg's study in the *Chardin and the Still-Life Tradition in France* exhibition catalogue, by Weisberg and W. S. Talbot, Cleveland Museum of Art, 1979.

22. This connoisseur donated eleven paintings by Chardin to the Louvre in 1869.

23. See the letter from Bonvin published by G. Weisberg, *op. cit.*, 1979, p. 46.

24. The two articles on Chardin were published in the *Gazette des Beaux-Arts*, December 1863 and February 1864 and in *L'Art du XVIII° siècle*, fasc. II, 1864.

25. Recent examples are *Histoire de la vie privée*, published under the direction of P. Ariès and G. Duby, in 1986; D. Roche's *La Culture des apparences*, 1989 and *La France des Lumières*, 1993. A. Farge mentions Chardin on several occasions in *Le Cours ordinaire des choses dans la cité du XVIII° Siècle*, 1994, particularly in the chapter devoted to 'Corps et l'Objet'.

26. F. Ponge, *Nouveau Recueil*, 1967, 'De la nature morte et de Chardin'.

27. *Ibid.*

Anne Vallayer-Coster. *Satyrs and Putti Playing with a Lioness*, 1776. Oil on canvas, 30 × 40 cm (11¾ × 15¾ in.). Private collection.

SELECTED TEXTS

DIDEROT
COCHIN

DENIS DIDEROT

Reports on the paintings exhibited at the Salons of 1759, 1761, 1763, 1765, 1767, 1769 and 1771.
These excerpts are translated from the edition of the *Salons* by J. Seznec and J. Adhémar, Oxford, 1957–67.

Salon of 1759

From Chardin there is a painting of a return from the hunt; some game; a young student drawing seen from the back; a girl doing some embroidery; and two small paintings of fruit. It is always nature and truth; you could take his bottles by the neck if you were thirsty. His peaches and grapes give one an appetite and beg to be picked up. I would much rather that these paintings were in your collection than in the collection of that miserable Trublet. This Chardin is a man of spirit: he understands the theory of his art; he paints in a manner which is unique to him and his paintings will one day be sought after. He gives such breadth to his little figures that it is as if they were cubits tall. The breadth of execution is independent of the size of the canvas or the size of its subjects. Reduce one of Raphael's holy families as much as you like and you would never destroy this breadth of execution.

Salon of 1761

From Chardin we have *Saying Grace*, some *Animals*, some *Lapwings* and other pieces. His imitation is always very faithful to nature and his execution is unique; he has a rough, almost harsh execution; and he renders a nature which is basic, ordinary and domestic. This painter has not finished anything for a long time now; he does not bother to complete feet and hands. He works like a man of the world who has talent and ability, who is happy to sketch out his thoughts in a mere four strokes of the brush. He heads the list of painters in a loose style, having completed a large number of paintings which have won him a distinguished place among first-rate artists. Chardin is a man of spirit and perhaps no one can discuss painting better than he. His reception piece, which is in the Académie, proves that he has understood the magic of colours. He has made use of this magic in several other compositions, uniting it with drawing, invention and extreme truth to nature, and it is the combination of so many qualities that already gives these works such value. Chardin has originality in his genre. This originality carries over from his paintings to his engravings. When one has

seen one of his pictures, one always remembers it and recognizes it everywhere. Look at his *Governess with her Children* and you will have seen his *Saying Grace*.

Salon of 1763

This man is truly a painter; this man is a true colourist.

At the Salon, there are several small paintings by Chardin; they are nearly all of fruit and the accompaniments for a meal. What we see is nature herself; the objects are quite separate from the canvas and are so true that they deceive the eyes.

There is one which you see as you climb the staircase which deserves a closer look. The artist has placed an old Chinese porcelain vessel on a table, with two biscuits, a jar full of olives, a shallow container of fruit, two glasses half-filled with wine, a Seville orange and a pie.

When looking at paintings by other artists, I feel that I need new eyes; when looking at paintings by Chardin, I need only use those which nature gave me and use them well.

If I were to direct my child towards painting, this is the painting which I would buy. 'Make me a copy of this', I would say, 'and then copy it again.' But perhaps nature is not more difficult to copy.

For this porcelain vessel is made of real porcelain, these olives are really separated from the eye by the water in which they are floating; one only has to reach out and take these biscuits and eat them, cut open this orange and squeeze it, take this glass of wine and drink it, or pick up this fruit and peel it, or cut this pie with a knife.

This is the true harmony of colour and its reflections. Oh Chardin! It is not white, red or black that you grind on your palette: it is the very substance of your subjects; it is air and light that you dip your brush into and transfer and attach to the canvas.

After my child had copied and recopied this piece, I would give him *The Skate* by the same master. The subject is disgusting, but it is the very flesh of the fish, its skin and its blood; seeing the thing itself would affect you in the same way. Monsieur Pierre, study this piece well when you visit the Académie and learn, if you can, the secret of using one's talent to redeem what is repulsive in nature.

This magic is incomprehensible. Thick layers of colour are applied one on top of the other, their effect seeping through from the bottom layer to the top. Sometimes it is as if a mist has been blown onto the canvas; and sometimes as if a light foam had been thrown over it. Rubens, Berghem, Greuze and Loutherbourg would explain this to you

better than I; all could open your eyes to the effect. Come close and everything becomes blurred, flattens and disappears; stand back and everything is created and takes shape again.

I have been told that Greuze was visiting the Salon and when he saw the painting by Chardin which I have just described, he looked at it and passed by, heaving a great sigh. This praise is shorter and more valuable than anything I could say.

Who will pay for paintings by Chardin once this rare man is no longer with us? You should know that this artist is still very able and that he speaks wonderfully of his art. Ah, my friend, forget the story of Apelles's curtain and Zeuxis's grapes. It is easy to fool an impatient artist and the animals are poor judges of painting. Have we not seen birds in the royal gardens crack their heads against the worst perspectives? But it is you and I that Chardin deceives when he wants to.

Salon of 1765

You have just arrived in time, Chardin, to restore my eyes, which your colleague, Challe, had so badly afflicted. Here you are again, you great magician, with your silent compositions. How eloquently they speak to the artist! Everything they say to him about the imitation of nature, the science of colour and harmony! How the air circulates around these objects! The light of the sun does not treat any better the disparate nature of the objects which it illuminates. You have scant regard for friendly colours and hostile colours!

If it is true, as the philosophers say, that nothing is real except our sensations; that the emptiness of space or the very solidity of bodies may be nothing, then let these philosophers teach me what they understand to be the difference between you and the creator, standing four paces back from the paintings.

Chardin is so true, so true and so harmonious, that although one only sees inanimate nature on the canvas, vases, cups, bottles, bread, wine, water, grapes, fruit and pies, his work stands out and sometimes even distracts you from two of the finest Vernets, beside which he did not hesitate to place his own work. This, my friend, is how it is in the world, where the presence of a man, a horse or an animal does not disturb the effect of a rock, a tree or a stream. The stream, the tree and the rock are certainly not as interesting as the man, the woman, the horse or the animal; but they are equally true.

My friend, I must tell you of an idea which occurs to me and which perhaps might not come to me again; this painting, which is known as genre painting, should be the reserve of old men or those who are born old. It requires only study and patience. No eloquence; little genius; hardly any poetry; much technique and truth, and that is all. Now, you know that the time when one begins to apply oneself to what is commonly called the search for truth, or philosophy, is exactly the time when one's temples are greying and when one would appear rather ungraceful writing a romantic letter. With regard to grey hair, my friend, I saw my own rather silver head this morning and I cried out like Sophocles, when Socrates inquired about his love life: 'A domino agresti et furioso profugi'. I am running from this wild and furious master.

I am enjoying myself talking to you, especially as I will say just one thing to you about Chardin, and it is this: choose his setting, place the objects into this setting as I will show you, and rest assured that you will have seen his paintings.

He has painted *Attributes of the Sciences*, *Attributes of the Arts* and *Attributes of Music*, as well as *Refreshments*, *Fruit* and *Animals*. There is hardly anything to choose between them. They are all equally perfect. I will give you as brief a description of these as possible.

45. *Attributes of the Sciences*
On a table covered with a reddish cloth, going from right to left, I think, are books on a ledge, a microscope, a small bell, a globe half-hidden by a green taffeta curtain, a thermometer, a concave mirror on its stand, a lorgnette with its case, rolled up maps and the end of a telescope.

This is nature herself, as regards the accuracy of the shapes and the colours; the objects are quite separate from one another, advancing and receding as if they were real; there can be nothing more harmonious; there is no confusion, despite the number of objects and the small space which they occupy.

46. *Attributes of the Arts*
Here are some books lying flat, an antique vase, drawings, hammers, chisels, rulers, compasses, a marble statue, brushes, palettes and other similar objects. They are laid out on a sort of balustrade. The statue is taken from the Fontaine de Grenelle, Bouchardon's masterpiece. The same truth, the same colour, the same harmony.

47. *Attributes of Music*
On a table covered with a reddish cloth, the painter has spread out various objects in the most natural and colourful way. There is a music stand; in front of the music stand is a candlestick with two branches; behind is a trumpet and a hunting horn, with the concave opening of the trumpet placed over the music stand. There is an oboe, a mandora, sheets of music spread around, a violin with its bow, and books standing upright. If a dangerous living creature such as a snake were painted as realistically, it would be frightening.

These three paintings are three feet ten inches wide and three feet ten inches high.

48. *Refreshments*
Fruit and animals. Imagine a square structure of grey stone, a sort of niche with a sill and a cornice. As nobly and elegantly as possible, add in a garland of vine leaves along the length of the cornice, tumbling down on both sides. Within this niche, put a glass of wine, a bottle, a loaf of bread which has been cut, some carafes cooling in an earthenware bucket, a small jug, radishes, fresh eggs, a salt cellar, two steaming cups of freshly poured coffee, and you will see Chardin's painting. This structure of broad, smooth stone decorated with vine leaves is an object of the greatest beauty. It could be a model for the facade of a temple of Bacchus.

48. Pendant to the above painting
The same stone; around it a garland of large white muscat grapes; inside, peaches, plums, carafes of lemonade in a green tin bucket, a lemon peeled and cut in the middle, a basket of pastries, a masulipatan handkerchief, a carafe of barley water and a glass half full of water. So many objects! Such diversity of form and colour! And yet such harmony! Such peace! The fabric of the handkerchief is astonishingly soft.

48. Third painting of Refreshments to be hung between the first two.
If it is true that a connoisseur cannot do without at least one painting by Chardin, then this is the one he should have. The artist is getting older. He has sometimes painted as well, but never better. Imagine a water fowl hanging by its leg. On a sideboard underneath, imagine whole and broken biscuits, a jar of olives with a cork stopper, a decorated china bowl with a lid, a lemon, a napkin unfolded and tossed carelessly aside, a pie on a wooden board and a glass half full of wine. It is here that we see that there are no unattractive objects in nature and that the aim is to depict them. The biscuits are yellow, the jar green, the napkin white and the wine red; this yellow, this green, this white and this red, contrasting with each other, restore the eye with the most perfect harmony. And do not believe that this harmony is the result of a weak, soft and over-polished technique. Not at all – there are the most vigorous brushstrokes throughout. It is true that these objects never change in the artist's eyes. As he has seen them one day, so he finds them again the next. This is not the case for animated nature. Only stone is constant.

49. *Basket of Grapes*
This is the entire painting. Scatter around the basket a few grapes, a macaroon, a pear and two or three small apples; one will agree that the separate grapes, the macaroon, the pear and the small apples are not ideal in terms of their shapes or their colours; but look at Chardin's painting.

49. *Basket of Plums*
Place on a stone ledge a wicker basket filled with plums, with a miserable piece of string for a handle; add in some nuts, two or three cherries and a few bunches of grapes.

This man is the best colourist in the Salon and possibly the best colourist in painting. I will never forgive the impertinent Webb for having written a treatise on art, without mentioning a single Frenchman. Nor can I forgive Hogarth for having said that the French school did not even have a mediocre colourist. You have lied, M. Hogarth; it is either ignorance or platitudes on your part. I know well that your country is inclined to look down on an impartial author who would dare to praise us: but do you need to lower yourself for your fellow citizens at the expense of the truth? Paint, paint better if you can. Learn how to draw and stop writing. We and the English have two very different tendencies. Ours is to overrate English paintings; theirs is to undervalue ours. Hogarth was still alive two years ago. He had spent time in France. Thirty years ago, Chardin was already a great colourist.

Chardin's execution is quite individual. It is an uneven style in that close up one does not know what it is, and as one moves away, the subject reveals itself, eventually becoming nature herself. Sometimes it pleases as much close up as from a distance. This man is as far above Greuze as the sky is above the earth, but only in this respect. He has no style; no, I am wrong, he has his own. But since he has an individual style, he should sometimes be wrong, but he never is. Try to explain that, my friend! In literature, do you know of any style which is common to all? The genre which Chardin paints in is the easiest; but no living painter, not even Vernet, is as perfect in his genre.

Salon of 1767

38. Two paintings of musical instruments.

These are about four feet six inches wide and three feet high.

They are destined for the apartments at Bellevue.

Let us start by telling his secret. This indiscretion will be of no consequence. He compares his painting to Nature and he judges it to be poor if it has not maintained her presence.

These two paintings are very well composed. The instruments have been used tastefully; there is a sort of eloquence in their disorder; the artistic effects are designed to delight; everything is there for the maximum truth of its shape and colour. It is here that one learns how to combine strength and harmony. I prefer the one with the drums, perhaps because the objects form larger blocks, or perhaps because their arrangement is more piquant. The other would pass as a masterpiece without its pendant.

I am sure that when time has faded the rather hard and raw brilliance of the fresh colours, those who thought that Chardin did better on other occasions will change their opinions. They will look at these works again when time has painted its gloss over them. I say the same of Vernet and of those who prefer his early works to those which come from his later palette.

Chardin and Vernet envisage their works twelve years on from the time they are painted and those who judge them are as wrong as those young artists who go to Rome where they slavishly copy pictures which are one hundred and fifty years old; as they do not realize how the colours have been changed by time, they do not realize that the paintings by the Carraccis look different now to the way the Carraccis saw them on their easels. But who will teach these people to appreciate the effects of time? Save them from the temptation of copying tomorrow paintings from the last century? Good sense and experience.

I do realize that Chardin's subjects, the inanimate nature which he copies, do not change in place, in colour, or in shapes. And that in terms of equal perfection, a portrait by La Tour has more merit than a genre piece by Chardin. But a brush with the wings of time will not leave anything to justify the reputation of the former. The precious dust will have left the canvas, half dispersed into the air and half attached to the long feathers of old Saturn. One will speak of La Tour, but one will see Chardin. Oh, La Tour, *memento homo quia pulvis es et in pulverem reverteris*.

It is said that Chardin has a technique all his own and that he uses his thumb as much as his brush. I do not know what it is; what is certain is that I have never known anyone who has actually seen him paint. Whatever it is, his compositions are equally well liked by the ignorant and the connoisseur. There is an incredible strength of colour, a general harmony, a piquant and true effect, beautiful masses, a magic of execution that makes one despair and a mix of composition and arrangement. Stand back or come closer and you have the same illusion: there is no confusion, but no symmetry either, no flickering light; the eye is always restored, because there is calm and rest. One stops in front of a Chardin as if by instinct, like a weary traveller who sits down for a rest on his journey, hardly noticing that he has chosen a place which offers him greenery, water, silence, shade and coolness.

Salon of 1769

I should mention the paintings by Chardin and refer you back to what I said about this artist at the previous Salons. But I like to repeat myself where praise is concerned; I yield to my natural tendency. What is good generally affects me much more than what is bad. The bad, at first, makes me very angry, but this then passes. Admiration for what is good stays with me. Chardin is not a history painter, but he is a great man. He is the master of all in harmony, this quality which is so rare and which everyone speaks of and which so few know. Take your time in front of a beautiful Teniers, or a beautiful Chardin; absorb the effect into your mind; then relate everything which you see to this subject and rest assured that you have found the secret of rare satisfaction.

The Attributes of the Arts and Their Rewards

Everyone sees nature, but Chardin sees it well and exhausts himself in rendering it as he sees it; his *Attributes of the Arts* demonstrates this. How he has observed perspective here! How the objects reflect off one another! How definite his masses are! One does not know wherein the prestige lies, because it is everywhere. One looks for the shadows and the lights, and there certainly are some, but they are not striking anywhere. The objects are separate from one another quite naturally. Take the smallest painting by this artist: a peach, a grape, a pear, a nut, a cup, a saucer, a rabbit, a partridge, and you will find the greatest and most profound colourist. Looking at his *Attributes of the Arts*, the eye is satisfied and tranquil. When one studies this painting for some time, the other paintings seem cold, jagged, flat, rough and out of tune. Chardin is between nature and art; he makes other imitations seem third

rate. There is nothing in him which reminds one of the palette. One has no desire for further harmony; it creeps imperceptibly into the composition, into every part of the canvas; as theologians describe the spirit, it is present everywhere, yet is invisible everywhere. But to be fair, or sincere, his Mercury symbolizing sculpture appears to me to be a bit meagre, too bright and too dominant over the rest; it does not create the overall illusion that is possible. He should not have taken a new cast for a model; a dustier cast would have been more muted and a more fortunate choice; because he has not drawn an academic figure for a long time, he is no longer able and, so, this figure has not been well drawn. Chardin is an old magician from whom age has not yet taken away the wand. This painting of *Attributes of the Arts* is a repetition of the picture which he painted for the Empress of Russia and it is better. Chardin makes copies willingly, which makes me feel that his works must cost him a lot.

Girl Returning from the Market

This kitchen maid who is returning from the market is again a repetition of a picture which he painted forty years ago. This is a fine little painting. If Chardin has a fault, because he keeps to his individual execution, you will find it everywhere; for the same reason, what is perfect, he never loses. Here, he is equally harmonious, it is the same harmony of reflections, the same truth of effects, a rare thing, because it is easy to create an effect when one takes liberties, when one creates a block of shadows without worrying about its source. But to be strong and principled, a slave to nature and a master of art, to have taste and to be correct, is the devil. It is a pity that Chardin applies the same style to everything, so that in going from one object to another, it sometimes becomes heavy and sluggish. There is marvellous reconciliation with the opaque, the matt and the solidity of inanimate objects; but not so with the living and the delicacy of animate things. Look at the style used in the bread and other items here, and judge if it works equally well on the face and arms of this servant, who seems to me to be quite colossal in proportion and rather mannered in her pose.

Chardin is such a rigorous imitator of nature, such a harsh judge of himself, that I have seen one of his paintings of game which he never completed because the little rabbits which he was using as models had rotted and he despaired of achieving the harmony which he had in mind with any others. All the other rabbits brought to him were too dark or too light.

Two bas-reliefs

The models for these two small bas-reliefs were a poor choice, as the sculpture is mediocre; despite this I admire them greatly. One sees here that it is possible to be both harmonious and a colourist in the objects which least require it. They are white and yet there is neither black nor white; no two tones are similar and yet there is perfect harmony. Chardin was quite right to ask a colleague, a dull painter: 'Does one paint with colours?' – 'With what then?' – 'With what? With feeling.' It is he who sees the light ripple and the reflections on the surface of a body; it is he who seizes these and who renders with I know not what the inconceivable confusion.

Head of a Wild Boar

Here is the *Head of a Wild Boar* which does not tempt me. The masses are good, but the brushwork is heavy, there are details missing and the sides of the animal have neither the ease or the eloquence which I would like.

Two paintings of fruit

His two small paintings of *Fruit* are very pretty. Chardin needs only a pear or a bunch of grapes in order to sign his name. *Ex ungue leonem*. And bad luck to those who cannot recognize the animal by its claw.

What is this partridge? Do you not see it? This is a partridge. And that one? That is also one.

There you are my friend – six letters and eight painters sent off. Now say that I am not a man of words!

Salon of 1771

38. A painting of a bas-relief: *Children's Games*
One can recognize the great man anywhere. M. Chardin uses a different magic here; this piece is much less finished than his previous works, but nevertheless has as much effect and truth as all of his work; the strength of the illusion here is immense and I have seen more than one person fooled. It seems to me that one could say that Nature has taken M. Chardin and M. Buffon into her confidence.

39. Three studies of heads in pastel
It is still the same sure and free hand, the same eyes accustomed to looking at nature, to seeing it well and to extricating the magic of its effects.

CHARLES NICOLAS COCHIN

Essai sur la vie de M. Chardin, 1780

Jean Siméon Chardin, painter famous in his genre, was the son of a cabinet-maker who had distinguished himself with his talent for making billiard tables; he was in charge of those which were made for the King. This talent was passed on through the generations of his family and his younger son, who is still practising as a cabinet-maker today, continued it with similar success. J.-S. Chardin was the eldest child; his father, who had many children, wanted him to join him in his profession, but he was loath to do so. He felt a spirit driving him towards greater talents. His father accepted his inclination for painting and apprenticed him to Pierre Jacques Cazes, a history painter, then one of the most skilled painters. Since M. Chardin the Elder, who had a large family, could not have hoped to leave his children an adequate inheritance, as it would have to be split up between them, he tried only to give them enough skills to enable them to earn a living. This is why he did not concern himself with making them learn the classics, which would have taken up a part of their youth, without actually leading them to the goal which he had in mind for them. M. Chardin often regretted that he had not had the help of a first-rate education, which seems to be more and more necessary, although it is true that it delays the study of the arts. He studied painting and history at M. Cazes's studio and he achieved only very ordinary success there. M. Cazes's studio was not suitable for training pupils, as one never painted from nature. Pupils copied the paintings of the master and drew at the Académie in the evenings. M. Cazes never had sufficient funds to pay models. He painted his finest pictures purely from practice, using a small number of studies which he had made in his youth and figures which he had drawn at the Académie. He drew accurately, in a style which was superior in many ways, yet which was rather too mannered. There is reason to believe that this fault can be attributed to the system in force during his century and his routine, which was always the same, to this unfortunate saving which he had to make to economize on the costs which using a model would have incurred.

At this time, the art of painting, without support or protectors, was slow and difficult work. With the exception of M. Le Moyne, M. de Troy and some portrait painters, all of the rest lived in a mediocre way, close to poverty. Very few paintings were commissioned by individuals, paintings for churches were rare and then at a price which was so modest that one would have difficulty living even frugally. Payment for the paintings for Notre Dame (for which two copies of everything had to be made, one large and one small version) was only 400 *livres*. The same applied to those which were subsequently made for the abbey at Saint-Germain des Prés. Nevertheless, such work was much sought after, because this was the only means of making one's talents known. The exhibition of paintings at the Salons was not yet established and one could say that this happy institution revived painting by making known new talents and by inspiring the taste for art in a number of people who would otherwise never have thought of it.

M. Chardin was not yet very advanced when he left the school of M. Cazes and it is the path which he has taken since, by observing nature, which has developed his abilities and shown that he is truly a born painter. However, this knowledge, which he himself discovered, came too late for him to apply it to history painting, which would have required of him sacrifices in terms of time and money which he was unable to make. However, the seed had been planted. The studies of heads which he made in pastel in his last years have shown that he had the sensitivity of a great master and the warmth and generosity of execution which characterizes history painting.

It may be interesting to point out how he learnt the need for an exact study of nature in the art of painting. He was invited to work for M. Noël Nicolas Coypel, who needed a young man to help him with some work. M. Chardin was first given the task of painting the gun in the portrait of a man dressed as a hunter. M. Coypel took care to place the model in a certain light, which was to be reproduced in the painting. He told M. Chardin to copy this exactly. The latter was astonished to see such precautions taken, as he had never before seen these so strictly applied. At the time, M. Chardin was of the persuasion that the painter should paint from his head and that one did not need nature unless one was lacking in imagination. However, he tried to execute this object and rendered it well, but not as easily as he had at first imagined. He realized then that the accuracy of colour and the effects of light which are present in nature are difficult to achieve and thoughts which this effort provoked made him what he subsequently became.

At about this time, in his early youth, a surgeon friend of his father's asked the young artist to make him a signboard to hang outside his premises. In it, he wanted to include various surgical tools, such as scalpels and trepans. But this is not what the young M. Chardin had in mind. Unbeknown to the surgeon, he painted a composition filled with figures. The subject of the painting was a man who had been wounded by a sword and brought to the surgeon who was dressing his wound. The police commissioner, the watchman, women and other figures animated the scene which was composed with a good deal of life and action. Although this painting was only a sketch, it was treated very well and had a very striking effect. One day before anyone had risen at the surgeon's home, M. Chardin hung his signboard. When he awoke, the surgeon was surprised to find passers-by stopped in front of his door. He went out and saw the signboard. Although his first instinct was anger that M. Chardin had ignored his suggestion, the praise which he heard coming from all sides soon made him ashamed of his lack of taste and he did not dare complain except in the mildest way. With this painting the young M. Chardin's talents become known to all at the Académie; the painting caused such a stir that everyone made a point of going to see it.

The first lessons which M. Chardin had learnt from nature made him study it very assiduously. One of the first things which he painted was a rabbit. The subject in itself was not important, but the way that he wanted to paint it forced him to study it seriously. He wanted to paint it with the greatest accuracy possible in all respects and yet with taste, without any evidence of it having being slavishly copied, which would have made his painting dry and cold. He had never before tried to paint an animal's fur. He knew that he should not try to paint it in a calculated way or to render it in too much detail. He said to himself 'Here is an object which needs to be painted. In order to render it as accurately as possible, I need to forget everything that I have seen and even the way in which similar subjects have been treated by other artists. I need to place it far enough away from me so that I no longer see the details. Above all, I need to concentrate on copying, as well and as accurately as possible, the general masses, the colour tones, the volume and the effect of light and shade.' He succeeded and the painting demonstrates the ability and magical technique which have since distinguished his talents. After that, he found himself painting all sorts of inanimate objects and still life. To these, he added living animals which he painted very successfully and as these works were praised by all of his colleagues, he found himself as if irresistibly drawn to painting in this genre.

I am ahead of myself now and I do not want to leave out a particular anecdote from Chardin's youth because it honours the memory of Jean Baptiste Van Loo, elder brother by several years of the famous Carle Van Loo, who acted as a father to him. He was the father of Louis Michel Van Loo and Amédée Van Loo. Jean Baptiste Van Loo was responsible for restoring a gallery at the Château of Fontainebleau. In order to carry out this work he brought with him some of the best students from the Académie, including M. Chardin. The agreement was that he would pay them 100 *sous* per day (a decent fee at that time) and that he would cover all their expenses. At the end, Van Loo, who was very satisfied with their work and their enthusiasm, gave them all an excellent dinner and paid them double the agreed price.

This was not the only time that M. Chardin benefited from Van Loo's generous nature. M. Chardin had exhibited, either at the Salon or in the Place Dauphine – I don't remember exactly where: since the Salons had only begun in 1737, before this happy event the best artists used to exhibit their paintings in the Place Dauphine. In any case, M. Chardin had exhibited a painting of a bronze bas-relief, which he had imitated perfectly and painted in the best possible taste. Van Loo asked him how much the painting cost. M. Chardin quoted quite a low price, which he was not optimistic about getting from anybody because up until that time he had not yet had the good fortune to have been paid well for any of his work. 'It's mine', said M. Van Loo, 'but it is worth more than that', and, in fact, he paid him more. Nothing is more flattering for an artist than such a mark of esteem coming from a famous man such as Jean Baptiste Van Loo.

M. Chardin's father was very keen that his son become a master painter at the Académie de Saint-Luc. This ordinary middle-class man, a former master and syndic of his guild, who was not *au fait* with the Arts, believed that a man had no standing unless he was a master in his profession. Without consulting his son, who was not at all keen, he paid whatever was necessary and had him received. Master painters, on occasions when they are showing off about their guild and trying to persuade others that their guild acted as a seed bed for future members of the Académie Royale, often gave M. Chardin's name as an example. However, for a long time now his was the only name they have been able to use.

M. Chardin did not remain a member of this guild for long. Encouraged by the praise which he received from many artists, in 1728 he submitted his application to the Académie

Royale. However, he was keen to gauge the true opinion of the chief officers involved in selecting new members. He therefore used a little trick, perfectly permissible, to reassure himself about their favourable opinion of him. He arranged the paintings he had to show in one of the first rooms, apparently haphazardly, and went into the next room. Monsieur de Largillierre, an excellent painter and one of the best colourists and the leading theoretician on the effects of light, went to see him. He stopped to look at the paintings before entering the room where M. Chardin was. Going in he said to him 'you have some very good pictures there. They are surely the work of some good Flemish painter. The Flemish school is an excellent school for colour. Now let us see your works.' 'You have just seen them', replied M. Chardin, 'What, these pictures here?' 'Yes, Monsieur.' 'Oh my friend', said Largillierre embracing him, 'introduce yourself boldly.' M. Cazes, who was similarly taken in, was hurt by his pupil's trick, which had elicited from him the highest praise. However he forgave him quickly, gave him much encouragement and helped with his application.

M. Chardin was accepted into the Académie to general approval. Before he was accepted, as Louis de Boullongne, Director and First Painter to the King mentioned to the Assembly, M. Chardin had said to him that the ten or twelve paintings submitted were all his and that if the Académie liked any of them they could have them. 'He has not yet been accepted', said M. de Boullongne, 'and he is already speaking of his reception. However you did well to speak about it to me.' He made the proposal, which was accepted with pleasure, and the Académie took two of his paintings. One was of a sideboard laden with fruit and silver and the other was that painting of a skate and some household utensils which is still admired very much by all the artists. Effectively, M. Chardin has never painted a picture whose colour is stronger and whose execution and effect is more magical.

At about this time M. Chardin had by chance been invited to a little middle-class dance where he made the acquaintance of a very respectable girl to whom he was attracted. They quickly became engaged, but as M. Chardin's situation was not yet very secure, the marriage was put back for a time and for various reasons it was delayed for several years. In the meantime the girl's father's financial situation took a turn for the worse and it happened that instead of quite a decent fortune which the girl had been counting on, she no longer had anything. However, despite this set-back M. Chardin

268

married her. This situation, coupled with the delicate state of his wife's health, caused him a great deal of distress which he hid with courage. A few years later she died of tuberculosis. This situation meant that he was not able to use his talents to the full.

In any event, his work was not very lucrative. He painted pictures in various genres and sold them for whatever people would give for them. Up until about 1737 he had never attempted to paint any pictures of figures. How he finally came to try this is quite unusual. M. Aved, a portrait painter, was a very good friend of his. He often sought M. Chardin's opinions about things, which he respected. However, one day M. Chardin's comments were a little harsh and M. Aved said to him crossly: 'You think that this is as easy to paint as stuffed tongues and saveloys'. M. Chardin was extremely annoyed with this retort. However he said nothing at the time. But the very next day he began a painting with figures: a servant who was drawing water from a cistern. The result was extremely satisfactory. There followed a number of very attractive paintings, whose subjects were improved by a more sophisticated choice of figures. These included his paintings of a governess and of a woman amusing herself in different ways.

These paintings took up a lot of his time, because he was not content merely to imitate nature closely; instead he tried to achieve the greatest truth possible in his tones and his effects. He painted his pictures over and over until he had achieved that breaking down of tones produced by the distance of the object and the reflections of all the surrounding objects, until he finally achieved this magical harmony which so distinguished his work.

Long practice, a good deal of effort and thought combined to give him an excellent knowledge of theory and this made the advice which he gave to others extremely useful. Several times, without actually touching the work of other artists who had trusted him, he taught them methods of giving much greater harmony to their paintings, which had been previously lacking in this respect. It was as if he gave them a type of sauce which would improve their dishes and make them taste much better – if I may express myself in such terms. He held as a principle that shadows are all the same, and that in some way the same tone should serve to break them all up. This truth is known only to painters who are colourists. Also, although in general his brushwork was not very attractive and was rather rough, there are very few paintings which could stand up alongside his and, as Restout the Elder said of him, he was 'a dangerous neighbour' to have.

His paintings also had an extremely rare quality, that of truth and naivety, both in his expressions and in his compositions. Nothing seems to have been done deliberately, either in his compositions or for producing his effects. Nevertheless, he manages to fulfil all of these conditions with a skill which is all the more admirable for being so discreet. Besides this truth and strength of colouring, his very simplicity, which is so natural, charmed everyone. In general, the public hardly notices the efforts of imagination which it takes to create the effects which we call picturesque. In truth, they sometimes have a real merit. But too often they are not natural and the impression which they make is false. It is truth and nature which most people seek out – this is why M. Chardin had so much success at all of his exhibitions.

His reputation caused many painters, even history painters, to emulate his work. The artists who were working in this highest genre were easily persuaded that if one were a successful history painter one could easily succeed in the so-called minor genres, which are only minor if they are handled in a minor way. How difficult these are is proven when one considers how difficult it is to achieve such a degree of perfection. These competitors had so little success that they were forced to abandon their efforts and to leave each artist to continue in his own speciality.

M. Chardin's success was the fruit of his profound study of nature; however this also had the effect of cramping his imagination, so that he found it very difficult to paint anything that satisfied him in the absence of nature. However it seems that he was judging himself too harshly. It was not a lack of imagination, but something else; a cruel severity in chastising himself which is natural for an educated man who does not allow himself to take any liberties and who is very difficult to please.

I would like to come back to M. Chardin's domestic life. His first wife had borne him a son and I will speak of him at the end. He remarried a kindly and honest widow. She was quite well off and this helped him greatly until the end of his life. Without her help, the painter would not have had a very comfortable life. At the time paintings did not achieve the kind of prices which they do now and, although there were paintings of his in almost all of the collections in Europe, he did not gain much from that. The most that he ever received for a painting, even at the height of his fame, was 1,500 *livres*. There were no children from the second marriage.

As I have already said, M. Chardin was accepted and received into the Académie in

1728. He became a Counsellor in 1743 and became Treasurer of the Académie in 1755, after M. Portail's death. He was willing to take on the responsibility of hanging the exhibitions free of charge and, although this was a difficult task and took up a huge amount of time, he did this for almost twenty years.

In about …, the Marquis de Marigny obtained for him rooms in the Louvre galleries. He made this request not thinking that it would be granted, because although he was quite a confident person, he was a very modest man and made few assumptions about himself. However, his name and his talent were too well known for him to have to wait a long time for a reply. He was delighted and surprised when he received the letter confirming that he had been awarded rooms and, throughout his life, he maintained respect for the Ministry which granted him this favour and which, in addition, had granted him pensions later in life which were increased on an ongoing basis, as circumstances allowed. These rooms gave him the greatest pleasure because not only were they very pleasant, but living there he found himself at the centre of the artistic community and among the artists who were all his friends.

When M. Chardin became the Treasurer of the Académie, he found it to be in a very poor financial situation. This was because its previous caretaker had become bankrupt and it was he who had been in charge of all of the collections. However, thanks to the order which he restored and with the help of some favours which the Marquis de Marigny granted to the Académie, this situation was resolved. He kept this post up until 1774. At that point, however, the burden which it imposed both on him and especially his wife was exhausting and he retired from this position.

His presence in the Louvre galleries meant that he and M. Cochin, Secretary of the Académie, became very good friends, a friendship which endured until the end of his life. His fondness for Cochin exposed him to a number of vexations which were to bother him a great deal later in life.

Seven years before his death, he suffered a number of illnesses which made him practice more rarely his talent for painting in oil. At this stage he made his first attempts to use pastel which he had never thought of previously. He did not choose pastel for his usual genre subjects, but instead he used it for life-size studies of heads. He made several of these of different individuals, young people, old people and others. He was very successful due to his skill and his manner which was broad and easy – in appearance, on the surface at least, for in fact it was the fruit of a great deal of reflection and he was a hard man to satisfy.

These works show that he had a feeling for greatness and that he could have been a history painter had he so desired. I believe that it cannot be denied that had he treated his subject matter in the same way as Michelangelo da Caravaggio he would have had even more success.

He suffered a personal tragedy which upset him greatly – this was the death of his son. The latter had been an art student and, frustrated that he himself had not had the opportunity in his youth to learn Latin and its literature – for which he had only been able to make up through reading – he never ceased to encourage his son to study the classics. He had hoped that his son would achieve a certain distinction as a painter.

M. Chardin's son won the painting prize at the Académie. In truth, he won it too easily as his painting was too weak. However, this was not unjust, because the competition was even weaker. Undoubtedly, it would have been better not to have awarded a prize at all that year. However, it is forgivable for a father to be blind to the talents of his own son and at any rate it is not easy to ignore the feelings of a man as highly regarded and well loved as his father, M. Chardin the Elder.

M. Chardin the Younger was still quite weak when he left for Italy and he did not make great progress. However, on his return he did practice in a different genre in many respects to that of his father, but which would have its reward, especially as he did have some of his father's talent, mainly in colouring and in the intelligence of his effects. However, insecurity and a perpetual restlessness meant that he was never able to use his talents fully. He could not be reproached for having any particular vice. He had spirit and good sense, but he had a rather unusual character which was harmful to himself. During the years when he stayed in Paris it was almost impossible to see any painting of his which could be regarded as finished. He began paintings which held great promise but was unable to finish them.

The Marquis de Paulmi was travelling to Venice as Ambassador, and he wanted to take with him an artist. Doyen, a professor at the Académie, suggested that he take M. Chardin the Younger and this was agreed. He stayed there with Paulmi throughout his time as Ambassador, but he did not return with him at the same time. Instead, he stayed in Venice and a few years later it became known that he had fallen into a canal and drowned.

I would like to come back to M. Chardin the Elder. In the last year of his life, he experienced a degree of satisfaction which meant a great deal to him. For over forty years he had never failed to exhibit at any of the Salons and it can truthfully be said that we have never seen an old man sustain his talents for so long. His final paintings still maintain the fire of those of his youth. At the Salon of 1779, among other paintings, he exhibited the head of a young boy which he had painted in pastel. Madame Adelaide de France was very taken with the power and the truth of this painting. She enquired how much the picture would cost, as she was keen to acquire it. M. Chardin did not want to name a price and instead declared that he would be extremely flattered by the honour which the Princess was paying to his old age and that this favour would mean more to him than anything. She then presented him with a very fine snuffbox and he was filled with gratitude.

M. Chardin had been suffering from a gallstone for a very long time. However, it had not yet fully formed and manifested itself as small flakes. He also suffered from other infirmities. In these last days his legs became very swollen; dropsy finally reached his chest and he died on 6 December 1779, aged eighty.

M. Chardin was a small man but very strong and muscular. He had spirit and above all a great store of good sense and excellent judgment. He had a singular ability to express his ideas and make them understood, even in those areas of art which are most difficult to explain, such as the magic of colour and the various reasons for light effects. He frequently had lively and surprising conversations. One day an artist was making a great show of the means which he used to purify and perfect his colours. M. Chardin, who was irritated by this chatter coming from a man whose paintings he knew to be executed in a cold and highly finished fashion, said to him 'Who told you that one paints with colours?' 'With what then?' replied the astonished man. 'One uses colours', M. Chardin said, 'but one paints with feeling.' It was once said in front of him that a particular artist had a noble disposition. 'I have never noticed that', he said; 'it is not possible: I have only ever found him to be insolent.' M. Chardin was an extremely sensitive man. He was very grateful for the favours he received, but he was also very irritated by bureaucracy when he suffered under it. This manner which he had of being rather bitter at the end of his days, when he took a few disagreements a little too much to heart, was unfortunate.

His passing was regretted not only by fellow members of the Académie, but also by students whom he had received with affection and to whom he had willingly given the most helpful advice. He leaves the memory of a good man and a great artist.

CATALOGUE
OF ENGRAVINGS
AFTER CHARDIN

ENGRAVINGS AFTER CHARDIN

It would appear that nothing further needed to be added to the catalogue of engravings after Chardin's work which was compiled by Emile Bocher in 1876. However, since Bocher followed the order in which the plates are filed in the two volumes of Chardin's œuvre in the Cabinet des Estampes of the Bibliothèque Nationale (*Db 22*, in fol.), neither the chronology of the engravings nor the sequence of engravers is treated systematically, which can sometimes make consulting it difficult.

The solution to this practical problem adopted here is to arrange the engravings after Chardin's paintings according to their date of publication. For each engraving – which has been given a Roman numeral – Bocher's catalogue number (B.) is also given, as well as the relevant 'T.O.P.' number of the painting from Pierre Rosenberg's *Tout l'Œuvre peint de Chardin* of 1983. The chronological list of these engravings is followed by an alphabetical list of the engravers.

The title of each engraving where it appears on the plate is given in italics with its original spelling. Where the engraver has not used a title, I have followed Bocher. For each engraving, I give the signatures, the title, the collection to which the original belonged when the engraving was made (when this is mentioned), and the verses with which most of the engravings are accompanied. If the sale of the engraving was announced in *Mercure de France*, I have given the date of this announcement, which frequently enables the engraving itself to be dated. Where the date does not appear with the signature on the engraving and there was no announcement in *Mercure de France*, the engraving may be dated according to when it was exhibited in the Salon.

I *Le Faiseur de châteaux de cartes* or *Châteaux de cartes* (Building Houses of Cards, or Houses of Cards), 1737
Chardin Pinx. – Fillœul Sculp.
Vous vous moquez à tort de cet adolescent / Et de son inutile ouvrage / Prest à tomber au premier vent / Barbons dans l'âge même où l'on doit être sage / Souvent il sort de vos serveaux / De plus ridicules châteaux.
The painting was also engraved ('with variations' according to the handwritten catalogue in the Cabinet des Estampes of the Bibliothèque Nationale, *Ef 27*, no. 3), by Marcenay de Ghuy, under the title *L'Enfant qui joue aux cartes* (Child Playing Cards).
B. 20 – T.O.P. 102

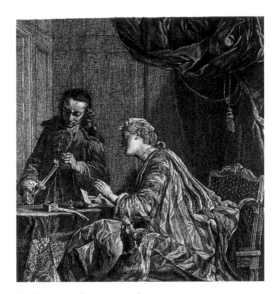

II *Dame cachetant une lettre* (Lady Sealing a Letter), 1738
Chardin Pinx. 1732. – E. Fessard Sculp.
Hâte-toy donc, Frontain: vois ta jeune Maîtresse, / Sa tendre impatience éclate dans ses yeux; / Il lui tarde déjà que l'objet de ses vœux / Ait reçu ce Billet, gage de sa tendresse. / Ah!

Frontain, pour agir avec cette lenteur / Jamais le Dieu d'amour n'a donc touché ton cœur.
Engraving announced in *Mercure de France*, May 1738.
B. 12 – T.O.P. 79

III *Le Jeune Soldat* (The Little Soldier), 1738
Peint par Chardin. – Gravé par C. N. Cochin
Sans souci, sans chagrin, tranquille en mes désirs, ! Un moulin, un tambour, forment tous mes plaisirs.
Bocher pointed out the existence of a counterfeit in reverse of this plate, with some additions and different lettering, published by Basset in Paris (B. 31).
Engraving announced with the following one in *Mercure de France*, July 1738.
B. 30 – T.O.P. 90

IV *La Petite Fille aux cerises*
(Little Girl with Cherries), 1738
Peint par Chardin. – Gravé par C. N. Cochin.
Simple dans mes plaisirs, en ma colation, /
Je sçais trouver aussy ma récréation.
Engraving announced with the previous
one in *Mercure de France*, July 1738.
B. 43 – T.O.P. 91

VI *La Fontaine* (The Copper Cistern), 1739
The signatures and the note about the
La Roque collection are identical to those
of the previous engraving.
Engraving announced with the previous
one in *Mercure de France*, June 1739.
B. 21 – T.O.P. 80

VIII *Les Osselets*
(Game of Knucklebones), 1739
Chardin pinx. – Fillœul Sculp.
Déjà grande et pleine d'attraits / Il vous est peu
séant, Lisette, / De jouer seule aux osselets, / Et
désormais vous êtes faite / Pour rendre un jeune
amant heureux, / En daignant lui céder quelque
part dans vos jeux.
Engraving announced with the previous
one in *Mercure de France*, December 1739.
B. 39 bis – T.O.P. 98

V *La Blanchisseuse*
(The Washerwoman), 1739
Painted by Chardin. – Engraved by
C. N. Cochin.
D'après le tableau original, du Cabinet de
Mr le Chevalier de La Roque
Engraving announced with the next one
in *Mercure de France*, June 1739.
B. 6 – T.O.P. 81

VII *Les Bouteilles de savon*
(Soap Bubbles; lit. 'Soap Bottles'), 1739
Chardin Pinx. – Fillœul Sculp.
Contemple bien, jeune Garçon / Ces petits globes
de savon: / Leur mouvement si variable / Et leur
éclat si peu durable / Te feront dire avec raison /
Qu'en cela mainte Iris, leur est assez semblable.
Engraving announced with the next one
in *Mercure de France*, December 1739.
B. 8 – T.O.P. 97

273

XIII *La Maîtresse d'école*
(The Schoolmistress), 1740
Peint par Chardin – Gravé par Lépicié 1740
Si cet aimable enfant, rend bien d'une maîtresse/
L'air sérieux, le dehors imposant, / Ne peut-on
pas penser que la feinte et l'adresse / Viennent au
sexe, au plus tard en naissant. – Lépicié.
Engraving announced in *Mercure de France*,
October 1740.
B. 34 – T.O.P. 104

IX *La Gouvernante* (The Governess), 1739
Peint par Chardin – Gravé par Lépicié, 1739
Malgré le Minois hipocrite / Et l'air soumis
de cet enfant, / Je gagerois qu'il prémédite /
De retourner à son volant – Lépicié.
Engraving announced in *Mercure de France*,
December 1739.
B. 24 – T.O.P. 117

XI *Le Garçon cabaretier*
(The Cellar Boy), 1740
Same signatures and provenance as the
previous engraving.
B. 22 – T.O.P. 113

XII *Le Jeune dessinateur*
(The Young Draughtsman), 1740
Chardin pinxt. 1737 – J. Faber fecit 1740.
The happy Youth whose strength of genius fires;/
Who, smit with sciences, to fair Fame aspires, /
Thro' all her Windings nature, must pursue; /
Nor quit the nymph till he obtain the clue. –
Lockman.
B. 28 – T.O.P. 112

X *L'Ecureuse* (The Scullery Maid), 1740
Peint par J. S. Chardin. – Gravé par C. N.
Cochin.
Du Cabinet de Mr le Comte de Vence.
B. 16 – T.O.P. 114

XIV *La Mère laborieuse*
(The Diligent Mother), 1740
J. B. Simeon Chardin Pinxit. –
Lépicié Sculpsit 1740.
Un rien vous amuse ma fille, / Hier ce feuillage
étoit fait, / Je vois par chaque point d'éguille /
Combien votre esprit est distrait. / Croyez moi,
fuiez la paresse, / Et goûtez cette vérité, /
Que le travail et la sagesse, / Valent les biens
et la beauté. – Lépicié
Le tableau original est placé dans le Cabinet
du Roy.
Engraving announced in *Mercure de France*,
December 1740.
B. 35 – T.O.P. 118

XV *Le Négligé* or *La Toilette du matin*
(The Morning Toilet), 1741
Peint par Chardin. – Gravé par Le Bas 1741.
Tiré du Cabinet de Monseigneur le Comte
Tessin.
Avant que la Raison l'éclaire, / Elle prend du
miroir les avis séduisans. / Dans le désir et l'art
de plaire, / Les Belles, je le vois, ne sont jamais
enfans. – Pessélier.
Engraving announced in *Mercure de France*,
December 1741.
B. 38 – T.O.P. 121

XVI *Jeune Fille à la raquette,* or *au volant*
(Girl with a Racket, or Shuttlecock), 1742
Chardin pinx. – Lépicié Sculp. 1742.
Sans souci, sans chagrin, tranquille en mes
désirs / Une Raquette, et un Volant forment
tous mes plaisirs.
B. 29 – T.O.P. 108

XVII *La Pourvoïeuse*
(Girl Returning from the Market), 1742
J. B. Simeon Chardin pinxit. – Lépicié
Sculpsit 1742.
A votre air j'estime et je pense, / Ma chère enfant
sans calculer, / Que vous prenez sur la dépense, /
Ce qu'il faut pour vous habiller. – Lépicié
Engraving announced in *Mercure de France*,
November 1742.
B. 45 – T.O.P. 115

XVIII *Le Toton*
(Child with a Spinning Top), 1742
J. B. Siméon Chardin pinxit – Lépicié
Sculpsit 1742.
Cet aimable écolier, aussi fin que solide, /
Paroît méditer sur ce ton, / Des choses d'icy bas
le caprice décide, / Et tout prend le train du
Tôton. – Lépicié
Dans la main du Caprice, auquel il s'aban-
donne / L'homme est un vrai tôton, qui tourne
incessament; / Et souvent son destin dépend du
mouvement / Qu'en le faisant tourner la fortune
lui donne.
B. 50 – T.O.P. 111

XIX *La Ratisseuse*
(Woman Peeling Vegetables), 1742
J. B. Simeon Chardin pinxit. – Lépicié
Sculpsit 1742.
Quand nos ayeux tenoient des mains de la
nature, / Ces légumes, garants de leur
simplicité, / L'art de faire un poison de notre
nourriture / N'etoit point encore inventé.
Engraving announced in *Mercure de France*,
January 1743.
B. 46 – T.O.P. 116

XX *Le Dessinateur*
(The Draughtsman), 1742–43
Signed within the image, top right:
M Chardin P.; bottom left: *Gautier S.*
Bocher points out (B. 15/a) the existence
of a copy in reverse, signed E. Cécile
Magimel, said to be entitled *Les Principes*
des Arts.
This engraving was announced with
the next one in *Mercure de France*,
January 1743.
B. 15 – T.O.P. 85

XXI *L'Ouvrière en tapisserie*
(The Embroiderer), 1742–43
Signed on the wall in the background: top
left, *M. Chardin P*, bottom right, *Gautier S.*
B. 41 – T.O.P. 84
There is said to be a copy in reverse,
signed E. Cécile Magimel, with the title
L'Amusement utile.
Engraving announced with the previous
one in *Mercure de France*, January 1743.
B. 41 – T.O.P. 84

*Dans le dédale obscur des monumens Antiques, /
Homme docte, à grands frais pourquoi
t'embarrasser ? / Notre siècle à des yeux
vraiment philosophiques, / Offre assez de quoi
s'exercer – Pesselier.*
B. 2 – T.O.P. 94

XXIII *Le Peintre* (The Painter), 1743
*J. B. Simeon Chardin pinxit – P. L Surugue
filius sculp. 1743.*
*Le Singe, Imitateur exact ou peu fidèle / Est
un aminal fort commun : / Et tel homme icy bas
est le Peintre de l'un / Qui sert à l'autre de
modèle – Pesselier*
B. 42 – T.O.P. 93

De nos projets ou bien de vos châteaux – Lépicié
Engraving announced in *Mercure de France*,
September 1743.
B. 11 – T.O.P. 105

XXV *Le Château de cartes*
(House of Cards), after 1743
J. B. Simeon Chardin pinx. – Aveline sculp.
Same unsigned quatrain as for
the previous engraving.
B. 10 – T.O.P. 109

XXII *L'Antiquaire* (The Antiquarian), 1743
*J. B. Simeon Chardin pinxit. – P. L. Surugue
Filius Sculpsit. 1743.*

XXIV *Le Château de cartes*
(House of Cards), 1743
J. B. Simeon Chardin pinxit. – Lépicié sculpsit.
*Aimable enfant que le plaisir décide, /
Nous badinons de vos frêles travaux : /
Mais entre nous, quel est le plus solide /*

XXVI *L'Inclination de l'âge*
(The Inclination of Her Age), 1743
J. B. Simeon Chardin pinxit – P. L. Surugue
filius sculp. 1743.
Sur les frivoles jeux, sont s'occupe cet âge, /
Gardons-nous de jetter des regards méprisans ; /
Sous des Titres plus imposans, / Ils sont aussi
notre partage. – Pesselier
B. 25 – T.O.P. 110

XXVII *Les Tours de cartes*
(Card Games), 1744
Chardin pinx. – P. L. Surgue filius scul. 1744
Le tableau original est dans le Cabinet de Mr.
Chev. Despuechs.
On vous séduit foible jeunesse, / Par ces tours que
vous yeux ne cessent d'admirer; / Dans les cours
du bel age où vous alles entrer / Craignés pour
votre cœur mille autres tours d'adresse–Danchet.
Bocher mentions a state with four musical
staves at the bottom.
Engraving announced in *Mercure de France*,
April 1744.
B. 51 – T.O.P. 95

XXVIII *Le Bénédicité* (Saying Grace), 1744
J. B. Simeon Chardin Pinxit – Lépicié
sculpsit. 1744.
Le tableau original est placé dans le Cabinet
du Roi.
La Sœur en tapinois, se rit du petit frère, /
Qui bégaie son oraison ; / Lui, sans s'inquiéter,
dépêche sa prière / Son apétit fait sa raison –
Lépicié.
Another version of the engraving is signed
Renée Elizabeth Marlié Lépicié Sculpsit.
Engraving announced in *Mercure de France*,
December 1744.
B. 5 – T.O.P. 120

XXIX *Le Soufleur* (*sic*; The Philosopher
Reading), 1744
Peint par J. B. Siméon Chardin. – Gravé par
Lépicié 1744.
Malgré tes veilles continües / Et ce vain attirail
de chimique sçavoir / Tu pourrais bien trouver au
fond de tes cornues, / La misère et le désespoir. –
Lépicié.
Engraving announced in *Mercure de France*
of January 1745.
B. 48 – T.O.P. 99

XXX *Le Jeu de l'oye* (Game of Goose), 1745
Peint par Chardin. – P. L. Surugue fils, sculp.
1745.
Le tableau original est dans le Cabinet de Mr.
Chev. Despuechs.
Avant que la carrière à ce jeu soit finie /
Que de risques à craindre et d'écueils à franchir; /
Enfants, vous ne pouvés trop tôt y réfléchir ; /
C'est une image de la vie. – Danchet.
B. 27 – T.O.P. 96

XXXI *Les Amusements de la vie privée*
(The Amusements of Private Life), 1747
*Peint par J. B. S. Chardin en 1746. –
L. Surugue sculpsit 1747.*
*Dédié à Madame la comtesse de Tessin /
Senatrice de Suède / par son très humble et très
obéissant serviteur J.B.S. Chardin peintre du
Roi et Con[r] en son Académie.*
*Le tableau original est dans la Gallerie de
Brotningholm [sic] en Suède qui fait pendant à
un autre du même Auteur représentant une
Dame qui vérifie des livres de dépenses
domestiques. Peint en 1747.*
Engraving announced in *Mercure de France*
of June 1747.
B. 1 – T.O.P. 123

XXXII *L'Instant de la méditation*
(The Moment of Meditation), 1747
*J. B. S. Chardin Pinxit. – L. Surugue
sculpsit 1747.*
*Cet amusant travail, cette lecture aimable, /
Da la sage Philis occupent le loisir, / Quand on
sçait joindre l'utile à l'agréable / L'innocence est
toujours la baze du plaisir. – Lépicié.*
Some prints are marked: *Dédié à M. Le Noir
par son très humble et très obéissant serviteur et
son amy J. B. S. Chardin.*
Engraving announced in *Mercure de France*,
October 1747.
B.26 – T.O.P. 106

XXXIII *Dame prenant son thé*
(Lady Taking Tea), 1749 (?)
Chardin pinx. – Fillieul [sic] sculp.
*Que le jeune Damis serait heureux, Climène, /
Si cette bouillante liqueur, / Pouvoit échauffer
votre cœur, / Et si le sucre avait la vertu
souveraine / D'adoucir ce qu'en votre humeur, /
Cet amant trouve de rigueur.*
It is generally accepted that this engraving
was made by Fillœul long after that of its
pendant, *Building a House of Cards*, which
had been engraved in 1739, and 1757 has
been suggested as the date of this
engraving. However, in 1749 it featured
with its pendant in the catalogue of the

sale by Le Bas of some prints which he
himself had not made. In that context,
both were announced at the price of one
livre each in *Mercure de France* in December
1749, at the same time as *The Morning
Toilet*, sold at 1 *livre* 10 *sols*.
B. 13 – T.O.P. 101

XXXIV *La Serinette*
(The Bird Organ), 1753
Peint par Chardin. – Gravé par L. Cars.
*A Monsieur de Vandières, conseiller / du Roy
en ses conseils, directeur [etc.]*
*Ce Tableau est tiré du Cabinet de Monsieur
de Vandières. / Par son très humble et très
obéissant serviteur, Chardin.*
Engraving announced in *Mercure de France*,
November 1753.
B. 47 – T.O.P. 133

279

XXXV *L'Œconome*
(The Household Accounts), 1754
Chardin pinx. – J. Ph. Le Bas Sculp. an. 1754
Tiré du Cabinet du Roy de Suède desiné par
Renn d'après le Tableau original.
Quel prodige! une femme a des soins plus
flatteurs / Dérobe un temps qu'elle donne au
ménage. / Ce Tableau simple du vieux âge, /
Est pris dans la nature et non pas dans nos
mœurs.
B. 39 – T.O.P. 124

XXXVI *L'Etude de dessein*
(The Drawing Lesson), 1757
Chardin pinxit 1749 – Le Bas Sculp.
A Sa Majesté – la Reine de Suède. / Le Tableau
est dans le Cabinet de sa Majesté – Par son trés
humble et très obéïssant serviteur Chardin.
B. 18 – T.O.P. 126

XXXVII *La Bonne Education*
(The Good Education), 1757
Chardin pinx. 1749 – Le Bas Sculp.
A Sa Majesté – la Reine de Suède. / Le Tableau
est dans le Cabinet de sa Majesté – Par son trés
humble et très obéïssant serviteur Chardin.
B. 7 – T.O.P. 127

XXXVIII *Le Dessinateur*
(The Draughtsman), 1757
Gravé d'après le tableau original de M. Chardin
/ Peintre ordinaire du Roy: Conseiller et
Trésorier de l'Académie royale de Peinture et de
sculp.re / By Jean Jacques Flipart in 1757.
A Paris chez Laurent Cars.
This engraving was made after a different
painting to that engraved by Gautier
Dagoty in 1742 (c.f. XX above), which is
in reverse: here, the young artist is facing
towards the right. But it is apparent that
the engraving is reversed compared to the

painting. as he is holding his pencil in his
left hand – and he is copying a male nude
whose arms are outstretched, rather than
folded. There is a plaster bust to his left,
which is not in the earlier version of the
painting. A palette is hanging on the wall
and the thin lines around the engraving
form a frame. The two paintings belonged
to Laurent Cars – which is why the
engravings were sold by him – were
exhibited at the Salon of December 1757.
Engraving announced with the next one in
Mercure de France, December 1757.
B. 14 – T.O.P. 85

XXXIX *L'Ouvrière en tapisserie*
(The Embroiderer), 1757
Same lettering as the previous engraving.
As with the previous number, the
engraving is in reverse compared to that
by Gautier Dagoty (XXI).
Engraving announced with the previous
one in *Mercure de France*, December 1757.
B. 40 – T.O.P. 84

XL *Portrait d'André Levret*, 1760
Peint par Chardin en 1746. – Louis le Grand.
[1760]
Text around the medallion:
ANDREASLEVRET
ECOLLEG.ETACAD.REG.CHIRURG-
PARIS.–ANNO DOMINI.M.D.CCLIII.
And on the base: *Viro in arté obstetricia*
celebri.in Germanae amicitiae Tesseramponit /
Henr.Crantz Med.Doct.S.M.Imp.Pens.
B. 32 – T.O.P. 122

XLI *L'Aveugle* (The Blind Man), 1761
Peint par Chardin. – Gravé par Surugue fils.
Hélàs, tu ne vois point la splendeur du soleil /
A ton sort déplorable il n'est rien de pareil; /
Pour moi, tout ce qui fait le malheur de ma vie, /
C'est d'avoir trop bien vu la beauté de Silvie /
Dont mon ardent amour et ma fidélité, /
De plus en plus augmentent la fierté. – Moraine.
B. 4 – T.O.P. 89

XLII *Portrait d'Antoine Louis*, 1766
Peint par J. S. Chardin Ptre du Roy –
Gravé par S. C. Miger, en 1766.
Text under the medallion: *Ant.Louis*
Secrétaire perpétuel de l'Académie Royale de /
Chirurgie, Professeur et Censeur Royal,
Chirurgien consultant des / Armées du Roy, de
la Societé R.le de Sciences de Montpellier &3 /
Inspecteur des Hôpitaux militaires et de Charité
du Royaume, / Docteur en Droit de la Faculté de
Paris, Avocat au Parlement.
Bocher indicates the existence of a smaller
version in reverse, drawn and engraved by
Dupin and presented to M. Louis in 1778
(B. 33/c) as well as another one based on
the latter (B. 33d).
B. 33 – T.O.P. 134

XLIII *Autoportrait de Chardin aux besicles*
(Self-Portrait of Chardin with
Spectacles), *c.* 1775?
Peint par lui-même en 1771. –
Gravé par Chevillet Graveur de leur Maj.
Imp. et Royale.
Jean-Baptiste-Siméon Chardin / Peintre du Roi
Conseiller et Ancien Trésorier / de l'Académie
Royale de Peinture et Sculpture. / De l'Acad.
Roy. des Sciences Belles Lettres et Arts de
Rouen / …
B. 2 – T.O.P. 191

This plate was dated to the beginning of
the nineteenth century, clearly because of
the reference to 'His Imperial Majesty';
but the existence of a portrait of
Marguerite Siméone Pouget (B. 44),
engraved by Chevillet in 1777, in which
the engraving of *Self-portrait with Spectacles*
appears, would lead one to believe that this
engraving should be dated *c.* 1775, and that
the print catalogued by Bocher was a
reprint of the early nineteenth century
with altered lettering.

CHARDIN'S ENGRAVERS

Pierre Aveline (1702?–60?)
XXV *Le Château de cartes* (House of
Cards)

Laurent Cars (1699–1771)
XXXIV *La Serinette* (The Bird Organ)

Juste Chevillet (1729–1802?)
XLIII *Autoportrait de Chardin aux besicles*
(Self-Portrait of Chardin with
Spectacles)

Charles Nicolas Cochin the Elder
(1688–1754)
III *Le Jeune Soldat* (The Little Soldier)
IV *La Petite Fille aux cerises* (Little Girl
with Cherries)
V *La Blanchisseuse* (The Washerwoman)
VI *La Fontaine* (The Copper Cistern)
X *L'Ecureuse* (The Scullery Maid)
XI *Le Garçon cabartier* (The Cellar Boy)

John Faber, Junior (1684–1756)
XII *Le Jeune dessinateur* (The Young
Draughtsman)

Étienne Fessard (1714–77)
II *Dame cachetant une lettre*
(Lady Sealing a Letter)

Pierre Fillœul (1696–after 1754)
I *Le Faiseur de châteaux de cartes*
(Building Houses of Cards)
VII *Les Bouteilles de savon* (Soap Bubbles)
VIII *Les Osselets* (Game of
Knucklebones)
XXXIII *Dame prenant son thé*
(Lady Taking Tea)

Jean Jacques Flipart (1719–82)
XXXVIII *Le Dessinateur*
(The Draughtsman)
XXXIX *L'Ouvrière en tapisserie*
(The Embroiderer)

Jacques Fabien Gautier Dagoty
(1706–85)
XX *Le Dessinateur* (The Draughtsman)
XXI *L'Ouvrière en tapisserie*
(The Embroiderer)

Jean Phillipe Le Bas (1707–83)
XV *Le Négligé* or *La Toilette du matin*
(The Morning Toilet)
XXXV *L'Œconome*
(The Household Accounts)
XXXVI *L'Etude du dessein*
(The Drawing Lesson)

XXXVII *La Bonne Education*
(The Good Education)

Louis Le Grand (1723–1807)
XL *Portrait d'André Levret*

François Bernard Lépicié (1698–1755)
IX *La Gouvernante* (The Governess)
XIII *La Maîtresse d'école*
(The Schoolmistress)
XIV *La Mère laborieuse*
(The Diligent Mother)
XVI *Jeune Fille à la raquette*, or *au volant*
(Girl with a Racket, or Shuttlecock)
XVII *La Pourvoïeuse*
(Girl Returning from the Market)
XVIII *Le Toton*
(Child with a Spinning Top)
XIX *La Ratisseuse*
(Woman Peeling Vegetables)
XXIV *Le Château de cartes*
(House of Cards)
XXVIII *Le Bénédicité* (Saying Grace)
XXIX *Le Soufleur*
(*sic*; The Philosopher Reading)

Cécile Magimel
XX *Le Dessinateur* (The Draughtsman),
under the title *The Principles of the Arts* (?)
XXI *L'Ouvrière en tapisserie*
(The Embroiderer), under the title
The Useful Pastime (?)

Antoine de Marcenay de Ghuy
(1724–1811)
I *L'Enfant qui joue aux cartes*
(Child Playing Cards)

Simon Miger (1736–1820)
XLII *Portrait d'Antoine Louis*

Louis Surugue (1686–1762)
XXXI *Les Amusements de la vie privée*
(The Amusements of Private Life)
XXXII *L'Instant de la méditation*
(The Moment of Meditation)

Pierre Louis Surugue (1717–71)
XXII *L'Antiquaire* (The Antiquarian)
XXIII *Le Peintre* (The Painter)
XXVI *L'Inclination de l'âge*
(The Inclination of Her Age)
XXVII *Les Tours de cartes* (Card Games)
XXX *Le Jeu de l'oye* (Game of Goose)
XLI *L'Aveugle* (The Blind Man)

BIBLIOGRAPHY

L'Age d'or flamand et hollandais – Collections de Catherine II, Musée de l'Ermitage, Saint-Petersbourg, exhibition catalogue, Musée des Beaux-Arts de Dijon, 1993.

Bachaumont, L. P. de, *Mémoires secrets pour servir à l'histoire de la République des Lettres en France, depuis 1762 jusqu'à nos jours*, London, 1777–89, 36 vols.

Baillet de Saint-Julien, Baron L. G., *Réflexions sur quelques circonstances présentes contenant deux lettres sur l'exposition des tableaux au Louvre cette année 1748, à M. le comte de R°°°*, n.p., 1748.

———— *Lettre sur la peinture à un amateur*, Geneva, 1750.

———— *Lettre a M. Ch[ardin] sur les caractères en peinture*, Geneva, 1753.

———— *La Peinture, ode de Milord Telliab, traduite de l'anglois par M°°°, un des auteurs de l'Encyclopédie*, London, 1753.

———— *Lettre à un partisan du bon goût sur l'exposition des tableaux faits dans le grand Sallon du Louvre*, n.p., n.d. (1755).

———— *Caractères des peintres actuellement vivans*, n.p., 1755.

Baxandall, M., *Patterns of Intention*, Yale, 1985.

Beaulieu, M., *Robert Le Lorrain*, Paris, 1982.

Bellier de la Chavignerie, E., 'Notes pour servir à l'exposition de la Jeunesse. Les artistes français oubliés ou dédaignés', *Revue universelle des Arts*, 1864, vol. XIX, pp. 38–67.

Bjurström, P., *Carl Gustaf Tessin och Konsten*, Stockholm, 1970.

Bocher, E., *Jean-Baptiste Siméon Chardin* in *Les Gravures françaises du XVIIIᵉ siècle*, 3rd fascicle, Paris, 1876.

Boilly, J., 'Billet de Ch. N. Cochin à Belle le fils', *A. A. F.*, 1852–1853, p. 128.

Bois, Y. A., J. C. Bonne, C. Bonnefoi, H. Damisch, J. C. Lebensztejn, 'The Skate', *Critique*, August–September 1973, no. 315–316, pp. 679–683.

Bridard de la Garde, Abbé P., 'Observations sur les tableaux, sculpture et gravure, exposés au Sallon du Louvre le 25 août 1767', *Mercure de France*, September 1767.

Bryson, N., *Looking at the Overlooked – Four Essays on Still Life Painting*, London, Cambridge, 1990.

Burollet, T., *Le Musée Cognacq-Jay – Peintures et dessins*, Paris, 1980.

———— *Le Musée Cognacq-Jay – II – Porcelaines*, Paris, 1983.

Cailleux, J., 'Three portraits in pastel and their history', *The Burlington Magazine*, supplement to 'L'art du XVIIIᵉ siècle', November 1971, no. 27, pp. II–VI.

Campardon, E., *Madame de Pompadour et la cour de Louis XV*, Paris, 1867.

Carritt, D., 'Mr Fauquier's Chardins', *The Burlington Magazine*, September 1974, no. 858, vol. CXVI, pp. 502–509.

Chaperon, P. R., *Traité de la peinture au pastel*, Paris, 1788.

Cochin, C. N., *Lettre à un amateur en réponse aux critiques qui ont paru sur l'exposition des tableaux*, Paris, 1753.

———— 'Réflexions sur la critique des ouvrages exposés au Sallon du Louvre', which appeared under the title of 'Extraits des Observations sur la Physique et les Arts', *Mercure de France*, October 1757, II, pp. 170–184.

———— *Réponse de M. Jérôme, rapeur de tabac, à M. Raphaël*, Paris, 1769.

———— *De l'illusion dans la peinture*, text written between 1765 and 1770, published in *Recueil de quelques pièces concernant les arts*, vol. II, 1771, read to the Académie in 1772.

———— 'Essai sur la vie de M. Chardin' (1780), published by C. de Beaurepaire in *Précis analytique des travaux de l'Académie des Sciences, Belles-Lettres et Arts de Rouen*, 1875–1876, vol. LXXVIII, pp. 417–441.

———— 'Lettres adressées par Charles-Nicolas Cochin fils à Jean-Baptiste Descamps, 1757–1790', edited by C. Michel, *Correspondances d'artistes des XVIIIᵉ et XIXᵉ siècles – Archives de l'Art Français*, nouvelle periode, vol. XXVIII, 1986.

———— *Troisième discours: les moyens de se diriger dans l'étude de la nature*, text sent to the Académie de Rouen in 1778 and delivered in 1779.

Colson [?], J. F. G., *Observations sur les ouvrages exposés au Sallon du Louvre ou Lettre à M. le comte de °°° S.t.*, n.p., 1775.

Conisbee, P., *Claude-Joseph Vernet, 1714–1789*, exhibition catalogue, London, 1976.

———— *Chardin*, Oxford, 1986.

———— *Soap Bubbles by Jean-Siméon Chardin*, Masterpieces in Focus, Los Angeles County Museum of Art, with a note on Materials and Techniques by Joseph Fronek, 1990.

Courajod, L., *L'École royale des Élèves protégés*, Paris, 1874.

Courboin, F., *L'Estampe française*, Paris, 1914.

Crow, T., *Painters and Public Life in Eighteenth-Century Paris*, Yale, 1985.

Cuzin, J. P., *Jean-Honoré Fragonard*, Fribourg, 1989.

Dacier, E., *Catalogues de ventes et livrets de Salons illustrés par Gabriel de Saint-Aubin*, Paris, 1909–21, 6 vols.

Daudé de Jossan, *Lettres sur les peintures, gravures et sculptures qui ont été exposées cette année au Louvre, par M. Raphaël, peintre de l'Académie de Saint-Luc, entrepreneur général des enseignes de la ville, fauxbourgs et banlieue de Paris; à M. Jérôme, son ami, rapeur de tabac et riboteur*, Paris, 1769.

———— *Sentiments sur les tableaux exposés au Salon*, 1769.

Dayot, A. and J. Guiffrey, *J. B. S. Chardin*, Paris, 1907.

———— and L. Vaillat, *Chardin et Fragonard*, Paris, 1907.

Demoris, R., *Chardin, la chair et l'objet*, Paris, 1991.

Desfontaines, Abbé P. F. G., 'Exposition des tableaux de l'Académie', *Observations sur les écrits modernes*, vol. XXXV, 1741, letter 374.

Deville, E., *Index du Mercure de France*, Paris, 1910.

Diderot, D., *Salons*, ed. J. Seznec and J. Adhémar, Oxford, vol. I, 1957, vol. II, 1960, vol. III, 1963, vol. IV, 1967; ed. Hermann, *Salons de 1759, 1761, 1765* (by J. Chouillet), Paris, 1984, *Salon de 1765* (by E. M. Bukdahl and A. Lorenceau), Paris, 1984.

———— *Pensées détachées sur la peinture*, in *Oeuvres esthétiques*, ed. P. Vernières, Paris, 1968.

———— *Essais sur la peinture*, ed. Hermann, by G. May, Paris, 1984.

———— *Diderot et l'art de Boucher à David*, exhibition catalogue, Paris, 1984–85.

Dorbec, P., 'Le portraitiste Aved et Chardin portraitiste', *Gazette des Beaux-Arts*, 1904, vol. XXXII, pp. 89–100, 215–224, 341–352.

Duplessis, G., *Collection de pièces sur les Beaux-Arts imprimées et manuscrites recueillies par Pierre-Jean Mariette, Charles-Nicolas Cochin et M. Deloynes, conservées au Cabinet des Estampes de la Bibliothèque nationale*, Paris, 1881.

Engerand, F., *Inventaire des collections de la Couronne: Inventaire des tableaux commandés et achetés par la Direction des Bâtiments du roi*, Paris, 1901.

Estève, P., *Lettre à un ami sur l'exposition des tableaux, faite dans le grand Sallon du Louvre le 25 août 1753*, n.p., n.d.

Estève, P., *Seconde lettre à un partisan du bon goût sur l'exposition des tableaux faite dans le grand Sallon du Louvre*, n.p., n.d. (1755).

Falconet, E., *Réflexions sur la sculpture*, Paris, 1760.

Faré, M. and F., *La Vie silencieuse en France – La nature morte au XVIIIᵉ siècle*, Fribourg, 1976.

Farge, A., *Le Cours ordinaire des choses dans la cité du XVIIIᵉ siècle*, Paris, 1994.

Fontaine, A., *Les Collections de l'Académie royale de peinture et sculpture*, Paris, 1910.

Fréron, E. C., 'Exposition des tableaux', *Lettres sur quelques écrits de ce tems*, vol. XI, 1753, letter 8.

Fried, M., *Absorption and Theatricality, Painting and Beholder in the Age of Diderot*, Berkeley, Los Angeles and London, 1980.

Fuhring, P., 'The Print Privilege in Eighteenth-Century France', *Print Quarterly*, vol. II, no. 3, September 1985 and vol. III, no. 1, March 1986.

Furcy-Raynaud, M., 'Correspondance de M. de Marigny avec Coypel, Lépicié et Cochin', *Nouvelles Archives de l'Art Français*, (1903), 1904, vol. XIX.

Gallet, M. and Y. Bottineau, *Les Gabriel*, exhibition catalogue, Paris, 1982.

Garrigues de Froment, Abbé, *Sentimens d'un amateur sur l'exposition des tableaux du Louvre et la critique qui en a été faite*, n.p., n.d. (1753).

Gersaint, E. F., *Abrégé de la vie d'Antoine Watteau*, Paris, 1744.

——— 'Neuf lettres au comte Carl Gustaf Tessin, 1743–1748', published by J. Heidner, *Archives de l'Art Français*, nouvelle période, vol. XXVI, 1984.

Gombrich, E., *Art and Illusion*, London 1971.

Goncourt, J. and E., *L'Art du XVIIIᵉ siecle*, 'Chardin', II fascicle, 1864, 'notules', XII fascicle, 1875.

Gougenot, Abbé L., *Lettre sur la peinture, la sculpture et l'architecture à M°°°*, n.p., 1748. Second edition, revised and with new notes, Amsterdam, 1749.

Guiffrey, J. J., *Livrets des expositions de l'Académie de Saint-Luc à Paris*, Paris, 1872.

——— *Collection des Livrets des anciennes expositions depuis 1673 jusqu'en 1800*, Paris, 1869–72, vol. I–V.

——— *Histoire de l'Académie de Saint-Luc, Archives de l'Art Français*, nouvelle période?, vol. IX, 1914–15.

Haak, B., *The Golden Age – Dutch Paintings of the 17th Century*, London, 1984.

Haillet de Couronne, 'Éloge de M. Chardin sur les mémoires fournis par M. Cochin', (2 August 1780), *Mémoires inédits* published by L. Dussieux, E. Soulié, et al, Paris, 1854, vol. II, pp. 428–441.

Haskell, F., *Rediscoveries in Art*, London 1976.

Heidner, J., *Carl Frederik Scheffer – Lettres particulières à Carl Gustaf Tessin, 1744–1752*, Stockholm, 1982.

Herdt, A. de, *Dessins de Liotard*, exhibition catalogue, Geneva and Paris, 1992.

——— *Histoire de la vie privée*, under the direction of P. Ariès and G. Duby, vol. III, Paris, 1986.

Huquier the Younger, *Lettre sur l'exposition des tableaux au Louvre avec des notes historiques*, n.p., 1753.

——— *Inventaire du fonds français – Graveurs du XVIIIᵉ siècle*, Bibliothèque nationale, vol. I, 1931, vol. II, 1934, vol. IV 1940 (by M. Roux), vol. VIII, 1955 (by M. Roux and E. Pognon), vol. IX, 1962 (by E. Pognon and Y. Bruand), vol. X, 1968 (by M. Hébert, E. Pognon, Y. Bruand), vol. XII, 1974, vol. XIV, 1977 (by Y. Sjöberg and F. Gardey).

Kemp, M., 'A date for Chardin's Lady Taking Tea', *The Burlington Magazine*, CXX, 1978, pp. 22–25.

Lacombe, J., *Le Salon, en vers et en prose ou jugement des ouvrages exposés au Louvre en 1753*, n.p., n.d.

Lacroix, P., 'Le nécrologe des artistes et des curieux. Éloge de Chardin', *Revue universelle des Arts*, 1861, vol. XIII, pp. 45–48.

La Font de Saint-Yenne, *Réflexions sur quelques causes de l'état présent de la peinture en France avec un examen des principaux ouvrages exposés au Louvre le mois d'août 1746*, The Hague, 1747.

La Font de Saint-Yenne, *Sentimens sur quelques ouvrages de peinture, sculpture et gravure, écrits à un particulier en province*, n.p., 1754.

Lagrange, L., *Joseph Vernet et la peinture au XVIIIᵉ siècle*, Paris, 1864.

La Live de Jully, A. L., facsimile reprint of the *Catalogue historique* (1764) and the *Catalogue raisonné des tableaux* (1770), by C. B. Bailey, Acanthus Books, New York, 1988.

Lastic, G. de, 'Nicolas de Largillierre, peintre de natures mortes', *Revue du Louvre et des musées de France*, 1968, no. 4–5, pp. 233–240.

Laugier, M. A., *Manière de bien juger des ouvrages de peinture*, Paris, 1771 (published posthumously and annotated by Cochin).

Lauts, J., *Karoline Luise von Baden*, Karlsruhe, 1984.

Locquin, J., *La Peinture d'histoire en France de 1747 à 1785*, Paris, 1925.

Mariette, P. J., *Abecedario pittorico*, published by P. Chennevières and A. de Montaiglon, *Archives de l'Art Français*, 1853–62.

Mathey, J., 'Les dessins de Chardin', *Albertina Studien*, 1964, no. 1/2, pp. 17–31.

Mathon de la Cour, C. J., *Lettre à Madame °°° sur les peintures, les sculptures et les gravures exposées dans le Salon du Louvre en 1763*, Paris, 1763.

——— *Lettres sur les peintures, les sculptures et les gravures exposées au Salon du Louvre en 1767*, n.p., n.d.

McAllister Johnson, W., 'Visit to the Salon and sculptors' ateliers during the Ancien Régime', *Gazette des Beaux Arts*, VI/CVV, July–August 1992.

——— 'La gravure d'histoire en France au XVIIIᵉ siècle', *Revue de l'Art*, no. 99, 1983.

McWilliam, N., V. Schuster and R. Wrigley, *A Bibliography of Salon Criticism in Paris from the Ancien Régime to the Restoration 1699–1827*, Cambridge, 1991.

Mesuret, R., *Les Expositions de l'Académie royale de Toulouse de 1751 à 1791*, Paris and Toulouse, 1972.

Michel, C., *Charles-Nicolas Cochin et l'art des Lumières*, Rome, 1993.

——— *Édition des lettres de Cochin à J. B. Descamps*, 1986. (See also Cochin).

Mirimonde, A. P. de, *L'Iconographie musicale sous les rois Bourbons. La musique dans les arts plastiques, XVIIᵉ–XVIIIᵉ siècle*, Paris, 1977.

Monnier, G., *Pastels des XVIIᵉ et XVIIIᵉ siècles au musée du Louvre*, Paris, 1972.

——— *Nécrologe des hommes célèbres de France*, 'Éloge historique de M. Chardin', vol. XV (1779), Paris, 1780.

Neufville de Brunhaubois Montador, Chevalier J. F. J., *Description raisonnée des tableaux exposés au Louvre, Lettre à Mme la marquise de S. P. R.*, n.p., 1738.

——— *Description raisonnée des tableaux exposés au Louvre, Lettre à Mme la marquise de S. P. R.*, n.p., 1739.

——— 'Notice historique sur M. Chardin, peintre ordinaire du Roi, conseiller et ancien trésorier de l'Académie royale de peinture et de sculpture, mort à Paris le 6 décembre 1779', *Journal de Littérature, des Sciences et des Arts*, 1780, vol. I, pp. 59–69.

Opperman, H. L., *J. B. Oudry*, exhibition catalogue, Paris and Fort Worth, 1982–83.

Oudry, J. B., 'Réflexions sur la manière d'étudier la couleur…', symposium held at the Académie on 7 June 1749, published in *Le Cabinet de l'Amateur et de l'Antiquaire*, III, 1844, pp. 33–52.

——— 'Discours sur la pratique de la peinture…', symposium held on 2 December 1752, published in *Le Cabinet de l'Amateur*, 1861–62, pp. 107–117.

Perrin, C., *François Thomas Germain, orfèvre des rois*, Saint-Rémy-en-l'Eau, 1993.

Pesselier, C. E., 'La Nature et l'Art. A M. Chardin'; 'Envoi', *Fables nouvelles*, book II, fable 16, Paris, 1748.

Pignatti, T., *L'Opera completa di Pietro Longhi*, Milan, 1974.

Piles, R., de, *Les Premiers Élémens de la Peinture pratique*, Paris, 1684, republished by Jombert, 1766.

Pinault, M., *L'Encyclopédie*, 'Que sais-je?', Paris, 1993.

Ponge, F., 'De la nature morte et de Chardin', *Nouveau Recueil*, Paris, 1967.

Pressouyre, S., 'La galerie François 1er au château de Fontainebleau. II. Les restaurations', *Revue de l'Art*, 1972, no. 16–17, pp. 25–44.

Proschwitz, G. von, *Tableaux de Paris et de la cour de France 1739–1742*, unedited letters of Count Carl Gustaf de Tessin, Göteborg, 1983.

——— *Procès-verbaux de l'Académie royale de peinture et de sculpture, 1648–1792*, published by A. de Montaiglon, Paris, vol. V, 1883, vol. VI, 1885, vol. VII, 1886, vol. VIII, 1888 and vol. IX, 1889.

Rambaud, M., *Documents du Minutier central concernant l'histoire de l'art, 1700–1750*, Paris, vol. I, 1964, vol. II, 1971.

Ratouis de Limay, P,. *Aignan-Thomas Desfriches*, Paris, 1907.

Rey, R., *Quelques satellites de Watteau*, Paris, 1931.

Roche, D., *La Culture des apparences*, Paris, 1989.

——— *La France des Lumières*, Paris, 1993.

Roland Michel, M., *Anne Vallayer-Coster*, Paris, 1970.

——— *Watteau, un artiste au XVIIIe siècle*, Paris, 1984.

——— 'Mode ou imitation : sculpture et peinture en trompe-l'–il au XVIIIe siècle', Proceedings of the symposium *Clodion et la sculpture française de la fin du XVIIIe siècle*, Paris, 1992, published 1993.

Rosenberg, P. *Chardin*, Geneva, 1963.

——— 'Le Concours de peinture de 1727', *Revue de l'Art*, no. 37, 1977, pp. 37–42.

——— *Chardin*, exhibition catalogue, Paris, 1979 (with S. Savina).

——— *Tout l'œuvre peint de Chardin*, Paris, 1983.

——— *Chardin: New Thoughts*, The Franklin D. Murphy Lectures I, Helen Foresman Spencer Museum of Art, The University of Kansas, 1983.

Rosenberg, P. and I. Julia, 'Drawings by Pierre Jean Cazes', *Master Drawings*, vol. 23–24, no. 3, 1985–86.

Rosenfeld, M. N., *Largillierre portraitiste du XVIIIe siècle*, exhibition catalogue, Montreal, 1981.

Schmid, F., 'The painter's implement in

eighteenth-century art', *The Burlington Magazine*, October 1966, no. 763, vol. CVIII, p. 519.

Schnapper, A., 'A propos de deux nouvelles acquisitions : "Le chef-d'œuvre d'un muet" ou la tentative de Coypel', *Revue du Louvre et des musées de France*, no. 4–5, pp. 253–264.

Snoep-Reitsma, E., 'Chardin and the Bourgeois ideals of his Time', *Nederlands Kunsthistorisch Jaarboek*, 1973, no. 24, pp. 147–243.

Taylor, S. J., 'Engravings within engravings: Symbolic Contrast and Extension in some 18th-century French Prints', *Gazette des Beaux-Arts*, VI/CVI, September 1985.

Thuillier, J., *Les Frères Le Nain*, exhibition catalogue, Paris, 1978.

Turner, E. H., 'La Serinette' by Jean-Baptiste Chardin: a study in patronage and technique', *Gazette des Beaux-Arts*, VI/XLIX, April 1957.

Watelet, C. H. and Lévêque, P. H., *Encyclopédie méthodique – Beaux-Arts*, 4 vols., Paris, vol. I in 2 parts, 1788, vol. II in 2 parts 1791.

Watin, *L'Art du peintre*, Paris, 1772.

Weisberg, G. P. and W. S. Talbot, *Chardin and the Still-Life Tradition in France*, exhibition catalogue, Cleveland, 1978.

Wildenstein, G., *Le Peintre Aved*, Paris, 1922.

——— *La Tour*, Paris, 1928.

——— *Chardin*, Paris, 1933.

——— *Chardin*, Zurich, 1963.

——— *Chardin*, English edition revised and enlarged by D. Wildenstein, Oxford and Zurich, 1969.

Wille, J. G., *Mémoires et Journal*, published by G. Duplessis, Paris, 1857.

INDEX

PHOTOGRAPHIC CREDITS